GOD'S POWER

GOD'S POWER

Traditional Understandings and Contemporary Challenges

Anna Case-Winters

Westminster/John Knox Press
Louisville, Kentucky

Book design by Gene Harris

First edition

Published by Westminster/John Knox Press
Louisville, Kentucky

PRINTED IN THE UNITED STATES OF AMERICA

9 8 7 6 5 4 3 2 1

Library of Congress Cataloging-in-Publication Data

Case-Winters, Anna, 1953–
   God's power : traditional understandings and contemporary
challenges / by Anna Case-Winters. — 1st ed.
       p.   cm.
   Includes bibliographical references.
   ISBN 0-664-25106-4

   1. God—Omnipotence—History of doctrines.   2. Calvin, Jean,
1509–1564—Contributions in doctrine of divine omnipotence.
3. Barth, Karl, 1886–1968—Contributions in doctrine of divine
omnipotence.   4. Hartshorne, Charles, 1897–   —Contributions in
doctrine of divine omnipotence.   5. Feminist theology.   6. Process
theology.   I. Title.
BT133.C37 1990
231'.4—dc20   90-34544

Contents

GOD'S POWER

Preface

Many serious challenges have arisen against the assertion that God is omnipotent. The most troubling of these challenges presents itself in the form of the theodicy problem: If God is omnipotent, why is there evil in the world? Many thinkers, ancient and modern, have insisted that the concept of God's omnipotence stands in need of reassessment in the face of the problem of evil. This observation has become fairly commonplace in recent studies. Works such as David Griffin's *God, Power, and Evil: A Process Theodicy* undertake this task. In these studies, the end in view—redefining omnipotence in such a way that God is not seen as indictable for evil—is largely determinative of the form that redefinition takes. Redefinitions tend to alter the concept in the direction of restricting "how much" power is implied in the term "omnipotence." They work primarily with the *scope* of the concept.

The present project differs from works of this sort in suggesting that prevailing concepts of omnipotence are problematic in themselves, even prior to consideration of the problem of evil. A different set of questions, related to the meaning of the concept, is posed. What do we mean by omnipotence? How may this term be applied to God? With what understanding of power are we operating? What other alternatives present themselves?

The difficulties inherent in attributing omnipotence to God at all merit full consideration. One intent of the present project would be to expose the unclarity that exists in the definition and usage of the term "omnipotence." Some extant definitions of omnipotence can be shown to be inchoate, rudimentary, and even self-contradictory. This lack of clarity is symptomatic of the larger difficulty and leads to misunder-

standing and an uncritical acceptance or rejection of the term
as applicable to God.

That God is all-powerful, omnipotent, has been a central assertion of classical theism. Generally this has been taken to
mean that God can do all things. This assertion, however, has
been recognized as problematic since its inception and has pre-
cipitated a variety of philosophical and theological responses.

Challenges have been brought regarding the scope of the
concept of omnipotence. Does omnipotence mean that God
can do literally *anything?* Does this include things that are logically contradictory? Responses to those questions differ. Some
thinkers will admit no qualification whatsoever, while others
will admit certain types of qualifications. For Descartes, the
answer to both questions is yes. God can do literally anything.
God is not to be thought of as bound by the law of noncontra-
diction. Rather, this law is decreed by God. For Thomas
Aquinas, however, the answers are yes and no respectively.
God *can* do anything, but a logical contradiction (e.g., a square
circle) is not properly a "thing." The problem is not that God
cannot do certain things but that they cannot be done. "God
can do everything except what cannot be done." Other thinkers have offered similar restrictions of greater and lesser degrees of seriousness upon the scope of omnipotence in hopes of
achieving a more coherent concept. Anselm, for example, proposed that there are things that even human beings can do that
God cannot do. He would insist that while human beings can
change, God cannot. This, however, does not represent a lack
of power on God's part but rather highlights our "impotence."
Ability to change is really a defect of power and not power in
the positive sense. Further specifications are introduced by
those who assume the moral perfection of God. It is argued that
omnipotence is only one of God's perfections and is qualified
by God's other perfections. The result is that divine self-consistency will qualify any single human concept such as power.
These qualifications represent a kind of self-limitation of God's
power which is internal to God.

Some thinkers will go farther to admit external limitations
upon God's power while still affirming "omnipotence." Most
often this position is articulated by those who are concerned
to allow for the genuine freedom of other agents in the world.
The case is made that for human beings to be morally accountable, God's power must be sufficiently subtle and indirect not
to negate their freedom. Thus it is proposed that there are
other agents that have a power of their own which is independent of God's power.

From these diverse interpretations it can be seen that there is no universal agreement on the scope of the qualifier "omni." The differences among these diverse interpretations may be seen to be primarily quantitative differences, centering around the question of how much power omnipotence entails. The more fundamental question of the *meaning* of power in this context is not addressed. There seems to be an underlying agreement as to what power is, with only superficial shifts of emphasis. What is the implied consensus at work regarding the meaning of power in general and of divine power in particular? What is the effect of attaching the qualifier "omni" to that meaning? What other alternatives present themselves? When the meaning is shifted, how does this affect the scope? These issues of meaning merit consideration.

Thus it can be seen that the problems of both meaning and scope of the concept of omnipotence are complex in nature, making the development of a coherent concept of omnipotence a difficult undertaking.

It must be acknowledged from the outset, however, that the challenge most often addressed to the assertion of omnipotence comes not in relation to the problem of the meaning and scope of the term but rather from another quarter. It is not so much the coherence of the concept that comes under fire as its religious viability. The protest is two-pronged. The religious viability of the traditional doctrine of omnipotence is called into question by its negative ramifications in the realm of human affairs, on the one hand, and its aggravation of the theodicy problem, on the other.

It is argued that the strong affirmation of omnipotence which we in fact find in the tradition cannot be reconciled with a concept of genuine human freedom. When God is seen as so totally in "control," any credible concept of freedom and autonomy for human beings is relinquished and human actions lose their real significance. Furthermore, attributing this kind of power to God has the unwelcome side effect of elevating (divinizing) power of this sort. The outcome is a legitimation and perpetuation of this kind of power in the realm of human affairs resulting in injustice and oppression. It is difficult to defend the doctrine of omnipotence in the light of these negative ramifications. The religious viability of the assertion of God's omnipotence is also rendered dubious in the face of the pervasive presence of evil in world process. This constitutes the severest challenge to a doctrine of God's omnipotence, making its affirmation religiously suspect.

Nevertheless the (assumed) incompatibility of "omnipo-

tence" and "freedom," on the one hand, and of "omnipotence" and "evil," on the other, presupposes a certain
meaning for omnipotence. Thus the issue of meaning must
necessarily be addressed before progress can be made in the
discussion. Hartshorne has argued convincingly for the necessity of this prior step of clarification of meaning. With regard
to the problem of evil, for example, he points out that when
we state the problem as a theodicy problem, certain questionable assumptions are already at work. This way of putting the
matter

> supposes that at least we know what divine power is, and only
> its use by divine justice is too deep for us. However, is not this
> idea of divine power already, just in itself, quite as mysterious
> as that of divine justice? The mystery is in both terms and not
> simply in one or simply in the other.[1]

Thus we are thrown back upon the question of meaning.
While the problem of evil may be uppermost in our minds as
making "omnipotence" a problematic assertion, the question
of meaning is really a prior and more fundamental question. A
necessary step in any attempt at resolution of the problem will
be an exploration of our concepts of divine "power" and divine "action." How are these terms meant?

> What does it mean to say, "God does something"? To accept
> such language as clear, but to find a puzzle in the divine mo-
> tive, *why* God does things, is as Berdyaev said, once for all, to
> treat as a mystery a problem which one has "already overra-
> tionalized." The puzzle begins one step earlier. Human
> "power" we know something about, but what sort of analogy
> enables us to speak of "divine power"? Until we have this anal-
> ogy straight, there is no clearly defined problem of evil.[2]

It is the thesis of this book that the underlying meaning of
power that the classical view of omnipotence presupposes is
the crux of the problem. This is the case whether we are dealing with the problem of coherency or the problem of religious
viability. Inheritors of the tradition who may differ in substantial ways from the classical view seem nevertheless to accept
this meaning of power as settled and to struggle instead with
the issue of *scope*. I am arguing that a theological critique of

---

[1]Charles Hartshorne, "The Mystery of Omnipotence," in *The Power of God: Readings on Omnipotence and Evil,* ed. Linwood Urban and Douglas N. Walton (New York:
Oxford University Press, 1978), p. 250.

[2]Ibid.

the meaning of power in the concept of omnipotence is prior to the issue of the scope of the term. Some resources found in contemporary theology assist this critique, and a constructive proposal is offered.

The Introduction explores the problematic nature of applying the term "power" to God. Problems of coherency and religious viability of the traditional doctrine of omnipotence are more fully presented there. The centrality of power to our concept of God is established and the meaning of the term is viewed from the angles of etymology and usage.

Part One focuses on uncovering the prevailing model for understanding power that is at work in the tradition. The central question being addressed here is, "What sort of power is being attributed to God?" In order to move more deeply into the model, its concrete expression in a representative figure (John Calvin) is closely examined. Elements of the model (i.e., its personal nature and political quality) and the way these elements shape the meaning are scrutinized. The particular meaning for power at work in the prevailing model seems to be power in the mode of domination and control, involving God's ability to bring about any state of affairs that God wills. Once this underlying meaning is exposed, the book proceeds to consider the effect of the application of the qualifier "omni" to this intended meaning. The major difficulties named above can be seen to arise at this point.

Part Two demonstrates how thinkers who work within the prevailing model, and who share the understanding of power operative there, seek to ameliorate its difficulties. One modification, which attempts to compensate by limiting the *scope* of omnipotence, is presented (Karl Barth). Some assessment is offered as to whether such (quantitative) modifications of scope are finally adequate to the task or whether more fundamental (qualitative) reconstruction as to *meaning* is needed.

Part Three of the book presents some alternative models for understanding power. The effect of applying the qualifier "omni" to these alternative meanings for power is very different from the effect when this qualifier is applied in the prevailing model. The alternatives that are appraised come from process theology and feminist perspectives. These alternative models are critically evaluated. The possibilities and the limitations of each are explored.

The conclusion of the book offers a reconstruction of the concept of omnipotence. This constructive proposal rejects the prevailing notion of power as "domination and control" in favor of a new meaning—elements of which will have been drawn from the alternatives explored. It is argued that attaching the qualifier "omni" to "power," meant in this new way, does not result in an aggravation of the theodicy problem or in negative ramifications for the realm of human affairs. This is because an altogether different kind of power is being attributed to God. This reconstruction is intended as both more coherent and more religiously viable.

In a project such as this, there are many collaborators. The work began as a dissertation at Vanderbilt University under the direction of Edward Farley. I want to express my deep appreciation to him first. His interest and encouragement in this endeavor have meant so much. He taught me (among many other things!) to delve deeply into the meaning of key terms and to pursue worthwhile questions with openness and tenacity. I have tried to do so in this book and now realize I have only made a beginning.

I am truly indebted to the members of my committee, Peter C. Hodgson (first reader), Sallie McFague (second reader), Eugene TeSelle, Walter Harrelson, and John J. Compton. Each one offered challenges and insights that broadened and enriched this work. Their provocative questions are with me still, enticing me to further work on what now appears to be a lifelong project.

The commitment and camaraderie of other students in the program at Vanderbilt University inspired and heartened me along the way. Serving as Associate Director of Field Education for the Divinity School while in graduate school proved to be not only a satisfying ministry and challenging learning experience but also a regular "reality check" for my theological reflections. Co-workers Don Beisswenger (Director) and Althea Gee (Program Secretary) lightened the load for me daily with their good humor, indulgence, and personal support.

As the dissertation becomes a book, I am now serving as Associate Professor of Theology and Church and as Associate Dean for Thesis Development at McCormick Theological Seminary. The seminary has been generous in granting me time and resources for continuing my research, reflection, and writing, and I am truly grateful. Colleagues and students at McCormick have been a continual source of inspiration. Their enthusiasm has been energizing and their insightful questions have helped me refine this work. In particular I want to thank my colleagues in the theology field, John E. Burkhart and Thomas D. Parker, who have taken care to affirm and nurture me in my continuing growth as a theologian.

Ongoing conversations with the Hyde Park Faculty Women's Reading Group (also known as The Feminist Theological Coalition!) have contributed much to this project. As we share our ongoing work with one another, this forum has provided a "clearing for freedom" in which some risky/original/from-the-heart thinking can take place. As I have ventured to struggle with the troubling questions raised in this book, their openness, critical questions, and genuine affirmation have strengthened me in this work.

Special recognition is due to Margarita Gonzales, whose capable staff support made it possible for me to take full advantage of the time I was granted for research and writing. I am very grateful to Trudy Priester for her willing and capable editorial assistance and to Carol Gorski for her careful reading and sound advice when it came time to reduce the lengthy dissertation to the book size.

I know with certainty that I would not have come to this point without the support of a loving family. The deep and abiding faith of my parents, Burton Case and Lucile Barksdale Case, has nurtured and sustained me and given my life its direction. They have always been there for me, conveying confidence that I could do whatever I set my mind to and that what I had set my mind to was worth doing. They have invested themselves sacrificially in my education through the years and I feel the deepest gratitude for all they have been and all they have done.

Life with our children has kept before me the urgency of our work. The hard questions of our time must be met and grappled with—for the children, for the future. They have each made distinctive contributions. My stepdaughter, Jennifer, has shown genuine interest in what must have seemed in her early years an odd preoccupation of mine (which has now lasted much of her life!). She has been supportive and ready to celebrate each small advance. My son, Michael, conceived about the same time chapters six and seven were conceived, can be credited with much of the inspiration for and experiential understanding of the image I have explored there.

My husband, R. Michael Winters III, has been an unfailing reservoir of loving support and encouragement throughout this whole endeavor. In our fifteen years together he has gone to great lengths—and done so willingly—to help me pursue my many and varied dreams. As these dreams become realities, I know who has been the "wind beneath my wings." I rely on his understanding and eager partnership in everything I undertake. My gratitude to him is more than words can express.

Abbreviations

OED	*Oxford English Dictionary*
Calvin	
(bk., ch., sec.)	*Institutes of the Christian Religion*
CO	*Calvini Opera* (in *Corpus Reformatorum*)
CEPG	*Concerning the Eternal Predestination of God*
TAL	*Treatise Against the Libertines*
Barth	
(vol., part, page)	*Church Dogmatics*
DO	*Dogmatics in Outline*
HOG	*The Humanity of God*
Hartshorne	
AD	*Anselm's Discovery*
CSPM	*Creative Synthesis and Philosophic Method*
DR	*The Divine Relativity*
LP	*The Logic of Perfection*
MVG	*Man's Vision of God and the Logic of Theism*
NTOT	*A Natural Theology for Our Time*
OOTM	*Omnipotence and Other Theological Mistakes*
PSG	*Philosophers Speak of God*

Introduction

I have chosen to reassess the traditional doctrine of divine omnipotence for at least two reasons. First, when this doctrine is affirmed, there are consequences that are problematic and in fact cause us to question its religious viability. In particular, the doctrine aggravates the theodicy problem and leads to negative ramifications in the realm of human affairs. Second, the doctrine has internal problems of meaning and coherency, and there is widespread confusion and unclarity regarding what we mean when we say God is omnipotent. Each of these problems will be taken up in turn.

The Question of the Religious Viability of the Concept

Aggravation of the Theodicy Problem

Perhaps the most troubling and at the same time unavoidable problem with which contemporary theologians must wrestle is the problem of evil. Why is there so much evil and suffering in the world? Anyone—believer or no—may ask this question, but the question becomes all the more poignant for persons who believe in a good and omnipotent God. The need to show how these realities are not inconsistent with one another becomes apparent. Unless God's existence and omnipotence are affirmed—while the problem of evil remains—no theodicy problem presents itself. However, as soon as we affirm the existence of an omnipotent God in the face of pervasive evil, the theodicy problem rears its ugly head.

The theodicy problem is most often formulated as a logical problem created by our holding three propositions simultaneously: that God is good, that God is omnipotent, and that there is evil in the world. There are many ways of posing the logical problem, but there are three basic expressions of it which are commonly found, and most of the others can be seen to be variations on these themes. Each statement of the problem is shaped by certain presuppositions and indicates a possible approach to resolution. In fact, it seems that the resolution anticipated determines the way in which the question will be put. Traditional approaches to the problem, for example, presuppose the goodness and omnipotence of God and pose the question in this way: "Since God is omnipotent and good, why is there evil in the world?" Here it is evil that is being called into question, and resolution to the problem is being sought through reexamination of the presence, origin, nature, and functioning of evil.

Another—more troubling—way of stating the problem might be, "Given the pervasive presence of evil, can we believe that a good and omnipotent God exists?" Here the presence and nature of evil as well as a particular meaning for "God" (as good and omnipotent) are presupposed. God's *existence* is what is at stake in this formulation.

There is yet another possible way of putting the question. "Given the pervasive presence of evil in the world, how are we to understand God's *power?*" This way of stating the problem presupposes both the existence of a "good" God and the presence of genuine evil in world process. Resolution to the problem is sought by a reexamination of "omnipotence" as an attribute of God. I am suggesting that this approach is the most promising one.

It is my contention that certain ways of understanding omnipotence exacerbate the problem and make it intractable, while other ways of understanding omnipotence make the problem more amenable to resolution. Further, I would propose that an understanding of divine power as operating *in the mode of domination and control* has led to the present impasse in discussions of the theodicy problem. When omnipotence is defined in this way, human freedom is compromised and we are forced either to pose the problem in the first way mentioned and deny the presence of genuine evil in the world or to pose the problem in the second way and deny the existence of God. The traditional definition of omnipotence presents us with a forced option reflected in these two most common ways of framing the theodicy question. This aggravation of the theodicy problem which we find here may cause us to raise questions concerning the religious viability of the traditional doctrine of omnipotence.

Negative Ramifications in the Realm of Human Affairs

Another challenge to the religious viability of this doctrine is coming to expression as feminist theologians on the contemporary scene scrutinize the traditional doctrine of omnipotence. The critique, which will be presented later at greater length, is two-pronged. On the one hand, it can be argued that the whole preoccupation of the tradition with power is a stereotypically male preoccupation. On the other hand, the case can be made that the meaning for power at work in the prevailing model is shaped by a male bias, and the resulting way of meaning and living out power has had negative ramifications in the realm of human affairs.

I would insist that this is an important critique and a damaging one. The way in which we conceive of God and the way we speak of God have real consequences in the realm of human affairs. The theological constructs we employ may be said not only to reflect and express values we already hold, but also to inform and determine our valuation. The particular images we use become divinized. Kingship, for example, gains in status when the metaphor of king is applied to God. As one of the central assertions of classical theism, the assertion that God is omnipotent (all-powerful) is an important instance of this interplay between theological constructs and values. Traditionally, the power implied here has been interpreted as power *in the mode of domination and control.* The ramifications of ascribing power to God and especially power in this mode are an admission that we prize power highly and that this is the kind of power we prize. Moreover, as this notion becomes divinized the exercise of this kind of power in the realm of human affairs is legitimated and promoted—with obvious disastrous results in the form of oppression, exploitation, and violence. A careful consideration of the feminist critique may cause us to reassess our heavy emphasis upon power as a divine attribute or at least to reshape the particular understanding of divine power that we promote. An alternative model, broadened by a valuing of stereotypically female powers (e.g., life-giving power), might offer a new vision and result in a richer and at the same time less problematic understanding of divine power.

The Question of the Meaning and Coherence of the Concept

A different set of problems concerning clarity of meaning and logical consistency may cause us to question the coher-

ence of the traditional doctrine. There seems to be considerable confusion and unclarity regarding what is meant when we
say God is "omnipotent." In common parlance, the meaning is
simply that "God can do anything." But this definition, as
soon as it is put forth, becomes entangled in a web of logical
inconsistencies. I will sum these up under four categories:
If God can do anything, then

1. God can do things that are *logically contradictory,* such
   as making the past not to have been.
2. God can do things that are *not compossible,* such as creating an object that is simultaneously all black and all
   white.
3. God can bring about states of affairs that, while logically
   possible, are de facto unachievable since they require an
   external determination of free human agency. This
   would mean that God *could* bring it about that there be a
   world in which human beings always freely chose the
   good.
4. God can bring about states of affairs that are *self-limiting.*
   This would include a whole category of things that,
   while not in themselves self-contradictory, are contradictory when predicated of an omnipotent being. To say
   this is to give an affirmative answer to the age-old conun-
   drum, "Can God create a rock that God cannot lift?"

As soon as the meaning of omnipotence is stated as "God
can do anything," we become locked in the "omnipotence
paradox." This problem is far from new, but it is also far
from settled. Many types of resolution to the problems of def-
initional unclarity and logical inconsistency confronting the
traditional doctrine of omnipotence have been proposed
throughout the history of the Christian tradition. Different
ways of resolving these sorts of dilemmas have resulted in
different ways of understanding the scope of omnipotence. As
a consequence, there is no precision or uniformity regarding
the meaning or use of the term.

There are at least two ways of avoiding altogether the obstacle of logical inconsistency. One way is simply to assert
in defiance of all contrary considerations that omnipotence
means that God can do anything whatsoever, including things
that are logically impossible. In this approach, concern for
coherence and reasonable grounds for assertion are set aside.
One steps outside the domain of rational discourse and in-
quiry. Another option is to conclude that, because the concept of omnipotence here expressed is self-contradictory, it

should therefore be abandoned as irrevocably vacuous. One ceases to affirm divine omnipotence.

A middle way of proceeding seeks to hold on to omnipotence as a divine attribute but lets go of certain ways of conceiving omnipotence (as meaning that God can do *literally* anything) in favor of definitions that are more logically defensible. Placing multiple interlocking restrictions upon the scope of omnipotence may provide a method for achieving a more coherent definition. This third option is, of course, the one most often chosen.

Thinkers have approached the omnipotence puzzle in different ways and have made varied kinds of adjustments in an attempt to make things fit together, and each in turn is concerned to show why the adjustments do not create a deficiency in power. The outcome has been a multiplicity of definitions—each with its own qualifications—associated with the term "omnipotence."[1] The term has become "too amorphous, sprawling, or chameleon-like ever to be amenable to exact identification."[2]

One way of summarizing and illustrating the various proposed restrictions is to return to the common parlance definition of "omnipotence" (as meaning that "God can do all things") and see how its component parts are modified or qualified. We will begin with this very simplified and widely used definition and see how it turns in our hands as we work with it.

Some thinkers make modifications by working with the *subject* of the sentence. They might say that *God* cannot do all things, *other subjects* must do some things. For these thinkers, omnipotence does not imply that God has a monopoly on power, only that God is supremely powerful, having the maximum power any one being can have. This position makes room for the freedom, autonomy, and power of other agents/subjects.[3] This particular modification of the definition is conceived as an *external/metaphysical limitation*. It is a given of the way things are and not simply a matter of the divine

---

[1] I do not mean to imply that the logical problems are the sole cause of the diversity and the unclarity that exist, but they do present an occasion for revealing that diversity and unclarity.

[2] P. H. Partridge, "Some Notes on the Concept of Power," *Political Studies*, ed. Wilfred Harrison, 9/2 (1963): 107.

[3] Here omnipotence is being distinguished from *omnificence* or *universal agency*, which would hold that God has (personally) brought about every state of affairs that obtains or, even more comprehensively, every possible state of affairs.

choosing that at any moment could be revoked. For Hartshorne, as for process thought generally, actuality entails
power, so that if there is anything actual besides God, that
something necessarily has its own power (to do things).[4]

Other possible modifications focus upon the *verb* "can do."
There are restrictions related to the word "can." A distinction
is drawn between *being able to do* all things and *actually doing*
all things. Those who take this approach may affirm that while
God *can* do all things, God *does not* do all things. *Ability* and
will (and consequently action) do not coincide. God may do
only what God wills to do.[5]

Barth argues along these lines.[6] For him, God's power is not
to be conceived as abstract power; it is power working for
God's loving purposes. God's sovereignty is the "sovereignty
of God's love." This provides a kind of *internal limitation*
(though Barth would not have used the word "limitation" in
this connection) to the exercise of God's power. There can
also be a *voluntary self-limitation* of God's power, such as that
which we see in the incarnation. This is a decision of the will
and therefore constitutes a *moral limitation* as opposed to an
external, metaphysical limitation or an internal limitation imposed by a given within God's nature.

Diversity in our understanding of "God can do all things"
may be further illustrated by examination of what it is af-

---

[4]A different kind of modification of this subject component of the definition is
proposed by Paul Tillich. Tillich rejects the popular notion of God as a highest being
and with it the accompanying definition of omnipotence as the quality of a highest
being who can do whatever he or she wants. He argues that this anthropomorphism
leads to a view that is "magical" and absurd. This notion, he entreats, must be rejected, religiously as well as theologically, because it makes God into a being alongside other beings. It further subjects God to the potentiality-actuality split which is
the heritage of finitude and leads to senseless questions about God's power in terms
of logically contradictory possibilities. It tends to identify the divine power with
actual happenings in time and space and thereby suppresses the transcendent element in God's omnipotence. Tillich finds a more adequate definition of divine omnipotence as "the power of being which resists nonbeing in all its expressions and which
is manifest in the creative process in all its forms." Paul Tillich, *Systematic Theology*, 3
vols. (Chicago: University of Chicago Press, 1951–1963), 1:273.

[5]Thomas, for example, draws a distinction between God's "absolute power" and
God's "ordinate power." Everything possible lies within God's power (absolute
power), but not everything lies within God's will (ordinate power). God does not act
from a necessity of nature. God's will is the cause of all things. "We conceive of God's
wisdom as directing, God's will as commanding and God's power as executing."
Thomas Aquinas, *Summa Theologica* (New York: McGraw-Hill Book Co., 1963), vol.
I, q. 25, art. 5, ad. I, p. 163.

[6]Though Barth does so without using Thomas's distinctions in the way Thomas uses
them.

firmed that God can "do." Some of the options include affirmation that God can bring about desired effects and states of
affairs; cause things to come into being, produce things by
creative effort; control and govern; and act upon and affect.
Most often, as the definition is drawn out further, it emphasizes God's "doing" in the sense of either creating/causing to
be or in the sense of governing/controlling.

For John Calvin, for example, *governance/control* seems to
be the primary category. In Calvin's doctrine of particular
providence, God is seen as the world ruler ordaining each
event and watching over every creature. God's doing is not
contained in the natural order, nor is it "action at a distance";
it is, rather, a manifestation of personal care, omnipotence of a
"watchful, effective, active sort, engaged in ceaseless activity" (1.16.3). Nothing falls outside God's purview, being left
to chance. "Each year, month, and day is governed by a new,
a special, providence of God" (1.16.2).

Others focus primarily upon *causation* (final and/or efficient) as the way God's omnipotence is manifest. William of
Ockham sees God as "the immediate cause of all things."[7]
Friedrich Schleiermacher's primary understanding of omnipotence as "omnicausality" is also in this vein.

> In the conception of the divine Omnipotence two ideas are
> contained: first, that the entire system of Nature, comprehend-
> ing all times and spaces, is founded upon divine causality,
> which as eternal and omnipresent is in contrast to all finite cau-
> sality; and second, . . . everything for which there is a causality
> in God happens and becomes real.[8]

In addition to approaches that qualify the subject or the
verb, some qualify the object of the sentence. Some limit or

---

[7]William of Ockham, *Philosophical Writings*, ed. P. Boehner (Edinburgh: Thomas
Nelson & Sons, 1957), p. 129.

[8]Friedrich Schleiermacher, *The Christian Faith* (New York: Harper & Row, 1963),
vol. I, p. 211. It is interesting that Schleiermacher speaks against some of the possible
modifications of the definition that have been or will be mentioned in this exploration. He rejects the modification proposed in our distinction between what God *can
do* and what God actually *does*, as well as Thomas's distinction between God's "absolute power" and "ordinate power." He also rejects the rendering of the definition as
"can do all things that are *possible*—not self-contradictory." In Schleiermacher's
view, when it comes to divine power, there can be no distinction between "can" and
"will," "possible" and "actual." These can apply only in the finite realm of time and
space and cannot apply in the case of God's omnipotence which is eternal and omni-
present. All things happening in space and time have their determinations from outside in space and before in time.

reject the term "all." God cannot do *all* things. According to Anselm, God cannot change even though human beings can. This, however, does not represent a lack of power on God's part but rather highlights our impotence. For Anselm, ability to change is really a defect of power and not power in the positive sense. God cannot do all things but only those things which are consistent with divine perfection.

Restrictions can also be placed upon the last term in the definition, the object "things." Thomas, for example, would argue that self-contradictions (i.e., a square circle) are not properly "things." Therefore they present an impossibility. He notes that power is a relative term, relative to what is possible, and it is because divine power can do everything that is possible that it is termed omnipotent. "God can do everything except what cannot be done."[9]

This brief exploration of the common parlance definition and of the many ways in which it has been qualified, modified, and restricted has revealed that even the most commonly used definition of omnipotence—"God can do all things"—is not one definition but many. It is obvious that a process of clarification is needed.

Before we begin this process, we need to ask a fundamental question: Why do we attribute omnipotence to God in the first place? It is obvious from any study of the doctrine of God that this particular attribute holds a central place. Why is this the case?

The Centrality of Power as an Attribute of God

Why is power so basic to our concept of God? What is at work here? There are at least two ways in which these fundamental questions have been addressed. On the one hand, it may be argued (as Ludwig Feuerbach would argue) that human need is the chief cause for the imputation to the divine of great power (as well as other attributes). Because we want our needs to be met and our prayers to be answered, we project an image of an all-powerful God who is able to do so.

---

[9]Thomas Aquinas, *Summa* I, q. 25, art. 5. Thomas comments further that things are said to be impossible in three ways: in one way on account of a defect of the active power, in another way because something resists or impedes the action, and in a third way because what is said to be impossible cannot be the terminus of an action. God can do impossible things in the first two senses but not in the third. This is not due to a defect in God's power nor to an impediment God cannot overcome but to a lack of possibility.

On the other hand, it may be argued that genuine experience and perception of the divine as powerful are what lead to the attribution of power to God. We "find ourselves in communion with a life and a power other and stronger than ourselves which 'ecstasizes' us, carrying us out of ourselves (exalting or subduing) which we cannot but personify as superhuman and divine."[10] Hence we see beyond (and purify) our projections and wish fulfillment to a God who is wholly other than ourselves and not our own creation.

In the Judeo-Christian tradition the notion of redemption can be introduced in this vein. Whether in the exodus or in the Christ event, we encounter a God who saves *mightily*. Our experience of redemption and the accompanying reorientation of our lives and way of being in the world are of such a nature that we cannot account for them without reference to some concept of an omnipotent God. Any lesser God would not have the power requisite to break the power of evil in our lives and "save" us in this way. We experience this salvation as being decidedly not "of ourselves" and not from some mundane entity in the world. It is experienced as coming from an "other" who is supremely powerful. From this experience we form a concept of God as "omnipotent." The attribution of omnipotence or supreme power to God elemental in the Judeo-Christian tradition is also pervasive in religious experience as such.

Rudolf Otto, in his book on "the holy," describes an experience that is both terrifying and at the same time fascinating, as we stand before the *mysterium tremendum,* this majesty that betokens an overwhelming superiority of power. The numinous manifests power of quite another order *(ganz andere)* than that found in nature.[11]

Many others confirm the centrality of power with comparable descriptions. As Gerardus van der Leeuw has observed:

> The first affirmation we can make about the Object of Religion is that it is a *highly exceptional* and *extremely impressive* *"Other."* . . . There arises and persists an experience which connects or unites itself to the "other" that thus obtrudes, that this Object is a departure from all that is usual and familiar; and this again is the consequence of the *Power* it generates.[12]

---

[10]Gerardus van der Leeuw, *Religion in Essence and Manifestation,* 2 vols. (Gloucester, Mass.: Peter Smith, 1967), 1:16.

[11]Otto, *The Idea of the Holy.*

[12]Van der Leeuw, 1:1.

In his thoughtful analysis, Van der Leeuw argues that religion in its essence and manifestation consists in "being touched by Power," "being affected by Power," "conducting oneself in relation to Power," and "participating in Power." Power is the predominating concept at work whether we are looking at dynamism, animism, polytheism, or monotheism. Van der Leeuw also notes that "worship always depends on the substantiation of power."[13]

Lewis Farnell maintains that power is a central concept in most religions.

> In Vedic and Vedantic theology, in the Hellenic, the Judaic, the Christian, the Islamic and the Zarathustrian systems, the multiplicity of divine attributes could be brought under the three great categories, *Potentia, Sapientia, Bonitas*—Power, Wisdom, and Goodness—which was the quasi-trinitarian formula summing up the medieval schoolmen's ideal of God.[14]

Farnell also points out that power as an attribute belongs to the earliest concepts of God (insofar as these may be uncovered by historical research). Earliest religious thought involved belief in supernatural agents more powerful than oneself (mysterious, capricious, formidable). "The gods or the spirits are imagined as powerful before they are recognized as beneficent or just."[15] This may indicate that power has a certain priority and is even more basic to our ideas of God than wisdom or goodness.[16]

It would appear that the centrality of power as an attribute for God is common to all religious experience. This has been found to be the case from earliest accounts and across religious traditions. Though understandings of the nature and operation of power may vary, the centrality of power for any concept of God seems a universal assumption.

If we look more closely at how this is manifest in the Judeo-Christian tradition in particular, we find that here the predominance of the attribute of power in the concept of God is extremely pronounced. Walter Grundmann observes that the essence of God for Judaism becomes located in "power." In the Targums, when God speaks in the first person, "power" is

---

[13]Van der Leeuw, 1:85 (see n. 10 above).

[14]Lewis Richard Farnell, *The Attributes of God: The Gifford Lectures* (Oxford: Clarendon Press, 1925), p. 11.

[15]Farnell, p. 224.

[16]This conclusion will be borne out by a presentation of the arguments around omnipotence.

one of the terms used. "Power" becomes a paraphrase of the divine names, a kind of euphemism for "God." God and power become almost synonymous. In Hellenistic Judaism a bit of a shift occurs with reference to the understanding of divine power. The idea of God in God's perfect transcendence becomes "pure being." At this stage, divine power becomes hypostasized and takes up a kind of independent, middle role between God and human beings.[17]

The Christian tradition to a large extent adopted the view of divine power that was bequeathed to it by Judaism. Power maintains the same centrality in the Christian concept of God and is of the same sort—personal, active power exercised by the divine world maker and world ruler. One need only refer to the Apostles' Creed for evidence of the continuing primacy of the attribute of power. "I believe in God the Father *Almighty (pantokratōr,* "all-ruling"), maker of heaven and earth." In contemporary Christian practice, we cannot help noticing that the appellation most commonly used of the deity as a form of address in prayer is still, "Almighty God."

But what do we mean by "almighty" God? In order to address effectively the question of what is signified by "almighty" or "omnipotent" as a description of divine power, we must first consider what it is that we mean by "power" as such. When we have reexamined meaning and usage of the term in the human sphere, perhaps we may be better able to judge whether and in what sense this same term may be applied to God. The section that follows will be a brief exploration of the term "power" as used in its contemporary

---

[17]Even a cursory review of names for God in the Old Testament proves interesting in this light. The name *Yahweh sebaoth* is rendered in the LXX not only by *kyrios sabaōth* ("Lord of Sabaoth") but also by *kyros pantokratōr* ("Lord all-powerful, all-determining") and *kyrios dynameōn* ("Lord of hosts" or "Lord of the powers").

Most biblical names for God imply power to act or to make, though the exact meaning of these terms is often under dispute. Abraham worships *el shaddai* ("God the almighty") in Gen. 17:1 and *el elyon* ("most high God" or "God eternal") in Gen. 14:18. *El* ("God") as found in *elohim* throughout the Old Testament means "strong God." God is also called "the mighty one of Jacob" (Gen. 49:24), "the creator of the heavens . . . the designer and maker of the earth" (Isa. 45:18), "the Lord of the whole earth" (Josh. 3:11, 13). Somewhat mysterious in meaning is the most proper name of God, "Yahweh." "Yahweh" probably meant originally "he who causes all things to be" rather than the later, more common rendering, "I AM WHO I AM" (Ex. 3:14). The particular understanding of power associated with Yahweh is of a personal, living power which acts in history prototypically in the exodus. It is "saving power" that can be depended upon by an individual or by a people. Grundmann, *"dynamai/ dynamis,"* in *Theological Dictionary of the New Testament,* 2:284–317.

applications. Even here the term "power" will be seen to be a "dynamic" concept and not one with a settled meaning.

Contemporary Meanings and Usages of the Term "Power"

According to the OED, the English word "power" is derived through Old French *poeir*, from Low Latin *potere*, for Latin *posse*, "to be able." It may signify:

1. The ability or capacity to act effectively.
2. A specific capacity or aptitude (faculty).
3. Strength or force exerted or capable of being exerted (might, force).
4. Ability or official capacity to exercise control over others (authority).
5. A person or nation having great influence or control.
6. From the natural sciences: a measure of the rate of work (i.e., horsepower), a current of electricity, a measure of magnification, etc.
7. From mathematics: exponents or, in statistics, the probability of rejecting the null hypothesis.

In this simplified collection of meanings we get a glimpse of the options available in common usage. Some of these meanings can be seen to be rooted in more ancient terminology.[18] An etymological study reveals, among other things, that the term "power" historically entailed both active and passive capacity. "Power" at some times has the character of *intrinsic ability* and at other times has the character of *extrinsic ability*—power that is granted (authority). These particular dimensions of the term (active/passive, intrinsic/extrinsic) will prove to be important for the larger theological exploration.

---

[18]In Greek philosophy, for example, the term *dynamis* meant "to be able." This entailed both active capacity and passive capacity (potentiality). The Milesians and their successors saw *dynamis* as an "active force" in things. Plotinus spoke of a "vital force," a *dynamis zōtikē*, in all beings.

The religious view of late antiquity, which came to hold that the transcendent immobility of the gods must be preserved, spoke of the gods as not acting directly upon the world but rather through their *dynameis*. These *dynameis* could be and were personified. *Dynameis* could also refer to powers or faculties of human beings.

A secondary Greek term for power was *exousia*, from *exesti*, which means "it is free." This term connotes that there are no hindrances to an action, that it may be done and is not forbidden. It is to be distinguished from *dynamis*, which implies intrinsic ability. *Exousia* may be granted (extrinsically) by a higher norm or court as "authority, permission, freedom." A parallel difference is to be noted between the Latin forms *potentia*, which means "capability, power, or force," and *potestas*, which refers to "authority."

In its contemporary application the term "power" is used differently in different fields. In physics, for example, it is primarily used in reference to what we might call "pure force," physical forces that are neutral and impersonal in nature. Natural sciences seem to use the term in a mechanistic sense, giving special attention to cause-and-effect relationships. For our purposes, the usage in the social and political sciences may be most illumining, since concepts of divine power are primarily drawn from analogy with human power. The power attributed to God is usually "personal" and "intentional" in nature. We are most concerned with power as a *capacity possessed* by a subject and power as *exercised* by that subject. This makes the use of the term "power" drawn from the social and political context more suited to our needs.

In sociopolitical sciences, there is no end to the disputes regarding definition and usage of the term "power." There is a whole host of terms that bear relation to the larger concept: influence, control, authority, force, constraint, freedom, coercion, ability, domination, prestige, compulsion. In ordinary language these are used loosely, now standing for one relation, now for another. Theoretically, there might be a point at which we would cease to use the term "power," but it is difficult to say where the line should be drawn. The situations to which we apply these terms seem rather to form a continuum, with the terms overlapping at the edges, shading into one another.[19] There is no agreement across the disciplines on the meaning of power, nor within any given discipline. In fact, we do not often find a high degree of consistency in the writings of any one individual. As in the preceding theological discussions, here also we find an absence of uniformity and precision in the definition of this term.

Instead of seeking a single analysis of power, we may find it more helpful to think of the diverse usages of "power" and its related concepts as instances of a "family of concepts," which do not all share any one particular characteristic but have various relations and resemblances by which they are recognizably kin.[20] The questions that follow show some of the difficulties that are encountered and some of the decisions that

---

[19]Partridge, p. 107(see n. 2 above).

[20]Stanley Benn has constructed a kind of paradigm of power in which five main "family features" are delineated: He suggests that when these things are present we have before us an instance of power: (1) an intention manifest in the exercise of power, (2) the successful achievement of this intention, (3) a relation between at least two persons, (4) intentional initiation of actions of one by actions of the other, and (5)

must be made in clarifying the meaning of power. It is hoped
that they will prove to be to the point as a method of interro-
gating various meanings for "power" at work in the thought
of certain theologians.

Does Power Necessarily Entail Intentionality?

Bertrand Russell defines power as "the production of intended effects."[21] Intentions rather than effects are the essential element in this concept of power. A tornado would not be
a "powerful" occurrence if this condition is admitted. To require intentionality is to limit the presence of power to intelligent beings.

Among intelligent beings, the quality of a relationship in
regard to power dynamics may not even be known to the persons involved. Can power that is exercised without awareness
be said to be "intentional"? In family relationships, for example, this is a commonplace with which psychoanalysts and
novelists are very familiar. A mother may have considerably
more "power" over her children than she intends. Similarly,
the wealthy, pacesetters of a society, may affect the masses
"powerfully" though unintentionally.

Instances of power such as these caused Robert Dahl to remove the element of intentionality from his definition of
power and to define power instead as "the difference in the
probability of an event given certain actions by A and the
probability of the event given no such actions by A."[22] Such a
definition broadens to include power as we find it in nature
and the unintentional exercise of power.

This view expands the definition beyond the common assumption that being powerful means "being able to have
one's own way." But expansion poses a difficulty in that we
would not ordinarily see the production of unintended effects—especially if the effects are contrary to our intentions,
as is often the case in demonstrations of power. Some thinkers
have proposed that this difficulty may be resolved by distin-

---

a conflict of interests engendering resistance which the initiator overcomes. Benn,
"Power," in *The Encyclopedia of Philosophy*, 6:424–426.

My approach in analyzing will be to begin with this paradigm, which I find very
helpful, and show the complications that accompany its application. Benn himself
admits that not all these elements will be present in every instance of power. The
paradigm is being used primarily as a conversation partner to provide an occasion for
posing a set of questions.

[21]Russell, p. 35.

[22]Dahl, p. 214.

guishing between *power,* which includes intentionality, and *influence,* which suggests causal relationship but does not imply intentionality. We might speak in this way of the influence of weather upon mood. Or, when our children make it a point to do the exact opposite of our instructions, we may speak of influence, but not power!

Is Power Present Only When Intentions Are Being Successfully Achieved, or May We Speak of Power in Terms of Potentiality as Well as Actuality?

In Russell's definition, power is limited to "the *production* of intended effects" (italics added). But does power not also entail the *capacity* to produce intended effects? This gives the definition a future orientation. One may be said to have *now* the power to do something in the *future*. P. H. Partridge uses the example of a group plotting revolution. Before proceeding, they seek to gauge the "power" of the dictator to put down a revolution and maintain the status quo. There is also the common expression, "Wealth is power." If we were to identify power solely with the production of intended effects, without including the issue of *capacity* to produce intended effects, we would make nonsense of many of our habitual usages of the term.

Is Power a Relation? Of What Sort Is the Relation?

In pursuing this query, we make the additional distinction between *social* and *nonsocial* power. If intentionality is not a prerequisite, we may speak of nonsocial power in which the relation is between things rather than persons. Much of the natural science usage of the term refers to power of this sort—"horsepower," the force of gravity, and so forth. All of these could be included in the broader definition.[23]

When we move to consider social power, we have an extremely complex phenomenon to examine. In the sphere of human relationships, one rarely encounters a simple and straightforward example of one person exercising power over another, with the former having power and the latter not. Rather, power is relative. None has absolute power, and none is absolutely powerless. We speak comparatively, quantitatively, in terms of more and less in a given context.

---

[23]Some would argue here that what we are describing is causal relation, nothing more, and to call it "power" is anthropomorphic.

Some helpful terminology for quantifying power is in use in the social sciences. There is, for example, the notion of the *power base.* This points to the fact that power is always in reference to a structure of relationships, the persons and agencies that may confer power. We may speak of a broad or a narrow power base. *Range of influence* is another helpful concept. Here we measure power by asking, How many other persons can this individual influence?

We may also quantify in terms of *zone of acceptance.* One may have great power within a certain zone of acceptance, and little in some other zone. Parents have a high level of power within the zone of their own home and family, but cannot exercise the same power in the zone of the next-door neighbor's home and family.

Intensity of power is another means of measurement. This assesses the degree of influence on a given individual or group. A person might have ability to influence someone to do one thing but not be able to persuade the same person to do some other thing that is more extreme. One might be able to influence a friend to copy a computer program (a common though illegal practice), yet one might not be able to influence the same friend to steal a computer. That would require a higher "intensity of power."

Partridge makes an important distinction between powers as they are sanctioned and institutionalized and power as real influence. These could be otherwise termed *authority* and *power* respectively. These two may coincide, though in some instances the powers one is given by the structure of things and the power one is in fact able to wield may not be the same. More often than not, these are not identical, but one is greater or lesser than the other. For example, the traffic cop who has the authority to stop traffic is not always able to do so. On the other hand, people often acquire power that exceeds their authority. Others endow them with power beyond what is authorized and defer to their wishes in other matters. This may be termed the "halo effect."

Some analyses of power work with what is referred to as a "zero sum" concept of power—that is, the assumption that increase of power at one point in a social system implies diminution at another. It presupposes that there is a finite sum of power to be distributed and that one can increase one's power only by restricting the power of others.[24] Many challenges

---

[24]C. Wright Mills, in his book *The Power Elite* (London: Oxford University Press, 1956), adopts a "zero sum" analysis.

may be brought to bear upon this way of thinking about power.[25] Partridge points to certain concrete examples that run counter to any "zero sum" explanation. In the election of a leader, he argues, we endow the leader with power, including power over ourselves, in hopes that in doing so we may augment our power to fulfill some desire or intention. Combining forces in this way is at one and the same time a giving up and an increase of power.

Must Power Necessarily Entail a Conflict of Interests Engendering Resistance Which Is Overcome?

It would be possible to arrange the whole family of power concepts along a kind of conflict scale ranging from influence, to authority, to domination. At the far left we might place *influence* which does not presuppose serious conflict. Here the power is expressed through rational persuasion of one party by another (presumably equal parties). The influence is not so much that of the person as the persuasiveness of the argument. *Authority* we might place more toward the middle range. Here, even in the face of conflict, one party has the power (whether charismatic or institutional) to move the other party to do willingly what may not be in accord with the latter's desires or perceived interests.

Toward the far right of the continuum we might place *domination*. This assumes an unequal relation. In the presence of conflict, the stronger parties are able to force the weaker parties (by one means or another) to cooperate against their will and against their perceived interests.

One could also plot along this continuum the *methods* of persuasion and coercion. On this scale from left to right there is increasing use of coercion as well as increasing ability to resolve conflict in the direction of the powerful agent's interests. From the far left, where rational argumentation is operative, we move through various subtle and hidden psychological mechanisms and manipulations; on to the imposi-

---

[25]Bernard Loomer offers a critique of the "zero sum" analysis from a different angle. He expresses concern about how this way of thinking affects human behavior. Its effect, he says, is the perception that our struggle for greater power can be achieved only if we are able increasingly to restrict the power of others. It leads to an essentially unidirectional, unilateral understanding of power as the capacity to influence without being influenced. It is a nonmutual, nonrelational understanding, the outcome of which is negative or even destructive. The "other" comes to be viewed as a means to an end or as an obstacle to be overcome in the attainment of our ends. Loomer, pp. 12–29.

tion of increasing sanctions and penalties for noncooperation; and then to the extreme of actual physical force.

One could also plot a measure of the extent to which the patient cooperates *willingly*. Even toward the extreme right end of the spectrum, the patient may be willing, but this is in relation to certain consequences that the agent is able to bring about. One may be *willing*, at gunpoint, to turn over one's money rather than possibly forfeit one's life, but one can hardly be said to have had a choice. Stanley Benn has observed that where the method used is rational persuasion, one may see influence at work but not power, whereas, when cooperation is obtained through threats of injury, one sees power at work but not influence.

There are two presuppositions held by many who work with a conflict scale that may be called into question. First, I would question the assumption that, as we move from left to right on the conflict scale, we are moving in the direction of ever-increasing power. Would we really claim that monarchs who must use physical force to obtain the cooperation of their subjects are more powerful than those who can obtain cooperation simply by making their wishes known to the people?

Second, I would question the more basic assumption that power can be said to be operative only where conflict is overcome. This would imply that the defining character of the situation in which power is at work is that one person's or group's desires and perceived interests are forced to yield to another's. This would seem at best a serious limitation in our understanding of power. What about the power at work in an inspiring sermon that enables us to enlarge our vision of "our own best interests" to include a concern for the well-being of others and enables us to act in accord with the highest and best that is in us? This is neither against our will nor against our perceived interest (as newly defined), yet we behave differently, and perhaps radically differently, than we would have, had we not heard the sermon. Reconsidered in the light of Dahl's definition of power as "the difference in the probability of an event given certain actions by A and the probability of the event given no such actions by A,"[26] the sermon is extremely powerful.

In this section, we have considered the meaning of power from a social science perspective. Ludwig Wittgenstein's analogy of "family resemblance" has proven appropriate as we

---

[26]Dahl, p. 214.

have examined the cluster of terms that make up and relate to the larger concept of power. I have argued that no one of the features presented in these questions is common to all members of the family. The "family resemblance" is not a result of any one feature common to all expressions of power or to the presence of the entire set of features in every instance. It is due, rather, to many features that overlap and crisscross. I have sought to go father and show that the features mentioned in the questions need to be expanded in some important ways to account for the broad range of concrete instances to which we apply the term "power." The questions used have been questions with which any proposed understanding of power may be interrogated, and they will reappear as various understandings of power are assessed. They represent options to be explored and decisions to be made in setting forth what it is that we mean by power. It will be important to examine them even more closely as we apply the term "power" to God.

As we proceed to consider the treatment of divine power by various theologians, several of the discoveries made in this introduction will prove useful in providing a framework for analysis. With respect to the questions posed above, for example, most of the thinkers under consideration will work with an understanding that divine power does entail intentionality and implies a relation of a personal sort. They will differ widely, however, in their approaches to the issue of whether divine power involves a conflict of interests engendering resistance which is overcome.

In the analysis and critique of the classical model for conceiving divine power which follows, certain distortions of the ordinary usage of the term "power" will be uncovered. It will be shown, for example, that Calvin exaggerates one particular dimension of the meaning of power (active power) to the neglect of the other dimension (passive power).

PART ONE

The Classical Model

1

Calvin

The Meaning of Omnipotence for Calvin

The tradition is by no means monolithic in its answer to the question of the meaning of omnipotence. Nor is John Calvin necessarily the example par excellence of the tradition's common wisdom on the subject. Neither of these points is being presumed, nor is either a necessary prerequisite for the line of argumentation being pursued here. Nevertheless there are within the tradition shared convictions that create a certain "family resemblance" in which Calvin, in his own way, participates. At a bare minimum, these convictions include the belief that God's power is expressed in creating the world, governing it, and bringing it to its "proper end." It is assumed that God is able (has the requisite power) to realize divine purposes in world process. Given this minimal expression of the tradition's perspective, Calvin can certainly be seen to be an instance of the larger view. There is, of course, a broad range of interpretations within this very general statement. Calvin's understanding is being identified as "classic" in the sense that it is representative of a way of thinking about divine power which was both widely held and strongly influential within the broader tradition. It will be argued that this way of thinking presupposes a meaning for divine power which can be characterized as *power in the mode of domination and control.*[1]

---

[1]"To control" means "to exercise restraint upon the free action of, to hold sway over, to exercise power or authority over; to dominate, command; to hold in check, curb, restrain from action, hinder, prevent; to overpower, overmaster, overrule" (OED). While this term in itself communicates well the way in which the power here described operates, it does not, by itself, ensure that the personal nature of the exer-

It is difficult to find a thorough analysis of Calvin's thought on this matter. His friends seem only to do description, exposition, and appreciation without much analysis or critique. His foes tend to caricature his position as being deterministic, projecting an absolute power, and leaving no room for human freedom. Calvin explicitly rejects all three accusations. A careful analysis will reveal that the caricature is indeed off base, but that it is not totally without foundation. (Calvin is not so bad as he is made out to be, but neither is he "innocent on all counts.")

A Preliminary Definition

Calvin's central conviction was indeed that God is omnipotent, but this does not yet tell us how he conceived divine omnipotence. At this point we will attempt a preliminary definition which will then be elaborated and defended. For Calvin, omnipotence means *the effectual exercise of the divine personal will in accomplishing divine purposes.* It necessarily entails the ability to control events and creatures and the active use of that ability. The questions delineated in the introduction on power may be helpful in further analyzing this definition of divine power. Power, in this definition, involves intentionality. It is exercised in the context of a relationship, and the relationship is of the personal sort. Active power is given primacy in Calvin's usage. The question as to whether conflict is present is a complex one and will be addressed more fully when the relation of divine power to human freedom is taken up.[2] In Calvin's view of divine power the actions of one party do initiate the actions of another.

What is the effect of applying the qualifier "omni" to "power" when we are presented with the above definition? Simply put, the scope becomes all-inclusive and unrestricted.

---

cise of this power—a key ingredient for the tradition—will be conveyed. Therefore the term "domination," which is rooted in the Latin term *dominus* (meaning "lord" or "master"), is added. These two terms taken together are used to describe the meaning for power underlying the traditional doctrine of omnipotence. The control that divine power will be said to exercise is personal ruling and controlling by virtue of superior power.

[2]In a sense we might say that no conflict is present, for Calvin would insist that God does not use creatures contrary to their will in accomplishing divine purposes. On the other hand, Calvin believes that God controls not only the actions of creatures but also their *willing*. What sense, then, would it make to speak of an absence of conflict where conflict has never been an option?

This is the case for all the quantitative terms we mentioned (power base, range of influence, zone of acceptance, intensity of power).

A closer study of Calvin's treatment of divine power will reveal that his conception was complex, nuanced and formed by diverse influences. A first step in this exploration will entail a consideration of the legacy of the Middle Ages which Calvin inherited and in the light of which—or, to some extent, over against which—he articulated his own view. A second step will seek to elaborate the positive content of Calvin's doctrine of omnipotence. Here we will look at the images Calvin uses for God and what these images convey about the nature of divine power. Then we will turn to consider Calvin's doctrine of providence which will show where he sees divine power displayed and how he understands its mode of operation in the world.

The Legacy of the Middle Ages: Alternatives Available on Calvin's Theological Horizon

Calvin did not begin his thinking and writing about divine omnipotence in a vacuum. A whole history of debate preceded him. He was fully familiar with this legacy, and it necessarily formed the matrix for his own position. If we are to understand the why and the wherefore of his conclusions, we must know something of the issues he inherited and how they had been previously addressed.

In the medieval debate over the scope of divine power, it was widely agreed that God was omnipotent, but there was real disagreement as to what this claim covered. Of particular import for the present project is the discussion of how omnipotence could be reconciled with other divine attributes such as eternity and immutability.[3]

Divine power is disanalogous to human power not only in the greater scope and intensity usually predicated of it, but also because with it is coposited divine "eternity." This intensifies the problems omnipotence presents. For example, if God is omnipotent eternally, then the past is as open to God's intervention as the future is. The past becomes contingent. Considered from another angle, omnipotence would seem to remove all contingency from the future: If God has deter-

---

[3]For much of the analysis that follows I am indebted to the study of Tamar Rudavsky, ed., *Divine Omniscience and Omnipotence in Medieval Philosophy*.

mined from some point beyond time what will take place, then the *future* would seem to have the same kind of necessity that we think of as characterizing the past. There is no "before" and "after" in God.[4] This presented the church with the problem of how it might conform the affirmation of the omnipotence of the eternal God to undeniable intuitions of the *necessity* of the past and *contingency* of the future. It was exceedingly difficult to see how God could be present to all time as an omnipotent agent.

A second problem was raised by the copositing of divine omnipotence with divine immutability. How could the concepts of actuality and potentiality be made applicable to an omnipotence that was *immutable?* The relationship of potentiality and power to time in the Aristotelian framework made it unclear what sense, if any, could be made of power anterior to and apart from its actualization. Thomas's view of God as *actus purus* is based upon these presuppositions. There seemed to be no place for potentiality; it seemed that God did not have power to do anything that God had not in actuality already done.

The questions were indeed vexing.[5] The most satisfactory movement toward resolution of this set of perplexing problems was found in two distinct and significant steps taken in the medieval thinking about omnipotence. The first step had to do with the definition of omnipotence. Omnipotence came to be defined in terms of what is *logically possible*. The standard medieval definition of divine omnipotence was, "God can do whatever is doable."[6] This definition was intended to settle satisfactorily such issues as whether God could alter the past. The past is, by standards of logical possibility, not alterable. The second step had to do with the advancing of a distinction between God's "absolute power" and God's "ordained power." The former signified divine power in itself, and the

---

[4]The extent to which divine "eternity" underlines the discontinuity between divine and human exercise of power becomes apparent as we consider particular instances. If a human being saves someone's life and a few years later breaks both arms of that person, we may speak of two acts, one good and the other evil. If God does the same thing (from the stance of eternity), it is *one* act, that of saving-a-life-while-arm-breaking. If this act in its totality is good, God has done no wrong. Rudavsky, p. 6.

[5]For a fuller discussion of specific questions, see my paper, "Perplexing Questions of the Middle Ages" (Paper to be delivered at the Sixteenth Century Studies Conference, October 1990).

[6]Rudavsky, p. 114. This resolved questions such as the one concerning God's ability to cause the past not to have been as well as any other questions involving logical contradictions.

latter signified divine power in connection with divine willing. This distinction made a place for both potential (absolute) power and actualized (ordained) power.

Calvin was unwilling to take either of these steps. His refusal might be characterized as stemming from *the primacy of the divine will* in his thought. With regard to the first of the medieval conclusions, he insisted that omnipotence cannot be defined simply as "the ability to do that which is logically possible." It must, rather, refer to God's "ability to do whatever God wills."[7] It is the divine will that *determines* what is possible, not metaphysical necessities. Calvin was unwilling to admit metaphysical limitations to divine power. *God's personal will defines God's power.*

It is on the same basis—the primacy of the divine will— that Calvin refused the distinction between "absolute power" and "ordained power."[8] He rejected the idea of "absolute power" because it was an abstraction. One could not speak of divine power apart from divine willing. For Calvin, God's power is coterminous with God's will. The freedom (power) of that will is freedom to act *in congruency with the divine nature.* The divine will, it should be remembered, is not being understood in some abstract sense but in a *personal* mode. It is not a neutral, blind force of nature; it is a personal will, and, like the will of any person, it is, to an extent, *determined.* It has a certain character. In God's case, it has the character of goodness and justice which are part of the divine nature. As Calvin says, "It is no more necessary for him[9] to be God than for him to be good" (2.3.5).

---

[7]In this, Calvin followed Augustine (whom he frequently quoted in his arguments), who said, "For no other reason is God truly said to be omnipotent except for the reason that if God *wills* to do any thing whatever, God can do it." Rudavsky, p. 195.

[8]Duns Scotus identified *potentia ordinata* with the present order of things but insisted that some other order could just as easily be established if God willed it. The emphasis that Scotus placed upon God's ability to act outside the present order and to change the present order cast the meaning of *potentia absoluta* as a type of power that God might actually employ. William of Ockham sought to reassert the earlier ("proper") meaning of the distinction as merely two *ways of speaking* of divine power. God acts only in *potentia ordinata; potentia absoluta* is a neutral sphere of unconditioned possibility. William Courtney, "The Dialectic of Omnipotence in the High and Late Middle Ages," in Rudavsky, pp. 243–260. Calvin is rejecting both of these ways of using the distinction. His position on omnipotence is badly misrepresented when it is equated with that of Duns Scotus or William of Ockham.

[9]While Calvin might not say that God is *literally* male (if he were asked point blank), nevertheless Calvin uses masculine pronouns and images in speaking of God almost exclusively. It will be my contention that this way of thinking and speaking has fundamentally affected Calvin's doctrine of God in general and his understanding of

The difference between Calvin's viewpoint and that of thinkers who accept the distinction can be further illustrated by examination of the sense in which Calvin's God is "above the law" as compared to the sense in which the God of Duns Scotus and William of Ockham is "above the law."[10] For Duns Scotus and William of Ockham, "Nothing is of itself good or evil, the free will of God being the Sovereign arbiter of what is so."[11] Calvin would not concur with this statement. In Calvin's view, we should not say that divine will *makes* something good; rather, we should say that it *shows* something to be good. For Duns Scotus and William of Ockham, "it is good because God wills it"; for Calvin, "God wills it because it is good." While Calvin would say that God is above the law and determines the law, God is not *ex lege* ("without law"). Rather, God's will is the most perfect norm of all the laws.[12] Calvin can be seen to reject the concept of absolute power or will without hesitation. Stating his position rather strongly, he said, "What the Sorbonne doctors say, that God has an absolute power, is a diabolical blasphemy which has been invented in Hell" (Sermons on Job, 23:1–7).

Some have argued that the concept is readmitted into Calvin's system in his usage of the term "inscrutable will." This was not at all Calvin's intention. There was a significant difference between what Calvin referred to as God's "inscrutable will" and the notion of absolute will or power with which his

---

omnipotence in particular. For this reason, I have left Calvin's language (as translated) uncorrected. This will make even more obvious the extent to which Calvin's God is male and exercises "male" power. All other quotations that use masculine pronouns for God or use "man" as a generic term are left unchanged for the same purpose throughout the book.

[10]In selecting Calvin as a classic example of the tradition's understanding of omnipotence, I have not chosen to elaborate the most absolute position on divine power. Other thinkers—e.g., Duns Scotus and William of Ockham—held to more extreme definitions of omnipotence. By comparison, Calvin's can be seen to be more moderate and perhaps, as a result, more representative of the larger tradition. At a later point it will be stressed that even this more "moderate" example of the tradition's understanding of omnipotence presents insurmountable problems (i.e., in exacerbating the theodicy problem and denying real freedom in the sense of self-determination to human beings).

[11]Hunter, p. 54.

[12]Calvin comments, "To make God beyond law is to rob Him of the greatest part of His glory, for it destroys His rectitude and His righteousness. Not that God is subject to law, except insofar as He Himself is law. For such is the consent and agreement between His power and His righteousness, that nothing proceed from Him that is not considered, legitimate, and regular. . . . I detest the Doctrine . . . that invents for God an absolute power. For it is easier to dissever the light of the sun from its heat . . . than to separate God's power from His righteousness" (CEPG, p. 179).

critics frequently confuse it.[13] The modifier "inscrutable" sig-
nifies that the divine will is beyond our knowledge and understanding; there is no implication that this "hidden" will might
be something other than or contradictory to God's "revealed"
will which, as noted above, is characterized by perfect goodness and justice.

> Not, indeed, that absolute will of which the Sophists[14] babble,
> by an impious and profane distinction separating his justice
> from his power—but providence, that determinative principle
> of all things, from which flows nothing but right, although the
> reasons have been hidden from us (1.17.2).

"Inscrutable," then, is only a commentary on our limited vision and understanding, not a characteristic of the divine will.

We have so far seen what Calvin does *not* mean by "omnipotence." He does not mean simply that "God can do whatever
is doable." It is the divine will that determines what is possible, not metaphysical necessities. Calvin is unwilling to admit any metaphysical limitations to the exercise of divine
power. Calvin also rejected any definition of omnipotence
that implied "absolute power." His reason for doing so seems
to have been his concern to maintain that God's power is not
independent of God's moral character; rather, it expresses it.
Calvin's God is not a morally formless being, constituting an
irresponsible center of energizing power.[15] God's personal
will is the cause of all things and is not determined by anything outside itself. But God acts by virtue of an inner necessity, in accord with divine nature.[16] God is like a monarch
whose power is unlimited but not arbitrary or capricious.[17] In
summary, while metaphysical limitations are excluded, moral
limitations—perhaps for Calvin moral *determinations* is a better word—are admitted.

The particular problems that the Middle Ages sought to
solve by the two conclusions that Calvin rejected reassert
themselves unresolved in Calvin's doctrine of omnipotence.
When the coherency of his proposal is evaluated, we will see
significant tensions between Calvin's understanding of how
divine power operates and his affirmation of divine eternity

---

[13]Gerrish, p. 203.

[14]"Sophists" is a term Calvin uses to refer to the Scholastics in a negative manner.

[15]Hunter, p. 53.

[16]Warfield, p. 405.

[17]"For when, in The Psalms, it is said that 'he does whatever he wills,' a certain and
deliberate will is meant" (1.16.3).

and immutability. Meanwhile, we will elaborate the positive content of his definition of omnipotence.

The Personal Model for Imaging Divine Power

As a first step in this elaboration it is important to present for consideration the model that Calvin used for God and the light that this model may cast upon his meaning. Calvin's model for God was drawn from analogy with human experience. He conceived God's power and activity primarily along the lines of human agency.[18] Calvin ascribed to God intelligence, will, and power to control events in accord with purposes. God was seen as an agent in ways similar to those of a human agent.[19] Admittedly, the characteristics of human agency were infinitely enlarged when attributed to God—to the point where the limitations we experience are overcome and the differences of *degree* become differences *in kind.* "Power" becomes "omnipotence" when the limitations are removed.[20]

The model, then, that Calvin employed is a personal model. He was not interested in some abstract notion of God or in investigating the divine essence. As he saw it, they are merely toying with frigid speculations whose mind is set on the question of what God is *(quid sit deus),* when what really concerns us to know is rather what kind of person God is *(qualis sit)* and what is appropriate to God's nature (1.2.2).[21] Before looking more closely at the specific personal images Calvin employed and their implications for his understanding of what "kind of person" God is, we may want to consider briefly some of the

---

[18]In doing so, Calvin follows the tendency toward anthropomorphism which (in varying degrees of critical consciousness) is inevitable in theological reflection. In most religious myths ultimate power is personified in some way.

[19]Calvin is concerned to keep this tendency in check to some extent. He cautions, "Let not God's majesty, which is far above the perception of the eyes, be debased through unseemly representations" (1.11.12). Wherever Calvin enumerates divine attributes, these are declared to exist in an infinite mode.

[20]Gustafson, p. 189.

[21]When Calvin says that the divine attributes describe, not what God is *apud se,* but what kind of person God is *erga nos,* he is not intending to deny that these attributes are true determinations of divine nature and reveal the "kind of person God is." Calvin is refusing all a priori methods of determining the nature of God and requiring that our knowledge be formed a posteriori from revelation in scripture and divine activity. God "is" as God "seems" to us in God's dealings with us. These are true determinations and constitute the sum of our real knowledge of God, but they do not reveal the divine essence. Warfield, pp. 400–403.

assumptions that necessarily accompany the use of personal images.[22]

In his essay "Personality: Human and Divine,"[23] Hastings Rashdall examines the meaning of the term "personality" and then asks in what sense the term may be applied to individuals and to God. Briefly put, its elements are *consciousness* (not merely sensation/sensibility but thought—more like the consciousness of a human being than the consciousness of a worm); a certain *permanence* (which is requisite for both thought and connected experience); *individuality* (the ability to distinguish oneself from objects and other selves); *willing;* and *acting.*[24] All of these elements are present in Calvin's notion of God and are fundamental to his understanding of God. God is to be viewed as supremely personal. This view certainly "thickens," as Will James would say, our idea of God, in contrast to poor and "thin," though lofty, abstractions which held no interest for Calvin.

Power, when one has a personal notion of God as Calvin does, is the power of the person who exercises it. Now it remains to consider "what kind of person" God is toward us. Here Calvin draws upon metaphors from family life ("Father") and from the political arena ("Lord" or "King") to convey what God is like. With these metaphors he communicates implicitly and explicitly what he means by divine power.

Calvin's Metaphors: "Father" and "Lord"

To Calvin, true religion always involves recognition of God as both "Lord" and "Father." When he speaks of God as "Lord" (or King) he is usually emphasizing divine power in its form of sovereign governance. The response appropriate for piety in acknowledging God as "Lord" is *fear* or *reverence.* When he speaks of God as "Father," Calvin is usually emphasizing divine power as it is expressed in God's creating (being

---

[22]For a helpful discussion of personalism, see Edgar S. Brightman, *The Problem of God* (New York: Abingdon-Cokesbury Press, 1930).

[23]Rashdall, p. 370.

[24]Rashdall makes several important observations in his essay. He comments that personality is a matter of degree. Higher animals possess in some rudimentary form all the characteristics held to constitute personality. Furthermore, these characteristics vary in their degree of presence from one human being to another. Thus Socrates might be said to be more of a "person" than a savage would be. No one human being can possess all these characteristics in their fullness. If such "personality" is to be achieved, it must be achieved in a *superior* being—in God, if at all. God might then be the chief exemplification of personality.

the source of all that is) and providential caring. The responses evoked by this image are *trust* and *love*. These two images belong together. Each interprets the other. The sense of divine "fatherhood" is as fundamental to Calvin's concept of God as the sense of divine lordship and sovereignty. Of course, he throws the strongest conceivable emphasis on lordship. The sovereignty of God is the hinge of his thinking about God. But this sovereignty is ever conceived by him as the sovereignty of "God our Father." It is a "loving" sovereignty. "Lord and Father"—fatherly Sovereign or sovereign Father—that is how Calvin conceived God.[25]

For the purpose of more precise analysis we will treat the two images separately, considering first the import of Calvin's identification of God as "Father." It has been observed that "no one has ever spoken or written with more warmth of genuine feeling about the Fatherhood of God and all that it implies of love and care and compassion."[26]

There is no assumption of biological connection implied in his usage; but Calvin's frequent allusions to God as "Creator" and "Source" of all that is are central to the intention of the term and help to fill out the content of "Father." Other aspects of fatherhood, the nonphysical aspects, are even more to the point for Calvin. An idealized understanding of fatherly perfection in terms of love, protection, watchful concern, provision for our needs, and discipline exercised for our own good are the main elements that Calvin picks up on in the metaphor. These are emphasized and exaggerated.

It must be noted, however, that the metaphor is not simply a "loving relationship" term in Calvin's usage—as is so often implied in treatments of the subject—but is in fact loaded with power connotations. Three factors should be kept in mind if we are to grasp fully the "power" content conveyed in Calvin's use of the metaphor "Father": (1) The role of a father in Calvin's day and in the context of the scripture passages from which he draws the metaphor is a much more power laden role than it is in our time. This is decidedly not an "equal relations" term describing the kind of relationship we might expect to have with our fathers when we are adults, and we cannot read these associations into Calvin's meaning without distorting it. (2) Furthermore, when the metaphor is applied to God by Calvin, its content is significantly affected.

---

[25]Warfield, p. 424.
[26]Hunter, p. 49.

God is a sovereign Father upon whom we are always absolutely dependent. This is a Father from whom we never
achieve independence; our status is perpetually that of a helpless infant. (3) Last, the metaphor does not stand alone. It is
shaped by association with the political model which Calvin
also employs.[27] Standing on its own, it might have carried
more single-mindedly the commonplace associations of care,
guidance, concern, and self-sacrifice. But coming under the
influence of the metaphors of "Lord" and "King" as it does,
"Father" begins to take on more of the character of *patriarch*.
Patriarchs "rule" their children, demanding obedience and
punishing disobedience.

The metaphors of "Lord" and "King" which Calvin also
used as images for God are even more obviously "power"
metaphors. Drawn from the political realm, they signify that
God has the requisite power and authority to accomplish and
enforce the divine will.

Calvin held a high view of political authority.[28] It is difficult
to tell whether this exalted view is a "halo effect" resulting
from Calvin's conceiving God's power in these terms or
whether this way of conceiving God's power is made more
attractive because of his exalted view of political authority.
Still, it is important to note that the influences at work are not
unidirectional; they flow both ways.

Calvin's particular slant on divine sovereignty can be
fleshed out by brief consideration of the sources from which
he is drawing the political images he applies to God. In forming his concepts of "Lord" and "King," Calvin is influenced
by imperial Rome and Roman law, medieval feudalism and
monarchy as he experienced it in his own day.

Calvin interacted with and appreciated Roman law. He employed to his own purpose the definition of public power
which he found functioning there. His concept of the majesty
of God may be a theological transposition of the political concept of majesty according to Roman jurists. Herein the ruler is
above the law (*princeps legibus solutus*), because the ruler is
the law personified (*lex animata*). This is the perspective Calvin would in fact adopt in his description of the relation between God and the law, against those who would have said

---

[27]For this insight and the substance of its elaboration, I am indebted to Sallie
McFague.

[28]As Calvin says, "No one ought to doubt that civil authority is a calling, not only
holy and lawful before God, but also the most sacred and by far the most honorable of
all callings in the whole life of mortal men" (4.20.4).

that God is above the law in the sense of being without law *(ex lege)*.

There are elements of the feudal relationship between lords and vassals which are clearly inappropriate as parallels to the divine-human relationship Calvin conceives, but at important points there are parallels. Those elements which seem to have been most crucial in helping Calvin flesh out his view of divine sovereignty include the covenant relationship which existed, the vassal's state of dependency, the expectation that the lord could and would protect "his own," the obligation of service, the giving of a trust (the fief) of which the vassal was "steward" and not owner, and the injunction to fidelity. These elements, taken together and intensified to a degree appropriate to the divine-human relationship, describe well the nature of the power relation Calvin was implying in using the title "Lord" for God.

Calvin also, though less often, made use of the title "King" for God. His usage of this term, like his usage of "Lord," is shaped by its meaning in his own political context. To understand what he intends in this predication, it is important to know something of his political outlook. Calvin's views are made known in many locations, particularly in his sermons. He says, "Kings, princes, and the highest magistrates are called sons of God because God has chosen to show forth in them especially his majesty" (Sermon on 1 Samuel 10). In a sermon on Job 34:10–15, he states his view even more strongly: "Kings are the hands of God." Kings are to be obeyed even if they are wicked, for God might send a wicked king to chasten us.[29]

Calvin's aristocratic character appears at every opportunity. He is conservative in orientation, a promoter of law and order. Hierarchical rankings are ordained by God, and each person should accept his or her lot in life as being God's will. To Calvin, the crowd was naturally seditious and destitute of reason or discernment.[30]

Calvin's allusions to politics in *De Clementia* reveal him to

---

[29]It is only when a moral conflict ensues that the Christian may disobey the duly constituted authority of kings (it is questionable whether tyrants may be considered "duly constituted authority"). Calvinists later went beyond Calvin in this. Knox is thought to be the father of the Puritan doctrine of resistance to tyranny. It is Beza who most strongly advocated popular sovereignty and the deposing of tyrants. Things implicit in Calvin's teachings were made explicit by his followers who met with persecution by hostile political forces. Submission to authority was more easily preached in Geneva, where the authorities were favorably disposed. Harkness, p. 221.

[30]Wendel, p. 30.

be a champion of royal power[31]—provided it be legitimate and moderated by moral considerations—but an enemy of tyranny. "A king is he who accedes to power by legitimate means and who serves the public good while the tyrant is either a usurper or an enemy of the public good" (CO 5:90). Given this definition, there is no way God can be accused of tyranny, for God has usurped no one (there being no contenders) and, Calvin would insist, uses power for our good (even when it does not seem so from our perspective). Clearly, it is not Calvin's intention to elevate the image of a "tyrant" as a proper analogy for divine power.

Kings may allow their subjects varying degrees of self-determination. A king, for example, might make certain laws to be observed throughout the kingdom but leave enforcement to local powers and allow subjects complete freedom as long as those laws are not violated.[32] On the other hand, a king might have more direct involvement and control of subjects. As Calvin uses the metaphor, it is his intention to portray God as King directly and personally controlling and determining everything, from the greatest to the least. It is this role of "controlling" that makes God the "Ruler" of the universe. This is why Calvin rejected the view that

> concedes to God some kind of blind and ambiguous motion, while taking from him the chief thing: that he directs everything by his incomprehensible wisdom and disposes it to his own end. And so in name only, not in fact, it makes God the Ruler of the universe because it deprives him of his control (1.16.4).

The power connotations of the metaphor, then, do entail power in the mode of domination and control.

To summarize, I am not claiming here that in using "King" as a metaphor, Calvin is equating monarchy and tyranny. It is not his intention to elevate the image of a tyrant as a proper analogy for how God exercises power. God is more like the good king whose power is legitimate and "duly constituted" and who exercises power benevolently—in a fatherly manner—serving "the public good." To view Calvin's model as a tyrant model is to read into Calvin's meaning something very different from what he intended.

---

[31]Nichols, 195–215.

[32]There could be variations in freedom allowed at any of these levels (number and scope of the laws laid down, discretion allowed to local powers, autonomy of individual subjects).

More needs to be said in order to avoid this negative caricature of Calvin's political model. It should be noted that—like
the metaphor "Father"—the terms "Lord" and "King" do
not mean for Calvin what they mean for us. Because of our
democratic orientation we tend to equate kings and lords with
tyranny. Calvin's political context and the political context of
the scriptures from which he drew these metaphors would
take a different view. For example, kingship had certain appealing features that are easily forgotten in our context. A
good king brought such desirable qualities as unity, order,
justice, and protection to the people of the realm. Ancient
Israel gloried in the Davidic monarchy. The power of the king
was not something to be opposed; the more powerful the
king, the more able he was to bring unity, order, justice, and
protection—thus the mightier the better!

In applying the metaphors of "Father" and "Lord" or
"King" to God, Calvin has simply made use of the personal/
political metaphors that he finds close at hand: in scripture
and in the context of his own experience. In his use of them he
has conveyed, among other things, a certain way of conceiving
divine power. The metaphors themselves, of course, convey
much more than a set of power connotations, and the power
connotations they do carry are not fully exhausted in the notion of controlling power. Nevertheless it is arguable that
power in the mode of domination and control is a central
meaning conveyed by these metaphors and that this meaning
is problematic as a way of conceiving divine power.

The Nature and Operation of Divine Power: Calvin's Doctrine of Providence

The next step in our analysis will be to elaborate further the
positive content of Calvin's doctrine of omnipotence. Having
explored the power connotations of the images Calvin used,
we now turn to a consideration of Calvin's doctrinal expressions, specifically the doctrine of providence, as a way of describing the nature and operation of divine power.

In the Geneva Catechism (Q. 23), the question is asked, "In
what sense do you accord him the attribute 'almighty'?" The
response given is "that he has all things under his power and
hand; so that he *governs all the world by his providence*, constitutes all things by his will and rules all creatures as seems to
him good." Clearly, providence is a centerpiece in Calvin's
understanding and articulation of the meaning of divine
power. Prior to examining the doctrine itself, we need to view

providence against the backdrop of the wider display of divine power.

Where Divine Power Is Displayed

Calvin found divine power displayed in the creation, governance, and final disposition of the world. Creation *ex nihilo*[33] was very important to Calvin as evidence that God's power is effectual without the agency of any creature.[34] There is, for Calvin, a qualitative distinction between Creator and creation. That God is "Creator" and all other things "created" underlines God's self-existence and eternity[35] in contrast to the dependent being of the creature. This creative power of God is not seen as having operated in the past but no longer being operative. God's present creative activity is manifest in three ways: God sustains the created order in being (if it were not so, the creation would dissolve into nothingness), bestows on all things effective reality, and guides and disposes all things so that they may achieve the end for which they were created (1.16.3–4).

Creation and governance are inseparably joined for Calvin. It is not a matter of energy divinely bestowed from the beginning being sufficient to sustain all things. Nor is it a matter of an impersonal natural law being set in place to order all things. Calvin insists that we can only confess God as the Creator of all being if at the same time we appreciate God's power as effectively at work *in the present*.[36] The exercise of divine power in the present is thought of primarily in terms of *governance*.[37] God, we are told, sustains the world by his immense power, governs it by his wisdom, preserves it by his goodness, rules over the human race especially by his righteousness and justice, bears with it in his mercy, defends it by his protection (1.1.1). Thus divine sovereignty means power exercised in active governance of the creation both universally and in its particulars.

Finally, God's power is displayed as having a teleological

---

[33]"God by the power of his Word and Spirit created heaven and earth out of nothing" (1.14.20).

[34]Niesel, p. 63.

[35]It is necessary that he from whom everything derives its origin should himself be eternal and have the ground of his being in himself (1.5.6).

[36]Niesel, p. 70.

[37]As often as we describe God as the creator of heaven and earth, we must remember that the *government* of all things which God has created *is in God's power and control* (1.14.22).

thrust.[38] God is seen as guiding the whole process along according to the divine will, fulfilling foreordained purposes. Nothing escapes the all-encompassing divine willing and purposing, not even the smallest of matters. Calvin was fond of quoting Matt. 10:29: "Not even a little sparrow, sold for half a farthing, falls to the ground without the will of the Father (Mt. 10:29)" (CEPG, p. 163). There is no standing in the way of these purposes. In Calvin's description of God's relation to the church he remarked, "God has unlimited power to secure the existence of His church, and since He controls all creation, cannot be prevented by any resistance from fulfilling His purposes" (CO 32:184). The final accomplishing of God's will and purposes is certain; divine power cannot be frustrated.

The Values at Stake in Calvin's Doctrine of Providence

It may be that the best vantage point from which to view Calvin's concept of divine omnipotence is from the perspective of his doctrine of providence.[39] Here we see "what kind" of power is at work in the world, the scope of the power Calvin attributed to God, and how that power functions in world process. Calvin developed and expounded his particular view of providence in full awareness of the competing ideas in the philosophical context of his day. He confronted head on those ideas which he found most problematic, whether they originated in the philosophical arena (i.e., the Stoics and the Epicureans) or as alternative expressions of the Christian faith (i.e., the Libertines). In doing so Calvin fleshed out his own doctrine of providence, making very apparent what he was and was not saying about divine power in that doctrine.

One of the values that Calvin was determined to protect and promote was *the personal nature of God's exercise of power* in the world. He did not see God's power as operating immanently in neutral laws of nature set up and left to function independently. Instead, he saw direct intervention of a transcendent being whose active power continuously exerts

---

[38]There is, by God's providence, not only a continued order in creation but also an adaptation to "a definite and proper end" (1.16.7).

[39]This is the case whether we conclude, as many do, that Calvin's doctrine of providence is an a priori deduction from his concept of the sovereignty of God or whether we consider it to be derived a posteriori from Christian experience and interpretation.

itself to control and determine all things. For Calvin, "law of nature" was only a descriptive phrase connoting God's self-consistency in exercising power.[40]

Calvin was also concerned to promote *the particularity of God's care*. The scope of God's power is universal, but wherever it appears, it takes the form of particular, special care—as opposed to the form of a general ordering of things.

Calvin was eager to exclude both chance and necessity from his doctrine of providence. Here he displayed his concern for maintaining *the freedom of the divine will*. He sought a middle way between the *fortuna* of the Epicureans and the *necessitas* of the Stoics.[41] Divine power is all-inclusive, leaving nothing—not even the smallest detail—to chance. There is no necessity imposed upon God from outside that determines how God's power will manifest itself. The present section will seek to elaborate these convictions regarding divine power as demonstrated in Calvin's doctrine of providence.[42]

Calvin's Insistence Upon the Universal and Personal Particular Nature of God's Care: Chance Is Excluded

Calvin saw divine providence in three aspects of its operation: (1) universally, by ordering and conducting the natural world; (2) in the human race, by helping divine servants, punishing the wicked, and so forth; and (3) in the church, by living and reigning in the elect by the Holy Spirit. At all these levels divine providence is personally expressed and is concerned with particulars.

In Calvin's system, the scope of God's power is *universal*. God is working everywhere and always (panergism).[43] Calvin

---

[40]Calvin goes to great pains to preserve two truths he finds in scripture: God is active in nature and history and God is distinct from them both. If God is not the former, the Epicureans are right. If God is not the latter, the Stoics are right. Reardon, p. 525.

[41]Reardon, p. 525.

[42]The companion doctrine of predestination will be subsumed under this larger doctrine as one expression of it. In broad terms, providence is concerned with God's work and will in creation, while predestination is concerned with God's work and will in redemption. Calvin does not make a sharp distinction between providence and predestination. The unity of these two is analogous to the unity of God as Creator and Redeemer. Most researchers agree that Calvin's doctrine of providence is the theological basis of his doctrine of predestination. Partee, *Calvin and Classical Philosophy*, p. 145.

[43]"For he is deemed omnipotent, not because he can indeed act, yet sometimes ceases and sits in idleness, or continues by a general impulse that order of nature which he previously appointed; but because, governing heaven and earth by his prov-

also conceived of the divine power as acting continuously in nature. God's power is behind the existence and activity of all things. Nature is not to be conceived as a closed system operating independently and functioning with potencies and according to principles given it in creation.[44] God's action in the world is in no way bound by laws of nature; rather, the uniformity we perceive in nature and label as laws of nature is only God's self-consistent acting in the world. This divine self-consistency is the guarantee that the world will not lapse into chaos but will display a certain "lawfulness."

What we call a miracle is not a supernatural suspension of universal laws of nature but is only one more example of God's unceasing intervening activity.[45] Miracles are not outside the norm of God's operations. To multiply loaves and fishes is not qualitatively different from providing daily bread; it is just more calculated to strike the eye.[46]

Calvin perceives divine power to be operating universally and continuously. There is nothing outside its scope, and it is completely self-consistent, not characterized by occasional displays of power which happen in a manner qualitatively different from the usual mode of operation of divine power.

Another characteristic of God's providence that Calvin was eager to establish is its particularity. Unlike the philosophers of his day, Calvin was even more concerned with the particularity of God's care than with its universality. It is not as if God set the world in motion and now lets it run independently.[47] God governs every detail of the world's operation personally and directly. Even the course of the seasons is not automatic: "Each year, month, and day is governed by a new, a special, providence of God" (1.16.2).

Calvin went to great lengths to distinguish his position from the philosophical school that advocated a universal but "general" and "impersonal" providence. "We rightly rejected . . .

---

idence, he so regulates all things that nothing takes place without his deliberation" (1.16.3).

[44]Hunter, p. 56.

[45]Calvin finds complete continuity between what we call "miracle" and God's ordinary working in nature. In Calvin's exposition of the story of Jonah, when God stirred up a whirlwind to get Jonah cast into the sea, Calvin infers from this that no wind arises or increases except by God's command (1.16.7).

[46]Hunter, p. 57.

[47]As Calvin says, "We mean by providence not an idle observation by God in heaven of what goes on in earth, but His rule of the world which He has made, for He is not the Creator of the moment but the perpetual governor. Thus the providence we ascribe to God belongs not only to His eyes but to His hands" (CEPG, p. 42).

the opinion of those who imagine a universal providence of God, which does not stoop to the especial care of any particular creature" (1.17.6). We might be surprised to note the kinds of things Calvin attributed to God's direct determination. "Some mothers have full and abundant breasts, but others' are almost dry, as God wills to feed one more liberally, but another more meagerly" (1.16.3). In chapter 16 of Book 1, he named all the following particulars as being directly controlled and determined by God: lots, poverty and riches, the wind, the flight of birds, a branch falling from a tree, and each individual's death. Calvin conceived God's power as controlling and determining all things in a manner that is universal in scope but particular in application.

One of the chief benefits Calvin saw in this understanding of divine providence is that nothing is left to chance. Everything is "in the hands of a loving Father." In this confidence, all the faithful are to take comfort. By excluding chance, Calvin was refuting the position of the Epicureans. This philosophical school was influenced by Democritus, who held the universe to be only a purposeless interaction of atoms in an eternal, neutral world.[48] The highest good, in their view, is to seek pleasure—beyond which there is no more ultimate cosmic meaning. Calvin held this particular school of philosophy in low regard and consequently sought to underscore the difference between his view and theirs.[49] Calvin would admit that it *seems* as if some things happen by chance, but this is only because God's purpose in them is hidden from our view.[50] The upshot of Calvin's rejection of chance is that "there is no erratic power, or action, or motion in creatures, but . . . they are governed by God's secret plan in such a way that nothing happens except what is knowingly and willingly decreed by

---

[48]The Epicureans did not believe that the world is created by a god for human beings, or that it is the arena of the gods' activity, or that it has any purposeful goal (i.e., to glorify God). The gods live in perfect happiness unconcerned about human beings. Some things happen by a built-in necessity; most things happen by chance; few things are under our control.

[49]Partee, *Calvin and Classical Philosophy*, pp. 99ff. "Does nothing happen by chance, nothing by contingency? I reply: Basil the Great has truly said that 'fortune' and 'chance' are pagan terms, with whose significance the minds of the godly ought not to be occupied. For if every success is God's blessing, and calamity and adversity his curse, no place now remains in human affairs for fortune or chance" (1.16.8).

[50]"The true causes of events are hidden to us. . . . However all things may be ordained by God's purpose and sure distribution, for us they are fortuitous. . . . The order, reason, end, and necessity of those things which happen for the most part lie hidden in God's purpose, and are not apprehended by human opinion" (1.16.9).

him" (1.16.3). Herein lies comfort for believers which the Epicureans cannot share.

Calvin's Insistence Upon the Freedom of the Divine Will: Necessity Is Excluded

Just as Calvin excluded chance from his scheme, he also excluded necessity. This step may be the most important to elaborate because of the commonplace assumption that Calvin was a determinist.[51] He explicitly and vehemently denied this accusation. He saw two difficulties in the determinism of his day. First, a thoroughgoing determinism was problematic because it bound even God in its "Fate," thereby denying divine freedom. Second, determinism had the effect of denying human freedom and responsibility.

The Stoics had more in common with Calvin than did the Epicureans. Perhaps this is part of the reason that his view is more often confused with that of the Stoics. They did believe that the universe is governed by the providence of God who cares for human beings and desires our good. However, Calvin felt constrained to distinguish his position from theirs in no uncertain terms because they believed that God governs by fixed laws of nature, not by personal, particular providence. They posited a certain *necessitas* in all existence flowing from a "constant connection of causes." Their providence was contained in nature itself, and they tended to identify God with those natural processes.[52] This was the worst part of it for Calvin: that the Stoics viewed even God's causality as bound by necessity, while Calvin regarded God's free will as the "cause of causes" (3.23.8). The outcome of their program was a mechanistic cosmology that, in effect, denied both God's freedom and God's governance of all things. To Calvin's way of thinking, it was no doctrine of providence at all.

Just as Calvin in his debates with the Epicureans was willing to admit a certain sense in which there is contingency—that is, from our perspective (but not from God's) some things seem to happen by chance—so also in his debate with the

---

[51]The assumption that Calvin's position and Stoic determinism are virtually synonymous is, as Partee puts it, "not only superficial but an erroneous over-simplification of a complex issue." Partee, "Calvin and Determinism," pp. 123–128.

[52]For Calvin, providence could not be located in a temporal process, for its author was the eternal God. Calvin was later to call it an "eternal providence" because, for God, time does not exist. Calvin resolutely refuses to insert the notion of time into the notion of providence and consequently thinks in terms of "eternal decrees."

Stoics, Calvin was willing to admit a certain kind of necessity. What God wills must necessarily take place. There is necessity ("from God downward," so to speak), but it does not bind God. Things are not of themselves necessary, but they are necessary because God wills them.[53]

In Calvin's treatise "Against the Fanatic and Frantic Sect of Libertines Who Call Themselves Spirituals,"[54] he attacked determinism from another angle. Whereas, in debating the Stoic position, he was refuting a philosophical determinism that he felt compromised divine freedom (as well as God's personal/ particular providence), in his dealings with the Libertines[55] he was refuting an alternative expression of the Christian faith because he believed it compromised the freedom (and responsibility) of the human being. The Libertines believed that divine omnipotence directly determines all our actions. Evil is an illusion, since all that is, is of God. Therefore ethical questions become irrelevant.[56] The "abominable consequences" of this particular brand of determinism, according to Calvin, were that it "destroys the difference between God and the Devil," undermines conscience, and renders all moral judgment meaningless.[57]

In his "Treatise Against the Libertines," Calvin offered what is perhaps his most complete and most interesting interpretation of providence. Here he distinguishes among the

---

[53]"What God has determined must necessarily so take place, even though it is neither unconditionally, nor of its own peculiar nature, necessary. . . . Whence again we see that distinctions concerning relative necessity and absolute necessity, likewise of consequent and consequence, were not recklessly invented in schools" (1.16.9).

[54]In 1545 Calvin published this treatise which has been little noted in recent Calvin studies but was among his most successful in the sixteenth century. He was able to check the spread of this heterodox movement—which was flourishing in his day but has since slipped away into historical obscurity. As a result, the treatise itself now seems a historical curiosity. This has been a costly lack of attention, because the treatise is important for understanding Calvin's theology of divine sovereignty and human responsibility. Verhey, pp. 190–219.

[55]Verhey, p. 190.

[56]"In this they attribute no will to man, no more than if he were a stone, and they remove all discretion between good and evil, for to them no deed can be evil as long as God is its author" (TAL, ch. 13).

[57]As Calvin presents the second and third consequences, he offers what has always been the critical response to determinism, namely, we feel as if we are free and responsible. The witness of conscience is inescapable. We know of ourselves by experience that this is true. Even the pagans do. Furthermore, the Libertines themselves do not live as if there were no good or evil. They can be seen to apply moral judgments to others, just not to themselves. Calvin accuses them of being motivated by a desire to follow their appetites with impunity. TAL, ch. 15.

three aspects of the operation of providence and in each case carefully distinguishes providence from determinism.

The first aspect of providence is its universal operation in the ordering of nature. This is God's constant activity in the creation. God's action is not limited by the creation itself, but neither does it violate God's former work in creation. God "directs all creatures according to that condition and property which he gave them in forming them" (TAL, ch. 16). This universal operation does not hinder the creatures from following their own inclinations, and, for this reason, it is not deterministic. Providence is the work of God's freedom and power.[58] But, as noted elsewhere, this is not arbitrary omnipotence that may capriciously reverse the purposes established in creation. God's freedom/power is freedom/power to fulfill God's own purposes. "Such a freedom does not destroy creation, it preserves it. Such a providence does not subvert creation, it sustains it."[59]

The second aspect is God's "special providence." This is "divine ordering." It entails God's work in creatures to make them serve divine purposes, punishing wickedness, rewarding and chastising believers, and so forth. Neither good nor evil happens except by God's hand. Yet even this is not determinism. Two distinctions set it apart: (1) God does not work through human beings as if they were inanimate objects but uses them according to their nature as rational creatures and according to their willing—not against it. In this sense human beings are free agents even as God uses them to do God's bidding. (2) It cannot be said that God determines that someone will do evil. It is the intention of the heart that makes a deed "evil"; and intentions being the creature's own, they may be contrary to the divine intentions in one and the same action. God's motives and those of the wicked person are different. The wicked person is motivated by greed, ambition, envy, or cruelty and is rightly judged evil according to the affection of the heart and the goal in view. In the same act God's intentions are good because God's "motivations" and purposes are good.

The third aspect of providence is in God's governing of the faithful, living and reigning in them by the Holy Spirit. In this manner God abolishes our perversity and leads us into obedience (TAL, ch. 14). When we desire or do evil, that comes

---

[58]In this treatise, as in some other places, Calvin seems to use the terms "freedom" and "power" almost interchangeably.

[59]Verhey, p. 200.

from the corruption of our sin. When we do good, it comes from the supernatural grace of God "freeing us" in spite of our sinfulness and working in us to regenerate us. Even here God's determination of the believer is distinguished from a determinism that denies human freedom; it is, rather, a constituting of freedom. We are set free to do the good which, apart from divine grace, we could not do.

From Calvin's refutation of the determinism of the Libertines and the Stoics, it can be seen how highly he values freedom, both divine and human. The commonplace that Calvin was an absolute determinist has been challenged, and in the process a clue to understanding both divine sovereignty and human freedom has been discovered.

Freedom is a term Calvin used almost interchangeably with power. Earlier we saw that he defined omnipotence as "the effectual exercise of the divine personal will in accomplishing divine purposes." Divine freedom consists in being able to "effectually exercise the divine will" (which, as we have observed, has a certain character). Calvin had a clear idea of what he meant by freedom—a meaning somewhat different from the common view—and he applied it consistently to both divine and human. Freedom is not radical indeterminism, in which a neutral agent confronts and makes choices without rhyme or reason. It is freedom of a personal kind based upon the character of the will involved. It is the freedom to act according to that will. In God's case, that will is unqualifiedly good.[60] So also human freedom, imaging divine freedom,

> is inseparable from the establishment of one's very self. Such freedom has its genuine fruition in being established on God's own goodness. . . . God's freedom, for Calvin, is the basis of human freedom—not its contradiction.[61]

God created us as agencies and preserves that against destruction in the fall and regenerates it in us by the Holy Spirit. These insights provide a new way of viewing both divine sovereignty and human freedom. Here we see that "they are not contradictions which must be resolved in a paradox but are, like the knowledge of God and of ourselves, 'joined by many bonds.' "[62]

Thus Calvin rejected both the freedom-denying *determin-*

---

[60]Calvin would not say that God's freedom is limited by God's goodness but rather that it is constituted by and genuinely known in God's goodness. Verhey, p. 199.

[61]Verhey, p. 203.

[62]Verhey, p. 205.

ism of the Stoics and Libertines and the purpose-denying, radical *indeterminism* of the Epicureans. He sought to provide a kind of middle road up and out of the dilemma posed by two wrong theories: the theory that history is the product of sheer chance (Fortune) and the theory that history is the result of inexorable determinism (Fate).[63] His alternative was his doctrine of providence, that the world is ordered, not by chance or by necessity, but *personally,* by the constant and *particular* care of a "loving Father" who by effectual action controls and determines all things according to "his" good will.

---

[63]Partee, "Calvin and Determinism," p. 123.

2

A Critical Assessment
of Calvin's Position

Problems Inherent in Calvin's
Definition of Omnipotence

In the foregoing we have offered a preliminary statement of
the meaning of omnipotence for Calvin: "the effectual exercise of the divine personal will in accomplishing divine purposes." In seeking to understand what that definition entailed,
we considered both what Calvin was negating and what he
was affirming. We saw him rejecting the settlement of the
Middle Ages with its limitation of the scope of divine power to
that which is logically possible and its accompanying distinction between "absolute" and "ordained" power. The positive
content of Calvin's definition was fleshed out by our looking
first at the personal metaphors he used along with their power
connotations and then at Calvin's doctrine of providence
which proclaimed God's personal and particular care and the
freedom of the divine will.

The purpose of this chapter will be to expose further the
meaning for power which underlies Calvin's—and the larger
tradition's—definition of omnipotence and to show the negative consequences of attributing this kind of power to God. It
will be argued that the meaning for power presupposed here
and broadly accepted—in fact, treated as settled and therefore never reexamined—in the Christian tradition can be
summed up as "power in the mode of domination and control." The outcome is disastrous when power of this sort is
qualified by the term "omni" and then applied to God. The
negative consequences include problems of coherency and
problems of religious viability. The latter can be further specified as: (1) the severe curtailment, if not the complete denial,
of human freedom, (2) an accompanying aggravation of the

theodicy problem (making a credible "freewill defense" untenable), and (3) the promotion of oppression in the human community through the "divinizing" of power of this sort.

Power in the Mode of Domination and Control

Ruling and governing are central to Calvin's understanding of how divine power is exercised in world process. It is not enough that God be the "Maker and the Framer of the universe" (1.17.2); God must be clearly seen as its governor also. God's omnipotence is expressed primarily in the ability to rule and govern in such a way that what comes to be in world process directly corresponds with divine willing. God can and in fact does "dominate and control" all things.

This divine governance is not merely a setting of parameters and general laws in which the otherwise free and independent creation will make its way. Rather, it entails God's directly controlling everything without exception. The term "control" appears frequently in interpretive comments that Calvin makes regarding the meaning of omnipotence. In his comments upon the Stoic understanding of how God exercises power in world process, Calvin insists that in leaving out "control" the Stoics are leaving out the main thing in divine governance. Calvin rejected their view that

> concedes to God some kind of blind and ambiguous motion, while taking from him *the chief thing: that he directs everything* by his incomprehensible wisdom and disposes it to his own end. And so in name only, not in fact, it makes God the Ruler of the universe because it deprives him of his *control*. . . . What, I pray you, is it to have *control* but so to be in authority that you *rule* in a determined order those things over which you are placed? (1.16.4; italics added).

There is no hint in Calvin that this represents merely a capability in God, which God might or might not exercise. It is not the case that while God is able to dominate and control everything, God elects not to do so. We are not speaking here of latent power but of power that is actively and continuously exercised.[1] Power in this mode of operation is able to ensure

---

[1] "When the prophet speaks of the strength and power of God he does not mean power which is unemployed (*otiosam potentiam*), but that which is effectual and actual, which is actually *exerted on us* and which conducts to the end which he has begun" (Comm. Isa. 26:4).

the accomplishment of the divine purposes.[2] Whatever God wills, God can do. Nothing can obstruct God's purposes. The "purposing" of any other being is overridden.[3]

From the foregoing, we can see that God's governance is of central importance in Calvin's concept of omnipotence—as its primary expression. As he conveyed what this governance entails, "domination and control" were the substance of its meaning. The divine ruling requires the (actively exercised) ability to dominate and control the creation in such a way that world affairs (down to the minutest of details) are brought into correspondence with the divine will. The reality of this divine governance is so fundamental, not only to Calvin's concept of omnipotence but to his concept of God, that Calvin can say "If God resigns the supreme government of the world . . . he is no longer God" (Comm. Dan. 2:21).

Before launching into the problems created by such a meaning for omnipotence, we need to sound certain cautionary notes. It must be acknowledged that it was not Calvin's intention to promote "domination and control" for their own sake. Rather, this concept of power follows from certain other things he feels compelled to affirm about God. In Calvin's scheme, God must have power to dominate and control in order to achieve "the effectual exercise of the divine personal will in accomplishing divine purposes in world process" (creation, redemption, etc.).

It should also be noted that God's "domination and control" of creatures has a positive character: it is personal and particular care exercised in our behalf by a good and loving "Father." That Calvin's theology presents a *benevolent* omnipotent God is not in question in the criticisms that will follow. It is only the meaning for power underlying the term "omnipotent" that we are treating as problematic. (Domination and control exercised benevolently are still domination and control.)

Furthermore, it cannot be said that Calvin paints a picture of "domination and control" that entails an outside force violating the autonomy of independent creatures and coercing them to act against their will. In Calvin's picture, the creatures are not autonomous or independent to begin with. Rather, we are absolutely dependent upon God, who works

---

[2]"The will of God is certain, immutable and most efficacious, and . . . there [is] . . . nothing which it wills and is not able [to do]" (CEPG, p. 185).

[3]"God has unlimited power . . . and since He controls all creation, cannot be prevented by any resistance from fulfilling His purposes" (CO 32:184).

within us to bring us willingly to the fulfillment of the "true end" for which we were created.

With those cautionary notes in mind we now move to elaborate the problems created when power in the mode of domination and control is qualified by the term "omni" and then applied to God. We will deal briefly with the problem of coherency and then at greater length with the problem of religious viability.

The Problem of Coherency

Calvin's decision to reject the settlement secured by the Middle Ages, though well founded, was not without its complications, including problems of coherency. For example, because he refused to limit the scope of omnipotence to things that are logically possible, Calvin was left with the same sorts of puzzlements that caused the medieval theologians to propose that limitation in the first place. One such set of problems had to do with the relationship between omnipotence and divine eternity. If God is eternally omnipotent, then God stands in the same relation to past, present, and future; the past is as open to divine activity as are the present and the future. The past becomes contingent; God can "cause the past not to have been." It would have been easier simply to say that such divine activity would be outside the scope of the logically possible—"not that God cannot do it, but that it cannot be done."

A similar dilemma arises to call into question the coherency of Calvin's position when immutability is coposited with omnipotence. Calvin has been concerned to show the particularity of divine providence, which is presently, actively, personally, directly, determining all things in minutest detail. It is difficult to conceive how an immutable power could operate in this way. Yet Calvin took great pains to distinguish his positions from positions that would make immutable power more consistently conceivable. These positions, which Calvin repudiates, imply that God, having set things up in the beginning, now sits idly by as they run on their own, according to impersonal natural law. Yet, it is difficult to see how personal "Fatherly care" can be exercised without the kind of responsiveness that is inconceivable in conjunction with immutability. Here it would have been easier to distinguish between God's *absolute* power, which is "immutable," and God's *ordained* power, which is divine power as it actually operates in world process.

When Calvin refused the distinction between "absolute"

power and "ordained" power, as a means for making the concept of omnipotence more coherent, he was confronted with questions such as these: Does omnipotence entail that God can sin? Does it mean that God could significantly alter the created order? Can God change Godself? If one answers no, it seems that divine power is lessened. If one answers yes, other problems—the "what if" problems—confront us. Employing the distinction made it possible to answer yes and no in terms of God's absolute and ordained powers, respectively. Calvin does not have this option.

However, Calvin was not overly concerned with strictly logical problems; his interests were religious, not philosophical, in nature. Still, these problems of coherency go right to the heart of things he wanted to affirm from religious motivations. How could he give a coherent account of omnipotence exercised immutably, from eternity, in a manner that is at the same time *personal* and *particular* in orientation? Originating as they do from eternity, and being immutable (and therefore unalterable), divine determinations cannot in any way have their basis in a response to or interchange with world process.[4] There is never a capitulation on God's part or a necessary alteration of the divine will, originally differently disposed, as a result of human willing or acting. Does not the doctrine of providence that Calvin has laid out, and in which he has invested so much, chafe against the unresponsiveness we find here? Could Calvin give a coherent account of both "eternal and immutable decrees which determine all things," on the one hand, and "the attentive care of a loving Father," on the other?

Such problems cannot simply be passed over, but for the present we must be content simply to raise the questions. Other issues of coherency will arise related to the matter of religious viability, and these will receive more attention. We will question, for example, how Calvin could maintain both divine determination of all things and the reality and significance of creaturely freedom.

The Problem of Religious Viability

Denial of Genuine Freedom

Omnipotent power, when power is conceived in the mode of domination and control, seems to entail an accompanying

---

[4]Even prayer does not in any wise change the will of God or affect God's purposes but is itself instigated by God, as its answer or consequence has been eternally predetermined.

denial of genuine freedom to the creation. Calvin would not
accept this judgment. On the one hand, he held that whatever
is "had to be," and there is no escape from the chain of necessity imposed by the sovereign will of God. On the other hand,
he held that the human being is a free and responsible agent.
Calvin admitted, however, that it is impossible for the human
mind to maintain conceptually both that God is all-governing
and that the human being is free.[5] These insights "converge in
God," but in our own minds they remain a contradiction sur-
passed only in faith.

The relationship between the will of an omnipotent God
and the willing of free human beings has perplexed Christian
theologians throughout the centuries. Calvin's particular approach was to examine the meaning of freedom. He rejected
the ordinary concept of freedom as "freedom on the part of
the moral agent either to do or not to do; freedom of indeterminacy" (CEPG, p. 27). Calvin conceived of freedom (both
divine and human) as "the ability to act in accord with one's
will." Human beings have this ability, and, in this sense, are
free. The catch is that human will is determined by God.[6]
Even the divine will is not characterized by indeterminacy; it
is "determined" in the sense that it is constituted by unqualified goodness. The difference here, and it is no minor difference, is that the will of God is "internally" determined, while
the will of the human being is "externally" determined.

Calvin did not intend to deny freedom but rather to affirm
freedom as he defined it. The question is whether his definition is defensible as an account of "freedom." Can it really be
said that we are free if both our willing and our actions are
determined by God? Is this "genuine freedom"? It would
seem that if one or the other of these things (acting or willing)
were left to the control of the human being, there would be a
sphere in which we were indeed free, but Calvin insisted that
God is firmly in control of both. Concerning our acting, he

---

[5]Reardon, p. 523.

[6]Calvin is persuaded that we are only *truly* "free," in the best sense of that word,
when the will is determined by God. Freedom, for Calvin, does not mean indeterminacy but our being determined toward God. It is positive freedom to do the will of
God in obedient service. This is the understanding found in scripture, as Calvin interprets it, and he finds support for that interpretation in Augustine's treatment of the
matter. Augustine distinguished between *voluntas* ("will") and *arbitrium* ("choice").
The human being has *voluntas*, but only when the will is turned by grace to the good
can the human being make the "choice" of the good. The logical opposite of freedom, for Augustine, is not determinism but the choice of evil which results in bondage to evil.

said that God "specifically direct[s] the action of individual creatures" (1.16.4).[7]

Concerning our willing, Calvin's treatment was not entirely consistent. When seeking to make a theodicy argument, he claimed that our actions are governed by God but our motivations and intentions are our own. At other times, Calvin insisted that "the *will* not less than external works is governed by the determination of God" (CEPG X.10). "He governs the hearts of men. He bends their wills by His will either here or there" (CO 6:257).[8] Such an assertion would seem to compromise any theodicy argument grounded in the freedom of the will. Calvin's inconsistency on this point has the effect of destabilizing, or at least making less clear, Calvin's definition of freedom. In what sense can genuine freedom be said to exist if both the will and the action of human beings are determined? A freewill defense is credible only if one has a credible notion of free will.

The issue of whether Calvin was admitting genuine freedom on the part of human beings is further complicated by his conviction that divine omnipotence controls from the standpoint of eternity. This is seen particularly in his corollary concepts of foreknowledge and predestination.

With regard to foreknowledge, the Socinians had argued that, just as omnipotence can do only that which is logically possible to do, so omniscience can know only that which is logically possible to know. Future free actions are intrinsically unknowable; and what is unknowable is therefore not *fore*knowable even by God.[9] But for Calvin, divine foreknowledge is not a matter of foreknowing the actions of free beings; it is a matter of foreknowing how *God* will dispose such. That is knowledge assuredly available to God.[10] Not only are things determined by God but they are *pre*determined from beyond

---

[7]Interpreting Isa. 10:15, Calvin comments, "Justly therefore does Isaiah show that God presides over individual acts, as they call them, so as to move men, like rods, in whatever way he pleases, to guide their plans, to direct their efforts; and, in a word, to regulate their determinations, in order to inform us that everything depends upon his providence" (Comm. Isa. 10:15).

[8]Elsewhere Calvin says, "God works in the hearts of men to incline their wills just as He will, whether to good for His mercy's sake or to evil according to their merits, His judgment being sometimes open and sometimes concealed, but always just" (CEPG X.11).

[9]Danielson, pp. 66–75.

[10]God as the arbiter and governor of all things has "of his own wisdom, from the remotest eternity decreed what he would do, and now by his own power executes what he has decreed." Murray, p. 56.

time. The future is not contingent. Where, then, is the opening for freedom? Even divine freedom would seem to be limited by the noncontingency of the future.

Calvin's doctrine of predestination also represents divine decisions made from the standpoint of eternity. These decisions determine the destiny of human beings completely without reference to their acting or willing. This doctrine has the advantage of ascribing salvation totally to the grace of God, but it runs into difficulty when the "flip side" is presented. Since salvation is not grounded in the acting or willing of the human being, neither, consequently, is reprobation.[11] If it were, "the will of God would be overpowered by weak man—the weakness of man would be stronger than the strength of God, and God's omnipotence would be forfeit" (CEPG VIII.2). This doctrine seems to be more effective in protecting the omnipotence of God than it is in protecting the graciousness of God.

If we cannot simply accept at face value Calvin's definition of "freedom" as the authentic meaning of the term, we find ourselves asking fundamental questions. What does freedom entail? Almost any other definition of the term will include some degree of self-determination and autonomy. The logical consequence of defining human freedom in the way Calvin did is that all responsibility for "what is" (both the good and the evil) is placed squarely in God's court.

Aggravation of the Theodicy Problem

An unavoidable result of Calvin's conceiving power in the mode of domination and control and then attributing that kind of power (in unlimited scope) to God is the aggravation of the theodicy problem. If "whatever happens in the universe is governed by God's incomprehensible plans" (1.17.2), it would seem that God must bear responsibility for the evil that is in the world. To a great extent, Calvin was willing to accept this admission of divine responsibility for the sake of his doctrine of divine sovereignty. But while admitting that God is *responsible,* Calvin denied that God is *indictable.* He attempted a "freewill defense" which, as this section will argue, is unsuccessful precisely because, in his redefinition of freedom, he so severely curtailed—if he did not in fact deny—human freedom.

---

[11]Calvin makes the Augustinian affirmation in the negative, that those who perish are not found but *made* worthy of destruction (CEPG V.3).

Calvin's admission of divine responsibility for evil was conspicuous. He quoted Isaiah 45:7: "I, God, creating light and forming darkness, making peace and creating evil: I, God, do all these things." He spoke of God controlling the mighty powers of wickedness in history (1.5.8). This would entail divine responsibility for "moral evil" in world process. "Metaphysical evil" in the form of natural disasters[12] is also regulated by God.[13] Calvin did not take the easier path that some follow of attributing these evils either to God's "permission" or to the activity of other powers. Calvin contended that God is the "Author of all the things. . . . Nothing evil happens that he himself has not done" (1.18.3). The defense by appeal to divine permission he pronounced "a frivolous refuge."[14] Nor was he willing to attribute the presence of evil in the world to other powers. Any hint of dualism undermines both the creative glory and the sovereignty of God. In the final analysis, all the evil forces (both moral and metaphysical) that surround us serve God.

> The devil and the whole cohort of the wicked are completely restrained by God's hand as by a bridle. . . . The devil and his crew are not only fettered, but also curbed and compelled to do service. . . . Satan cannot carry out anything that he may contrive except with God's assent (1.17.11).

Another way theologians of Calvin's day tried to reconcile the omnipotence of God with the presence of evil in the world was to attribute *two contrary wills* to God, so that God was seen as decreeing some things by a secret plan that were openly forbidden by divine law. Calvin refused the assistance

---

[12]While the turbulent state of the world deprives us of judgment, God by the light of God's own right and wisdom regulates these very commotions in the most exact order and directs them to their proper end (1.17.1).

[13]Traditionally a distinction has been drawn between "moral evil" and "metaphysical evil." David Griffin's analysis is helpful in this regard. He notes that there are at least two different ways of drawing the distinction. Sometimes the distinction is based upon *agency*. In this case, "moral evil" is evil due to the misuse of freedom by a *rational* agent. Both the intentions and the effects are included in this definition of moral evil. "Metaphysical evil," on the other hand, is evil caused by *nonrational* agencies. The distinction, at other times, is drawn by taking "moral evil" to mean evil *intentions* (sin) and taking "metaphysical evil" to mean evil *effects* (suffering)—regardless of agency. In this latter case, both intrinsic and instrumental values must be considered. A given act may be intrinsically (morally) good but instrumentally evil. For purposes of this study, unless otherwise specified, the distinction is intended in the second sense. Griffin, pp. 20ff.

[14]"How foolish and frail is the support of divine justice afforded by the suggestion that evils come to be not by His will, but merely His permission" (CEPG X.11).

of this disclaimer also. God's will is one and simple[15] and appears manifold to us only because of our mental incapacity; we are unable to grasp how in diverse ways God wills and does not will something to take place (1.18.2). Calvin would talk about God's "hidden will." But this will is in no way "contrary" to God's revealed will. It is only hidden from our view.[16]

It is interesting that Calvin found in the affirmation of divine responsibility for evil a great source of comfort. The comfort, he proposed, comes from the knowledge that there is no sphere that is outside the realm of God's sovereign control. The chief outcome of this affirmation is assurance, freedom from fear. In the face of evil, whether moral or metaphysical, believers can take comfort in the knowledge that these things have no intrinsic power to harm us.[17] They are under God's command. If we suffer from them, we may take that as the strong chastisement of a "loving Father."[18]

It has been demonstrated that Calvin was willing to admit in fairly unreserved terms divine responsibility for evil. He bravely refused the refuge available in "divine permission," or in dualism, or in the argument that there are two contrary wills in God. He saw through these options to the diverse ways in which they compromise divine sovereignty. He even lauded this position as a source of real comfort for believers. In his admission of divine responsibility for evil, Calvin seems to have fully accepted the consequences of defining power as "control" and attributing this kind of power to God

---

[15]Perhaps the best example of the unity Calvin is upholding is seen in his defense of double predestination. Here in particular the divine will seemed, to some, to be divided. God's condemnation of the reprobate seems contrary to God's will made known in Jesus Christ, which wills to save and not to condemn. But Calvin maintained that the unity of the divine will is to be found in the "glory of God." God's glory is served equally well by salvation and reprobation. In the case of the first, God's grace and mercy are revealed; in the case of the second, God's justice is revealed. Both elect and reprobate stand in the same relation to the divine will.

[16]Calvin discusses God's "hidden will" in three main contexts: (1) the origin of evil (1.15.8; 3.23.4, 7, and 8), (2) God's use of the wicked (1.17.2; 1.18.3; 3.20.43), and (3) the double decree by which God withholds from some what God seems to offer to all (3.3.21; 3.22.10; 3.24.1–2, 8, and 15–17). Gerrish, p. 343.

[17]"We are superstitiously timid, I say, if whenever creatures threaten us or forcibly terrorize us we become as fearful as if they had some intrinsic power to harm us, or might wound us inadvertently, and accidentally, or there were not enough help in God against their harmful acts" (1.16.3).

[18]"In times of adversity believers comfort themselves with the solace that they suffer nothing except by God's ordinance and command, for they are under his hand" (1.16.3).

in an unqualified sense. But he was willing to do so only to a point. He admitted divine responsibility, but he then put forth various considerations calculated to provide qualifications that, while leaving God with ultimate responsibility, absolve God from guilt.[19]

Calvin's theodicy can be summed up in two main points: (1) God uses evil in the execution of good purposes. (2) The guilt for evil is to be attributed to the evil motives and intentions of human beings. After we briefly present these arguments, we will attempt to show that, as theodicies, they are unsuccessful.

Calvin's first line of defense is his insistence that God's purposes in using evil are always good and just. Evil is used as an instrument to do such things as punish the wicked[20] or correct and instruct believers. If only we could see from God's perspective or could know the final outcome of things, we would know that God has good reasons for using evil in the service of divine purposes (1.17.1). Because the divine purposes are good, God is not indictable for the instrumental use of evil.

Calvin's theodicy based upon the goodness of the divine purposes goes awry in three respects. First and most obvious, his argument is nonverifiable. The fact is, we *cannot* see things from God's perspective or know the "final outcome" of things.[21] "If only" is not a strong defense. Second, Calvin does not successfully establish or defend the goodness of God in his argument. Rather, he asserts it and takes this assertion as the point of departure and draws significant conclusions from it. The argument then is circular, arguing from God's goodness in order to establish God's goodness.

Another way in which Calvin's theodicy grounded upon the goodness of the divine purposes goes awry is in what, I will argue, amounts to equivocation regarding the meaning of goodness. A successful theodicy will give an interpretation of the three cardinal propositions that is plausible, if not demonstrably certain, and will do so in a way that also supports their

---

[19]Hunter, pp. 148–149.

[20]Against the argument that it seems the wicked prosper and the righteous suffer, Calvin offers this explanation: There is not to be a strict correspondence between the evil one does and the evil one suffers. God deals with each one personally in accord with the need for correction (which varies from one person to the next). Only God knows what is needed.

[21]Of course, Calvin does not even entertain the possibility that if we could see from God's perspective and know the final outcome, we might judge things to be otherwise.

mutual consistency.[22] But Calvin protected the omnipotence of God with apparent disregard for the interests of theodicy. When he later attempted to square the attribute of divine goodness with his primary postulate of divine sovereignty, he ended up using "goodness" in a sense not commonly attached to the term.[23] Calvin can be charged with equivocating at several points. For example, *all* events of life, including the most negative (those which we might ordinarily term "evil" happenings), were construed by Calvin to be expressions of God's goodness. We are forced to call "good" that which we experience as "evil" if we are to uphold Calvin's proposition. Furthermore, God's goodness has a direction to it that we would tend to identify as "discriminating." It is goodness directed toward the elect; what is worse, outsiders become mere instruments for the promotion of God's good purposes toward the elect. "The *goodness* of God shines forth the brighter in this, that on account of the favor He bears to one of His servants He spared not even whole nations" (Comm. Ps. 9:5). Such a statement makes it difficult to understand what exactly Calvin means by "goodness."[24] While asserting that God is good, Calvin alters the substance of the term so that God is "good" by definition only, and "God is good" is rendered devoid of content.[25]

Here Calvin seems to fall into a kind of theological voluntarism[26] that he elsewhere[27] seeks to avoid. Calvin did not wish to say that something is right because God wills it; rather, God wills it because it is right. God is not *ex lege*. Nevertheless Calvin did insist that we are not to seek for any cause beyond God's will (3.22.11). The will of God is the supreme rule of righteousness, so that everything which he wills must be held to be right by the mere fact of his willing it (3.23.2).[28] When

---

[22]Such criteria represent necessary rather than sufficient conditions for the success of a theodicy argument. Danielson, p. 9.

[23]Hunter, p. 51.

[24]Elsewhere Calvin says that "God cares for the world and for mankind in general only for the sake of that fatherly protection which He bestows upon His church" (CO 8:349). Such statements seem to so narrow the focus of God's "goodness" that it is no longer recognizable as *goodness*.

[25]Danielson, p. 8.

[26]Danielson, p. 8.

[27]See chapter 1 for the discussion of Calvin's response to the legacy of the Middle Ages. There Calvin is shown to be rejecting any notion of "absolute power" because it separates divine power from the divine goodness which is seen as constituting the divine will.

[28]It is interesting that Calvin has said elsewhere that to give one's will as the sole sufficient reason for an action is tyrannical in the case of human beings, but he denies

this is applied to particular instances, the offensiveness of what is being said confronts us. In giving an account of his doctrine of predestination, Calvin said that we must always return to the mere pleasure of the divine will, the cause of which is hidden in God (3.23.4). Nor ought it to seem absurd to say that God not only foresaw the fall of the first human beings, and in them the ruin of their posterity, but also arranged it (3.23.7). And to their posterity there is a universal call, by which God invites all alike to come to him, even those for whom God designs the call to be a savor of death, and the ground of a severer condemnation (3.24.8).

If our understanding of what is good and just and right is offended by the divine activity in relation to human beings, then, Calvin insisted, it is our standards and not God's that are in error. In this way Calvin ended up a voluntarist in practice, if not in theory.[29] Such a stance begs the theodicy question.

It would seem that Calvin's theodicy argument from the goodness of the divine purposes in using evil has failed. It has been shown above to be a nonverifiable argument, a circular argument, and an argument that involves equivocation regarding the attribute of divine goodness. If a successful theodicy argument is to be found in Calvin, it will have to be presented on other grounds.

Calvin also undertook to argue a theodicy based upon the "freewill defense." He attempted to show that culpability for evil is to be assigned to the evil motives and intentions of free human beings. The argument runs as follows: An act is, in itself, neutral; it is our intentions that make it good or evil. In one and the same action, God's participation can be good even while that of the human being is evil.[30] Our supposed freedom with respect to motivations and intentions is what makes us culpable.[31] A case in point, which Calvin used to illustrate his argument, is the Joseph story. Joseph declared to his brothers

---

that this principle can be applied to God. For us, the mere good pleasure of God is and must be an entirely sufficient reason: "He possesses by right such great power, that we ought to be content with His mere nod" (CEPG VIII.4).

[29]When asked, "Why did God do this? we must reply, Because he willed it. If one goes further and says, Why did he will this? that is asking for something greater and higher than the will of God which there cannot be" (3.23.2).

[30]"Whatever things are done wrongly and unjustly by man, these very things are the right and just works of God" (CEPG X.7).

[31]Between God's ordination and sin there stands the proximate cause of sin— human will. The intervention of this cause removes all guilt from God and leaves the human being liable with no cause to complain that God's judgment is unjust (CEPG, p. 19).

who sold him into slavery, "You meant evil against me; but God meant it for good" (Gen. 50:20).[32] This story provides an example in which both God and human beings are shown to be participants in the same act. In that act—as is the case in every such instance, Calvin would maintain—God's motives and intentions are good; only the human beings involved have evil motives and intentions. Therefore only they incur guilt; they are the ones accountable for the evil that is present in the act. This line of argumentation enables Calvin to say that "the will of God is the cause of all things that happen in the world; and yet God is not the author of evil."

> For even as the sun, when it shines upon a corpse and causes so much rot in it, does not derive any corruption from it . . . and does not by its own purity take away the stench and infection of the corpse, in the same way God, when he does his work through the wicked, does not at all justify them by the sanctity within himself, nor does the infection within them in any way contaminate him (TAL, ch. 14).

Even though God determines all human acting, human beings are shown to be indictable for evil. It is a matter of our evil intentions and motivations. We are not compelled to do evil "against our will."[33] We are accountable for the evil we do, because it is done willingly, though necessarily.[34] The intention of this line of argument is to show that while God may be seen as *responsible* for evil, since God is the author of all things, God is not *indictable* for evil.

This theodicy also runs aground. It is unsuccessful, because Calvin did not leave any space for the independent operation of the human will.[35] When Calvin wanted to argue that God is not the author of evil, he implied that the motivations and intentions of the human will are our own. However, in other places, he has made it clear that even the will of the human being is determined by God. We act in accord with our will; in that sense we do have freedom, but even our will is not our own. As he says, "God rules not only the whole fabric of the

---

[32]"For so great and boundless is his wisdom that he knows right well how to use evil instruments to do good" (1.17.5).

[33]"In this respect we should not think of any violent coercion, as though God led men into evil against their will" (CO 36:222).

[34]Danielson, p. 135.

[35]It is interesting that Arminius's ideas developed in the first place in an attempt to bring Reformation theology into line with the requirements of theodicy. Like Erasmus before him, he was concerned to make the "freewill defense" plausible. Danielson, p. 71.

world and its several parts, but also the *hearts* and even the actions of men" (CEPG X.1).[36] If God determines both human acting and human willing, it is difficult to see where any room is left for freedom (that entails any degree of independence) or the culpability that accompanies freedom (of that sort). Consequently, if there is evil, God is its author.[37]

Calvin was working from a position that we might characterize as "compatibilism," the position that freedom of the will does not preclude the external determination of the will and vice versa. His assertion that God determines the human will, yet determines it to work contingently and freely, is a case in point.[38] Here and there Calvin seemed to acknowledge the difficulty that compatibilism creates. But he was willing enough, having affirmed what he thinks must be affirmed, to attribute the complications that result to divine incomprehensibility or human incapacity. He seeks to rise above the apparent contradictions by using words like "marvelous," "ineffable," and "incomprehensible." Two examples will suffice. "In a marvelous and incomprehensible way He overrules all the impulses of men so that their free will remains intact" (CO 36:222). "Mighty therefore are the works of God and excellent in all His acts of will, so that in a marvelous and ineffable way that cannot be done without His will which is yet done contrary to His will" (CEPG IV). No matter what high-flown phrases Calvin uses to describe our present dilemma, it would seem that what we face here is a conspicuous contradiction.

Even if Calvin were able to find a convincing argument to show that these are indeed compatible, he still would not have a usable theodicy. If compatibilism is accepted, the "freewill

---

[36]Things we think of as proceeding from the will of the human being end up proceeding from God. Even such characteristics as "folly and prudence" are not *our* characteristics but "are instruments of the divine dispensation" (1.17.4).

[37]The line of argumentation pursued here might make it seem that while I delivered Calvin from determinism earlier, I did so only to return him to it here. This is not my intention. There is still a great gulf which separates what Calvinism is professing from the pure determinism of the Stoics. Calvin's position is more appropriately labeled "divine determination" than "determinism." The Stoics, on the one hand, depict God as bound up in a constant connection of causes (*necessitas*) and present the world as ruled by impersonal, fixed laws immanent in nature. Calvin, on the other hand, sees God as self-determining and ruling the world personally from a transcendent position by the free determinations of the divine will. While everything "from God downward" may be *determined*, this still is not synonymous with the *determinism* of the Stoics.

[38]We find illustrations of compatibilism in such statements as this one from the Westminster Confession (5.4): "Man therefore falls, providence so ordering, but he falls by his own fault."

defense" is radically undermined.[39] From a compatibilist position, theoretically God *could* have created a world of free
beings who always freely choose the good, or God could intervene—without compromising freedom—to prevent evil intentions from being acted upon whenever they arose.
Therefore God would be indictable for not having done so.
There is a fundamental inconsistency in Calvin's maintaining a
compatibilist framework and at the same time proposing a
freewill defense as a resolution to the theodicy problem.

Calvin's Answers to the Questions Raised

Calvin seemed convinced of his stance while he was arguing
for it, yet here and there he gave the impression of recognizing that his defenses were down or even pierced.[40] Then he
gave up on rational argument, which was his preferred approach, and made his appeals on other grounds. It is interesting, given the focus of the present project, to note the various
ways in which Calvin responded when he confronted a possible weakness in his arguments. His mode of defense provides
additional insight into his concept of divine power. It is fundamentally a call to submission before authority and before the
immensity of God's power.

In his attempts to reconcile his perception of God as all-
determining with his perception of the human being as free,
Calvin was especially hard pressed and at the same time especially obstinate. Calvin was apt to retreat behind an impregna-
ble wall of authority. He appealed to scripture, especially the
Pauline corpus, and to Augustine. He claimed—and rightfully
so—not to be entertaining novel ideas but only exposing what
is already present in Paul and Augustine. Given the scripture
principle with which Calvin was operating and his understanding of authority, he could not entertain the possibility
that Paul and Augustine might have been mistaken in their
views.

Another response was to remind the challengers of "who
we are." We are only human. Our capacity for understanding
is limited, and when we seek to understand divine omnipotence we are reaching for things beyond our ken.[41] Calvin
reminds us that our knowledge of God is fragmentary and in a

---

[40]Hunter, p. 141.
[41]"The predestination of God is indeed a labyrinth from which the mind of man can
by no means extricate itself" (Comm. Rom. 9:14).

manner exterior. We never know God in essence, only in relationship. This is a point well taken. However, it seems to be used by Calvin as license to state what is patently illogical and then appeal to faith and human incapacity (*imbecillitas*) or sluggishness (*hebetudo*) as a warrant to hold reason in submission. We are to assume that all apparent contradictions come together nicely in God's essence and all tensions are resolved behind the veil.[42] Calvin's doctrine of God, then, is "indeed a compound of very definite assertions and a pronounced agnosticism."[43]

Along these same lines of reminding us "who we are,"[44] Calvin at times simply pulled out all the stops and called names. It was a kind of defense by attack. It should be noted that this was a common approach in Calvin's day and that he was moderate in his use of this kind of defense in comparison with some of his contemporaries. Those who could not accept his strong position on the sovereignty of God, or saw it as entailing a serious theodicy problem, were called "impudent," "arrogant," "impious," and so forth. "Away," he said, "with this doglike impudence, which can indeed bark at God's justice afar off but cannot touch it."[45]

Another tack was to remind us "who God is." This seems almost in itself to be a sufficient answer to the theodicy question for Calvin (as it was for Job). God "dwells in inaccessible light," inscrutable and untouchable. The answer to the question of whether God is just is the non sequitur, "God is not subject to our judgments."[46]

At best this is a non-answer. What is demanded by the theodicy question is a moral justification. Calvin was claiming that our canons of morality cannot be applied to God. Calvin was rejecting the question by this approach—not answering it. Confronted with the question of God's justice, Calvin re-

---

[42]Hunter, p. 52.

[43]Ibid., p. 53.

[44]"O man, who art thou that repliest against God?" (CEPG III).

[45]1.17.5.

[46]Bramhall, in the Hobbes-Bramhall debates of the seventeenth century, had an appropriate answer to the tautological theodicy that justifies whatever ways one imagines to be God's ways. "It is the mode of these times to father their own fancies upon God, and when they cannot justifie them by reason, to plead His Omnipotence, or to cry, 'O altitudo,' that the wayes of God are unsearchable. If they may justifie their drowsie dreams, because God's power and dominion is absolute, much more may we reject such phantastical devises which are inconsistent with the truth, and goodness, and justice of God." Danielson, p. 137.

plied with the answer of God's "power."[47] Is it possible that Calvin is in fact applying a metaphysical solution to what is really a moral problem? God, he said, possesses such great power (*tantum potestatis*, not *talem potestatis*) as ought to content us.[48] At worst, this seems to become a "might makes right" argument. Even in Calvin's responses to the challenges and problems created by his strong view of divine sovereignty, he made appeals grounded in the very assumption in question—his dominant postulate of the sovereignty of God.

Where Calvin has no answer to "why" questions, he takes refuge in "for the glory of God." The maintenance and advancement of God's glory is the answer to all riddles.[49] We are called to humbly submit ourselves and all else to this higher good which is the divine glory. What Calvin understood by the glory of God was whatever God ultimately attains and achieves by the effectual exercise of the divine will freed from all restraints and guided by its own purposes. These purposes are incomprehensible to anyone but God and are therefore placed above question. The proper attitude is to give glory to God in the presence of all mysteries even when we see no glory in them.[50]

In this section we have sought to expose further the meaning for power that underlies Calvin's doctrine of omnipotence and to show the negative ramifications of attributing this kind of power to God in an unqualified sense. We have laid out problems related to coherency and problems related to religious viability. This strongly critical portion will need to be read through the lens of the portion that follows next in which we will explore the basis of Calvin's doctrine of omnipotence. Only with his motivations and valuations (yet to be presented) in full view can we understand why omnipotence was central for Calvin and why he held his particular view of it. Calvin's doctrine of omnipotence is not designed to answer in a distanced and objective manner the sorts of perplexing questions with which we have interrogated it. It is designed, rather, to give testimony to God, whose providential caring is personal, particular, and free (utterly gratuitous), whose purposes are

---

[47]"Will you assert that Paul is destitute of reason, because he does not drag God from His throne and set Him before you for cross-examination? . . . The holy apostle . . . restrains with fitting gravity the wild madness of those who do not shrink from impugning the justice of God. . . . To such blasphemy he opposes simply the power of God" (CEPG III).

[48]See Reid's introduction in CEPG, p. 31.

[49]Hunter, p. 58.

[50]Hunter, p. 61.

good, unswerving, and sure to be accomplished, and whose grace is invincible.

The Centrality, Basis, and Import of Divine Omnipotence in Calvin's Theology

In this section we will first simply observe the centrality of the doctrine of omnipotence for Calvin's theology. We will then seek to uncover the basis of this centrality and the reasons why his particular development of the doctrine unfolded as it did. What influences account for and give shape to Calvin's understanding of divine power? Why was it so important to Calvin to affirm omnipotence in the strong sense in which he did?

Calvin's particular meaning for omnipotence, as well as his unwavering commitment to the doctrine, was largely a function of his exalted view of the authority of scripture and his commitment to let his concept be determined by what he found there. The particular vision of God and of God's relationship with the world that Calvin found in scripture gives him warrant for his perspective on omnipotence. Nevertheless, Calvin did not simply *find* in scripture his particular perspective on omnipotence; in a sense he *brought it to* scripture. Certain religious considerations made it important to Calvin to affirm a strong doctrine of omnipotence, and the classicist worldview out of which he operated significantly shaped his way of thinking about divine power.

For Calvin, omnipotence is not one attribute alongside other attributes of God. Belief in the sovereignty of God undergirds and pervades all of Calvin's thinking and speaking about God. Nor is omnipotence some abstract principle applied to God; God *is* first and foremost the sovereign God. This sustaining conviction provides a central and unifying theme which runs throughout all Calvin's writings.[51] Calvin found in the sovereign will of God the source of all that is and the reason for all things being as they are. For him, the end of the whole creation is the recognition and adoration of the omnipotent and gracious God.[52]

The Scripture Principle: A Basis for and Corollary of Calvin's Doctrine of Omnipotence

Calvin did not construct this concept of an all-powerful God *de novo.* In his discussion of divine omnipotence, as with all

---

[51]Spykman, p. 186.
[52]Niesel, p. 64.

matters he treated, Calvin was seeking to set forth what he
found in scripture. His *Institutes of the Christian Religion* was
designed primarily to arrange the mass of biblical material
into a systematic order.[53] As Calvin himself said, "Our wisdom
ought to be nothing else than to embrace with humble teacha-
bleness . . . whatever is taught in Sacred Scripture" (1.18.4).
Scripture, for Calvin, had a certain facticity to it which made
it conceivable that he would use it in this way and which made
"speculation" in free-flown independence from scripture both
unnecessary and dangerous. Calvin's purpose, then, was not
primarily constructive or creative but interpretive. The centrality of omnipotence for his theology was a function of what
he saw in the biblical account of God. Furthermore, the particular shape his elaboration took and even the metaphors he
employed were dictated by scripture.

In the scriptures of the Old and New Testaments, certain
ways of understanding the nature of divine power are preferred to others.[54] In the picture presented there, we do not
see a neutral deity or an unconscious force that operates in
terms of immanent law. We see instead the power and might
of a personal God executing the divine will. In contrast to the
nature gods worshiped by surrounding peoples, the God of
Israel was God of history and *acted mightily in history.* Because the personalistic character of God is decisive and ab-
sorbs any underlying naturalistic elements, the predominant
feature is not simply force or power in a neutral sense but the
will which divine power executes and serves.[55] The unity of
the picture of divine power that Calvin appropriated from
scripture was that of personal power acting efficaciously in
history to fulfill the divine will.

The particular images that Calvin used to give content to
this concept of personal divine power also have their origin in
scripture. When he adopted the metaphors of God as "Father" and "Lord" or "King," he was simply incorporating the
language he found in scripture. The deity of the Pauline corpus is the lofty monarch. These personal models drawn from
family life and from the political arena are a given in scripture.

---

[53]It may safely be said that at not one point in the *Institutes* does Calvin discuss a
subject that is not explicitly derived from Holy Scripture. Forstman, p. 32.

[54]This description will of necessity be a generalization from what are, in fact, diverse perspectives within these writings. Nevertheless there is a certain unity to the
portrait painted by these different strokes. It is that unity which I am seeking to
present for purposes of this argument.

[55]Grundmann, 2:291.

Since, for Calvin, scripture was the utmost authority for theological reflection and construction, the language used there can be appropriated as fairly straightforward description—not of God's essence but of God's relationship to and mode of activity in the world.

It should be pointed out that there seems to be a kind of reciprocal influence between Calvin's doctrine of scripture and his doctrine of divine sovereignty. To illustrate, Calvin made certain assumptions regarding scripture: its divine-human nature, its unity, its clarity and sufficiency, and its self-authenticating nature. These assumptions themselves might be viewed as a direct result of Calvin's conviction of divine sovereignty.[56] The scriptures are divine in origin and there is a "principle of identity"[57] at work in them. That is, divine power ensures that there will be an identity between what God wills to communicate in these texts and what is in fact communicated. Clarity and sufficiency then follow logically.

Calvin probably subscribed to a dictation theory of inspiration, since he lived in a time when this view went unchallenged.[58] The whole of scripture, and sometimes the very words themselves, are seen by him as divinely inspired. Every part of scripture[59] carries the full weight of divine authority and validity for all times and places. There is a unity manifest that allows for synoptic viewing of Old and New Testaments (Calvin reads Christ into the Old Testament without hesitation) and enables one to "let scripture interpret scripture" whenever, because of a defect in our understanding, a passage seems unclear or seems to be in conflict with another.

On the other hand, Calvin cautioned that there are limits to what can be communicated in scripture. With respect to its ability to convey to us a knowledge of God, Calvin said scripture is like a mirror which gives a true reflection but does not impart the thing itself. Further, it is the content, not the form of scripture, that is divinely inspired.[60] Calvin was willing to admit errors in points of detail and "errors" in the personal lives of the authors that did not significantly affect the veracity

---

[56]It is interesting to note in this regard the terms that Calvin uses to talk about the witness of the Holy Spirit in scripture. They are verbs of coercive force: "The majesty of God will . . . *subdue* our bold rejection, and *compel* us to obey" (1.7.4; italics added).

[57]Farley, *Ecclesial Reflection*, p. 35.

[58]Forstman, p. 50.

[59]Farley has called this effect "leveling."

[60]Wendel, pp. 154–155.

of the teachings.[61] Perhaps the most significant restraint that Calvin placed upon literalistic use of scripture was the "principle of accommodation." The radical distinction between divine and human makes necessary a certain accommodation on the part of God in order to communicate with us at all. "For who even of slight intelligence does not understand that, as nurses commonly do with infants, God is wont in a measure to 'lisp' in speaking to us?" (1.13.1). This dynamic factor in Calvin's doctrine of scripture works against literalistic treatment and even against the granting of authority to any specific interpretation.

Given all these qualifications, literalism and verbal inerrancy are ruled out, as is any assurance that one has the definitive interpretation of a given passage. One relies upon the witness of the Holy Spirit, and competing interpretations are matters for public debate. Nevertheless, in keeping with the "logic of sovereignty" operative in Calvin's theology, the accommodation God does in order to communicate with us is *successful* accommodation. It makes possible a clear and comprehensible—though not comprehensive—knowledge of God. Our limitations do not present an insurmountable obstacle for God. By the illumining work of the Holy Spirit, our "internal teacher,"[62] God communicates to us what God wills to communicate.

Calvin's peculiar way of using the principle of accommodation is very revealing if we pay close attention to what things he took literally and what things he labeled "accommodation." When Calvin "demythologized" texts containing metaphorical language, he did so in an absolutizing direction, thereby revealing his underlying theological presuppositions.

The omnipotence and the sovereignty of God in fact function as a kind of hermeneutical principle for him, forming a dominating postulate that is largely determinative for his interpretation of scripture. Whenever an opportunity presented itself, Calvin interpreted scripture in the direction of maximizing the scope and the intensity of power to be attributed to God. It becomes clear from his exposition of certain passages that this theme is not simply something Calvin has found in scripture and consequently repeated; it is, rather, a presupposition that he brings to scripture. Many examples could be presented. Only one will be mentioned here. When Calvin

---

[61]"For we must always distinguish when we speak of the prophets and apostles, between the truth . . . which was free from every imperfection and their own persons" (Comm. Jer. 15:18).

[62]Forstman, p. 16.

reads that "God makes the winds his messengers and the flaming fire his minister, . . . makes the clouds his chariots and rides upon the wings of the wind" (Ps. 104:3–4), instead of pointing to the poetic and metaphorical character of the reference, he infers that "no wind ever arises or increases except by God's express command" (1.16.7). While the exposition could have gone in other directions, Calvin chooses to use the occasion to underline God's power which he sees as directly controlling every wind.

It is also revealing to examine Calvin's conclusions whenever he finds an apparent conflict in scripture and seeks to discover the underlying unity by "letting scripture interpret scripture." Statements that appear to limit God's power or make God responsive in any way to world process are always corrected by texts affirming divine omnipotence and immutability.[63] Correction never goes in the other direction, as it could, at least in theory. Here it becomes obvious that Calvin is attaching greater authority to certain texts than to others and interpreting scripture to agree with his most basic theological presuppositions.[64] It is ironic that with such a strong view of the authority of scripture, Calvin now and then denied outright the more obvious meanings of the particular texts.

Thus, two things become apparent: (1) Calvin's high view of the authority of scripture bound him to a perspective on divine power that we find expressed in the Old and New Testaments—that divine power is the power of a "personal" God who acts efficaciously in history to achieve divine purposes. Scripture also served as the source for the basic metaphors that Calvin used to flesh out divine power—"father" and "lord" or "king." (2) Calvin, because of his principle of accommodation, was able to exercise considerable freedom in his interpretation of the scripture upon which he relied. His presuppositions regarding divine power largely controlled his interpretations and may even have provided the rationale for the "scripture principle" itself.

---

[63]Calvin expresses concern that it seems from certain scripture passages "that the plan of God does not stand firm and sure, but is subject to change in response to the disposition of things below. . . . Hence many contend that God has not determined the affairs of men by an eternal decree." Calvin's response to this contention is to insist that such passages are to be taken figuratively. He then points to conflicting passages as stating the correct view (1.17.12).

[64]My point is not necessarily to fault Calvin for this. He is not the first or the last to treat scripture in this manner. My point is, rather, to uncover his commitment to more absolute ways of conceiving divine power as a dominating presupposition and to show the extent of its influence upon his thought.

This state of affairs leads us to ask the question, Why was divine omnipotence so important to Calvin? Calvin held an exalted view of the authority of scripture; yet in the final analysis, divine omnipotence sets the agenda for his interpretive efforts. Evidently his convictions concerning the power of God not only were based upon scripture but were in fact something Calvin brought to scripture. What were the values at stake here for Calvin? Why was his doctrine of omnipotence so central to and influential in his theology?

Piety: The Religious Considerations
That Make Omnipotence Important

In constructing his doctrine of divine omnipotence, Calvin was not concerning himself (primarily) with a systematic and logically consistent articulation of the doctrine of God. His purpose was religious—not philosophical. We do not find him adopting the stance of an impersonal inquirer doing abstract speculation. Rather, he was personally engaged in presenting, "with eloquent insistence," that which had laid hold of him.[65] His mental energy lay in his piety. He called the *Institutes* not a *summa theologiae* but a *summa pietatis*. He saw his task as that of expounding (in the language of his original title) "the whole sum of piety and whatever it is necessary to know in the doctrine of salvation."[66] If we consider what "piety" meant for Calvin, we may have some clue as to the driving force behind his insistence upon the omnipotence of God.

Piety, for Calvin, was that "reverence joined with love" which is induced by our knowing that "we owe everything to God." Consciousness of our absolute dependence upon the sovereign God is the very heart of Calvin's theology.[67] His theology was significantly shaped by the radical distinction between the Creator and the creature, between the self-existent being of God and the dependent being of the creature.[68] In fact, this distinction can be thought of as another way of stating the doctrine of the sovereignty of God—the intuition of our absolute dependence upon God has as its corollary an intuition of the absolute sovereignty of God.[69] All

---

[65]John T. McNeill in his Introduction to the 1960 edition of Calvin's *Institutes*, p. li.

[66]McNeill, p. li.

[67]Seeberg, *Textbook of the History of Doctrines.*

[68]This reformation distinction was later refined as the theological principle, *Finitum non est capax infiniti.*

[69]Leith, p. 108.

that we have and are is by the grace extended to us by this One—*sola gratia.*

The "all" may be subsumed under the gifts of our created existence and our salvation. Both these "benefits," as I will argue briefly, *require* that God be thought of as omnipotent. For God to create and to save in the way that Calvin understood *from scripture,* God must have the power requisite to do so—*omnipotent* power.

The creation story in its scriptural account presents a picture of the absolute dependence of all things upon God for existence. For this to be logically explicable, God must be omnipotent creator *ex nihilo.* God must be *omnipotent* Creator because, if there were some other power, then it would be conceivable that we might owe our existence to that power. Similarly, God must be creator *ex nihilo* because if God, in the act of creating, were only giving form to matter coeternal with God, then the fact of our material existence could not be credited to God; only the form of our existence could be credited to God. God must be omnipotent to be creator *ex nihilo.*

The second "benefit," that of salvation, seems to be even more basic as a driving force behind Calvin's doctrine of omnipotence. Ingredient in Calvin's understanding of the nature of the human being (as it is presented in scripture) is a sense of the desperateness of our fallen condition. Profoundly affected by original sin which we both inherit and perpetuate, we are "totally depraved." Our whole being is affected by our sinfulness; even our wills are in "bondage." The seriousness of our state requires a radical solution which can be wrought only by an omnipotent power. We are in no way able to save ourselves, and no one other than an omnipotent God has power sufficient to save us. Furthermore, for that salvation to be secure, there can be no competing powers at work in the world—much less equal powers—which could undermine God's salvific activity or take our salvation from us once it is given by God. The point is that God must be omnipotent to have the requisite "power to save."

If our state were not so serious, if sin affected us only superficially and not at the heart of our being (total depravity), then perhaps we could "cooperate" in our salvation. This was the perspective adopted by the Scholastics who preceded Calvin. This semi-Pelagian view held a less radical doctrine of sin and declared that salvation was dependent, at least in part, upon human efforts. Calvin was concerned that this belief compromised the gratuity of divine grace, degenerated into "works righteousness," and led to the assorted abuses in the Roman Catholic Church that he and the other Reformers vehemently protested. Thus he affirmed the Augustinian insistence that the human being is utterly helpless and wholly dependent upon divine grace.[70] "What have you that you did not first receive?" Grace is the *auxilium sine qua non* of salvation.

Calvin's concern to preserve the gratuity of grace and the invincibility of grace against our sinfulness led inevitably to an unwavering commitment to divine omnipotence. Given our state, three things are clear: the salvation we have experienced cannot be of ourselves; it can come only from One who is omnipotent—"strong to save"; and in order to be secure, it must be preserved by such a One.

The omnipotence prerequisite for both creation and redemption will necessarily be continuously applied. Having created the world *ex nihilo*, God does not then abandon it to the free play of creatures or to necessity's blind force, or to chance. God governs and controls all that thereafter happens in the creation. And so it is with salvation. It is inconceivable that God should act salvifically in Jesus Christ and then let the outcome of that action be determined by human autonomy and historical contingency. God both provides the means and determines the end—a double gratuity.[71]

Thus the origin of Calvin's unwavering conviction of divine omnipotence seems to lie in the scriptural presentation of the "benefits" we have received in creation and redemption. God's omnipotence is manifest in these benefits—neither of which would be explicable apart from the omnipotence of God. In creation and redemption we see established our absolute dependence upon an unconditionally sovereign God whose care is utterly gratuitous.[72]

Given the evidence he found in scripture, particularly in the accounts of creation and redemption, Calvin felt "under obligation to close the door to the notion that anything happens otherwise than under the control of the divine will."[73] He believed this position to be borne out both in scripture and in authoritative interpretations of scripture, such as that of Augustine. We have seen that there was a kind of reciprocal

---

[70]Augustine, *De Diversis Quaestionibus*, bk. I.

[71]Farley, p. 125.

[72]There is interplay here with basic tenets of the Reformation which were strongly influential for Calvin, namely, (1) the infinite distance between the creator and the creature (our absolute dependence), (2) *sola scriptura*, and (3) *sola gratia*.

[73]McNeill, p. lviii.

relation between Calvin's doctrine of omnipotence and the scripture principle which is both its basis and its corollary. It appears that the conviction of divine omnipotence is one that Calvin derived from scripture, on the one hand, and brought to scripture, on the other. Religious considerations further influenced Calvin to give this doctrine the place of a dominant postulate that would influence the whole of his theology.

The Classicist Worldview: The Driving Force Behind Calvin's Doctrine of Omnipotence

The previous chapter pointed to the context in which Calvin developed his doctrine of omnipotence as a shaping factor. He responded to the legacy of the Middle Ages by rejecting two moves that medieval theology made to ameliorate difficulties surrounding the concept of divine omnipotence. He rejected both the distinction between "absolute" and "ordained" power of God and the limitation of the meaning of omnipotence to "the ability to do those things which are logically possible." In his doctrine of providence, Calvin steered a middle course between the alternatives presented by the Epicureans, whose position seemed to deny purpose, and the Stoics, whose position seemed to deny divine freedom. He emphasized the universal exercise of God's personal and particular care (thereby excluding chance) and insisted upon the divine freedom in all things (thereby excluding necessity). In all these steps Calvin was formulating his own understanding of divine power in response to his theological/intellectual context and to his own concern to establish the primacy of the divine will. Calvin found a strong doctrine of omnipotence in scripture which he felt under obligation to expound, and certain religious considerations (i.e., that omnipotence is a necessary condition of the possibility of divine creating and redeeming) also made it important for Calvin to affirm a strong doctrine of omnipotence.

However, these things in themselves did not require that Calvin's way of thinking about divine power take the particular form that it in fact took—power in the mode of domination and control. It may be argued that there are certain elements in the classicist worldview that informed and set the parameters for Calvin's thinking about divine power and thereby shaped—and limited—the meaning for power that was realistically available to him. A brief review of certain elements of this worldview and particularly the doctrine of God that grew out of it may prove illuminating. This discussion will be subsumed under two overarching categories—"supernaturalism" and "perfection."

Supernaturalism

In the classical tradition, the concept of God was developed by the use of the *via negativa*. It was assumed that we cannot know God but can only know what God is not. We arrive at a concept of God by a process of denying, in succession, all the characteristics of the natural world and its effects. This perspective assumes, as the Greeks did, the unreality—and therefore the inferiority—of matter. The concept of God is formed in opposition to material nature; God is whatever material nature is not. Given this presupposition, relation with the natural world becomes problematic. Any portrayal of the historical activity of God tends to take the form of interventions that are a violation of nature. Calvin reflects this view when he insists that divine power is not to be thought of as immanent in nature, functioning through natural laws; rather, divine activity intervenes to control all things. What appears to be the outworking of natural laws is nothing more than the continuous and self-consistent operation of divine controlling power.

Another way of showing the import of supernaturalism for Calvin's unfolding concept of divine power is to examine Thomas's "five ways" that illustrate major contrasts drawn between material nature and the divine:[74]

1. Nature contains motion and is moved. Therefore there must be an "Unmoved Mover": God. This begins to set up the unidirectional flow that characterizes the exercise of divine power. God "moves" but is not "moved."

2. Nature is caused. Therefore there must be a "Causeless Cause": God. A cause is always greater than its effects and, in some sense, contains its effects within it.[75] Thus causality gains a certain priority in the doctrine of God in general and in the way divine power is to be construed in particular.

3. The world is temporal and contingent. Therefore there must be a Timeless Necessity: God. Clearly, it is difficult to conceive how an atemporal and necessary God may have real relationship with a temporal and contingent world. Perhaps the only relationship conceivable is one of divine world-

---

[74]Gunton, pp. 177–181.

[75]An analogy of proportion is being drawn here. God is, in respect to the universe, in a relation similar to that which obtains between cause and effect.

determination from outside time. This is a crucial ingredient in Calvin's understanding of divine power.

4. Nature is hierarchical in its degrees of perfection in goodness and truth. There must therefore be something that is Good and True in itself and is the epitome of perfection. This something could only be God. Of course, entities higher on the scale of being "naturally" ruled over the entities that were lower; social life and political life were structured in this way. God, as the apex of the pyramid, possessed supreme power and absolute right to reign. Thus, "ruling" comes to be regarded as a central element in the concept of God.

5. In nature there is order, and all things act for an end. Therefore there must be an "Orderer-Purposer": God. This concept gave primacy to divine control for the ordering and purposing of the natural world.

Even this cursory review of Thomas's five ways illumines some of the presuppositions and values that might have significantly shaped and limited Calvin's understanding of divine power. A kind of binary opposition is set up between the world and God, which results in many parallel oppositions: moved and mover, caused and cause, temporal and eternal, necessary and contingent, higher and lower, ruler and ruled, orderer and ordered. One side of each opposition was valued more highly and therefore ascribed to God. This valuation provided for the classicist the decisive framework for thinking about God, and this worldview substantially shaped and limited Calvin's understanding of divine power.

Perfection

The classical concept of perfection as "being complete and maximal in value" also shaped and limited Calvin's understanding of divine power. The Platonic argument held that a perfect entity could only change for the worse, which would be a defect. Therefore a perfect entity cannot change at all.[76] The doctrines of divine impassibility/immutability and independence were derived from this assumption, as was the conviction that God is *actus purus*. Denial of any of these conclusions admits the possibility of change in God and therefore "imperfection." These conclusions will only allow for a unidirectional flow of power. There are only active/causative dimensions to divine power; there are no passive/receptive

---

[76]Gunton, p. 3.

dimensions. The only option available to Calvin, as he worked out of this framework for thinking about "perfect" power, was unilateral divine determination of the world.

Conclusion

Thus the metaphysical presuppositions of the classicist worldview that Calvin accepted probably made it inevitable that he would think of God's power as controlling and determining. Through unilateral divine determination, God universally and in all particulars brings world process into conformity with divine willing. But given Calvin's priorities, such a view is problematic.

Such a doctrine makes difficult any concept of genuine *relationship* between God and the world—which in the ordinary meaning of the word would entail mutuality and reciprocity. In the classicist worldview this might not have been considered a serious deficiency, because in substance metaphysics reality is conceived in terms of substance rather than relations. But it becomes a serious deficiency when religious viability of the God concept is a consideration.

At one level, Calvin seems to adopt the classicist worldview wholeheartedly. He adopted supernaturalism as well as the classical understanding of divine perfection and did not anywhere formally dispute the logical conclusions of the accompanying presuppositions. At another level, however, he apparently recognized the inadequacy of this worldview and tried to make up for its deficiencies. Many of Calvin's theological affirmations presuppose a genuine relation between God and the world. He deals with this difficulty by "grafting onto" the classicist doctrine of God personal metaphors that enable him to speak in relational terms. The personal metaphors, however, cannot be coherently incorporated into the classicist worldview. Calvin's understanding of divine omnipotence seems to rely more heavily upon the classicist worldview than upon the personal metaphors which could have qualified the more extreme claims he ends up making. For instance, in human examples of "lord" or "king" and "father" we never find the kind of all-controlling power that Calvin ascribes to God.

The incipient breakdown of the classicist worldview, of which Calvin is one of the last good examples, may in itself have affected Calvin's presentation of the doctrine of omnipotence. Precisely because he was aware of the threats to this worldview, he may have buttressed his treatment of divine omnipotence. His is more elaborate and uncompromising than many. When one's worldview is crumbling, there is all the more need to affirm—and rely upon—God's being "in control."

The modern/postmodern world has rejected many elements ingredient to the classicist worldview that shaped and limited Calvin's doctrine of omnipotence: the scripture principle, the prescientific notion of divine intervention in world process, substance metaphysics, the hierarchy of being, predemocratic political theory, and so forth. These operative assumptions no longer prove persuasive for modern people. The dramatic changes in outlook (religious, philosophical, political), in addition to the previously explored problems of coherency and religious viability, urge us toward a reconsideration of the classical understanding of divine power. In Parts Two and Three we will look at certain attempts at reconstruction. We will consider carefully whether a simple modification of the classical model is what is needed or whether the problems presented require a more radical reassessment.

PART TWO

Modifications

3

Barth's Understanding of Divine Power

In the twentieth century we continue to struggle with the problem of omnipotence as bequeathed to us by classical theism. Some thinkers have attempted to ameliorate the difficulties surrounding human freedom and the theodicy question by introducing modifications in the scope of power that is attributed to God. In Part Two, I will present and explore one such attempt, that of Karl Barth.[1] I will argue that, although Barth does make efforts in the direction of modifying the *scope* of divine power, he leaves the *meaning* for power underlying the term "omnipotence" unaltered. Power is still being conceived as the ability to dominate and control. As a result, the fundamental difficulties that attend the doctrine of omnipotence remain in place. Furthermore, it appears that Barth himself does not consistently follow through on his own proposal and thus may not even succeed in significantly modifying the *scope* of the term. In Part Three, I will argue that other, more radical, alternatives that address themselves to the question of the *meaning* of power merit our consideration.

Before discussing Barth's modifications, we need to have

---

[1]There are several contemporary thinkers who are attempting to ameliorate the difficulties of the classical model while still working within it. It is beyond the scope of this book to consider them all. Barth is chosen as a representative example. This selection is made, at least in part, because of Barth's thoroughgoing treatment of divine power and related issues. There is an advantage also in being able to see how his modifications work themselves out in a full-blown systematic theology. It is worth noting, however, that some other thinkers have taken an important step that Barth did not—that is, the straightforward acceptance of the limitations imposed by logical possibility. To see the difference this step makes, the reader might refer to Austin Farrer's *Love Almighty and Ills Unlimited* (Garden City, N.Y.: Doubleday & Co., 1961) and Alvin Plantinga's *God, Freedom, and Evil* (Grand Rapids: Wm. B. Eerdmans Publishing Co., 1978). In my assessment, this step has some clear advantages, but—because it amounts to a limitation of scope and does not join the question of meaning—it does not finally enable these thinkers to avoid the pitfalls of the classical model.

some understanding of how he thinks knowledge of God is to be obtained. His basic presuppositions will set the framework for the discussions of omnipotence and will in themselves illustrate Barth's perspective on the way divine power operates.

For Barth,[2] all knowledge of God has its foundation in and derives from one and only one source—God's revelation of Godself in Jesus Christ. This point of departure determines everything that we can and must say about God. Barth does not attempt to substantiate this claim but takes it to be axiomatic. Ordinary criteria for human knowledge need not be applied. The canons of reason may be suspended. The validity of claims based upon divine revelation rests upon a divine guarantee of truthfulness.

Jesus Christ is more than a vehicle of divine self-revelation; he is in fact to be *identified* with God (I/1, p. 563). There is no other hidden or unknown God behind the God we encounter in Jesus Christ. However, in the act of self-revelation, God maintains control as "Lord" of both the *content* of the knowledge and the *process* of knowing. While Barth insists that it is really God who is known in revelation, he is not collapsing divine essence with divine self-revelation. To do so would be to make self-revelation necessary and Barth seeks to preserve divine freedom in this act.[3] God remains "Subject" and "Lord" even as the "Object" of human knowing. Divine control is further shown in that God both elicits and determines the human response to revelation (I/1, p. 516).

Barth rejects natural theology and any other position that implies that knowledge of God is a public and universally available possibility. The human being has no innate capacity to encounter and know God. God makes Godself known as "One who is utterly unknowable" in relation to any innate human capacity. Anything that human beings can know—and hence control—such as the concept of the Absolute or the concept of a Supreme Being, is not this God but an idol.

This presupposition is further illustrated by Barth's position regarding analogy. He holds that we cannot learn about God through analogy (*analogia entis*). The one exception—the analogy of faith (*analogia fidei*) is made possible only by divine

---

[2]In this analysis of Barth, I am indebted to the work of Sheila Greeve Davaney in her recent book *Divine Power: A Study of Karl Barth and Charles Hartshorne*. Direct quotations are footnoted.

[3]"God gives Himself to man entirely in His revelation. But not in such a way as to give Himself a prisoner to man. He remains free, in operating, in giving Himself" (I/1, p. 426).

action and can be appropriated only in relation to Jesus Christ. It is manifestly not a human capacity but a divine gift. It is never under our control but always under God's control. Barth will grant that human concepts and ideas must be used to think and speak of God. He would only insist that if words convey knowledge of God, it is not because they reflect divine reality but because God is Lord of words too.

In summary, we find in Barth a great emphasis upon divine control of the event of revelation—its occurrence, its content, and its reception. Furthermore, as we explore Barth's doctrine of omnipotence we will find that it is already prefigured in his doctrine of revelation. Barth's preoccupation with divine control will be even more obvious in his explicit treatment of omnipotence.

Since the matter of divine power is an all-pervasive presence in Barth's thought, we cannot examine every point where power is relevant. In this chapter, we will consider the points where Barth most clearly addresses the extent and character of divine power and the points where the problems of coherency and religious viability arise. In some instances we will draw upon Barth's explicit and formal analysis; in other instances we will draw upon his concrete illustration and application. We will begin with a discussion of the particular understanding of omnipotence that Barth advocates. As this understanding is analyzed it will become obvious that the fundamental meaning for power being presupposed by Barth's doctrine of omnipotence is "power in the mode of domination and control." We will look at some points of similarity and difference in Barth's position and Calvin's. Barth introduced two significant modifications of the traditional doctrine—one based upon the concept of divine self-limitation and the other based upon Barth's christological orientation. We will explore and evaluate these using coherency and religious viability as criteria. I will argue that because these modifications only address matters of scope without altering the underlying meaning, fundamental problems remain. The problems are compounded by Barth's apparent failure to follow through consistently with these modifications he proposed.

Barth's Treatment of the Meaning of Omnipotence

Barth's formal treatment of the meaning of omnipotence[4] comes in his discussion of divine perfections. Here Barth

---

[4]Barth uses a variety of terms that are all translated "power" in the English edition. They include *die Macht, die Kraft, die Gewalt, das Vermögen,* and *die Potenz.* The

seems concerned to protect two values: (1) the unity and independence of the divine being and (2) the *literal* rendering of these perfections. (They are not just metaphorical ways of speaking of God; they are real descriptions. God does not somehow exist behind them in utter simplicity.)

As with all other divine perfections, the descriptor *omnipotence*, for Barth, only restates what has been revealed in Jesus Christ, that God is "the One who loves in freedom" (II/1, p. 519). It does not add anything new but says the same thing in other words. Barth divides his discussion of the divine perfections between "perfections of love" and "perfections of freedom." The division, however, is only for purposes of discussion. Divine love and freedom presuppose and imply each other. God's freedom is loving, and God's loving is free. In this way the unity of the divine being is preserved. Nevertheless the location Barth chooses for omnipotence—under the rubric of perfections of freedom rather than perfections of love—does not seem to be merely arbitrary. At times freedom and power seem almost to be interchangeable terms for Barth. Much of what Barth says concerning power is repeated in his position on freedom.[5] At some points he even seems to reverse things and make freedom a subset of power.[6] Furthermore, freedom in God's case is never understood as empty freedom but always as efficacious, as able to effect its will.

Barth's location of the discussion of omnipotence under the perfections of freedom rather than the perfections of love proves significant in yet another way. His unfolding development of the doctrine seems more concerned with illustrating divine freedom than with illustrating divine love. The all-determining notion of power which Barth in fact develops demonstrates divine freedom well enough but sometimes makes divine love and even the possibility of genuine divine relationship with a real "other" more difficult to conceive. He does not seem to allow "love" to shape, define, and constitute what power means in the same way that "freedom" shapes, defines, and constitutes the meaning. When it comes to om-

---

term that Barth uses most frequently and almost exclusively in his formal analysis is *die Macht* which carries the sense not only of "strength" or "force" but also of "authority." Barth's term for omnipotence is almost always *die Allmacht*. When referring to nondivine power, Barth fluctuates between *die Macht* and *die Kraft* and uses other terms on occasion. Davaney, p. 29.

[5]"Thus God's power might also be described as God's freedom" (DO, p. 47).

[6]"Freedom means ability, possibility, power—power in its illimitability or its equality over against other powers" (I/2, p. 674).

nipotence, Barth's use of the phrase "the One who loves in freedom" stresses "freedom" more than "love."

Barth prefers to speak in terms of divine "perfections" rather than divine "attributes" because the latter implies qualities, characteristics, or capacities that are shared with others. Barth maintains that the perfections are God's alone in a singular and unique fashion. These perfections can be applied to other realities only in a derived and relative fashion. God not only *has* power, God *is* power, while everything else only has power (and has it only from God). For Barth, omnipotence is a term that applies to God in a literal, not a metaphorical, sense.

By way of delimiting his definition of omnipotence, Barth makes five important denials. Several of these denials limit the scope of power ascribed to God and the horizon in which "omnipotence" can be appropriately applied.

Barth denies that any neutral or abstract concept of omnipotence can be applied to God. It is not proper to begin with some general notion of what power is and then apply it to God in a preeminent sense. It is the divine Subject who must define the content and meaning of the predicate, and not vice versa. As a corollary of this conviction, Barth refuses to define God's omnipotence as "power itself."

Barth also denies that divine omnipotence is merely the power of might or physical force (*potentia*). It is always also *potestas*, which has the character of rightful, legitimate power, "authority." God's power is always both mighty and righteous.[7]

Barth denies that omnipotence is exhausted in omnicausality. Of course, there is no *other* independent power at work in the world—in that sense, God's power is omnicausal. But God's power is not to be understood solely in terms of God's activity within the world (II/1, pp. 526–528), nor is it to be identified and confused with the natural workings of the universe. The world would then become a prerequisite of God's omnipotence—a relationship of dependence that Barth finds unacceptable.

Barth straightforwardly denies that omnipotence implies

---

[7]"The power of God is never to be understood as simply a physical possibility, a *potentia*. It must be understood at the same time as a moral and legal possibility, a *potestas*. God's might never at any place precedes right, but is always and everywhere associated with it. . . . It is in itself and from the beginning legitimate power, the power of . . . holiness, righteousness, and wisdom. . . . What God is able to do *de facto*, He is also able to do *de jure*, and He can do nothing *de facto* that He cannot also do *de jure*" (II/1, p. 526).

unlimited power. God does not have the power to do everything but only those things which confirm and manifest divine
being (II/1, p. 522). In this sense, divine power is self-limiting. However, there are no external limitations upon divine
power.[8]

Last, Barth denies that omnipotence means that there are
no other powers than God. There are other powers, but these
have their basis and limit in God, who controls and determines
them. Their power is derived, not intrinsic.[9] Only God has
intrinsic power.[10] God is not to be thought of as the highest
power in a series of powers.[11]

We might summarize these five denials positively in two
affirmations of divine capacity that Barth finds implied in
omnipotence. Barth has described power in two ways: (1) As
God's power in relation to Godself, omnipotence is divine
self-determination and the capacity for God to be Godself.
Definitions based upon some abstract notion of power applied to God in a preeminent sense are excluded. Omnipotence either as unlimited power or as *potentia* apart from
potestas is thereby repudiated. (2) As power in relation to
the world, omnipotence entails but is not exhausted in omnicausality. It includes the capacity for *world-determination*,
the ability completely to determine all realities that are distinct (but not independent) from Godself.[12]

Having delimited his definition for omnipotence by these
five denials, Barth unfolds the positive content of his doctrine of omnipotence. In God's self-revelation in Jesus
Christ, God is encountered as a personal being who is *conscious* and *purposive*. For this reason, omnipotence must be
conceived and discussed in terms of the divine *knowing*
and *willing* (II/1, p. 543). In doing so, Barth is claiming
that this is omnipotent knowing (omniscience) and omnip-

---

[8]"God's will . . . is not conditioned from outside itself, by another. . . . Always and
everywhere His will is operative, and it is only conditioned and limited by itself, and
in this sovereignty it is the determination and delimitation of all things and all occurrence" (II/1, p. 596).

[9]Barth is claiming two things that seem to be in tension if not in direct contradiction with each other. On the one hand, he claims the reality of other powers. On the
other hand, he claims their complete determination by God.

[10]"God and God alone has real power, all the real power" (II/1, p. 531).

[11]"He is the Lord of all lords, the King of all kings. So that all these powers . . . are
a priori laid at the feet of the power of God" (DO, p. 47). The place of each of these
powers is the place that God chooses to give them.

[12]Davaney, p. 37.

otent willing (omnivolence[13]), but it really is knowing and willing.[14]

The relation of divine knowing and divine power is best illustrated in Barth's treatment of foreknowledge and omniscience.[15] God knows everything *as it is* and "in exactly the sense proper to it" (II/1, p. 553). Divine foreknowledge has absolute priority and is independent ontologically and is therefore not tied to the distinctions of past, present, and future. As knower, God is not passive but entirely active and is in no way dependent upon or determined by that which is known. "It is not that God knows everything because it is, but that it is because He knows it" (II/1, p. 559). Because divine knowledge is coextensive with the divine will, it is causative knowledge. Similarly, divine will has absolute priority and independence. God's will is definitive, embracing and determining all reality. It is a specific concrete will, never simply general.

Barth's central conviction is clear: divine knowledge and will, which are the positive content of divine power, are to be interpreted as independent, unconditioned, and causative in nature. They are never even partly determined by, dependent upon, or responsive to their objects. The repercussions of this assessment will be seen to be far-reaching.[16]

Omnipotence entails "the effectual exercise of the divine personal will in accomplishing divine purposes,"[17] for Barth.[18] Underlying this definition, as we have argued, is a concept of power as "domination and control." World process is seen as controlled by this personal will unilaterally.

---

[13]"Rightly understood it is as right and necessary to speak of God's 'omnivolence'—His willing all things—as of His omnipotence. For God's will also, being omnipotent will, is in its sphere a complete and exhaustive will, embracing and controlling not only being which has no will but all other wills" (II/1, p. 555).

[14]Because God's knowledge and will are seen as coextensive (each is Godself and each is the other), Barth is able to maintain the unity of God's being. At the same time, these are to be interpreted in a literal and radically personal sense. They are not "to be understood only as figurative; . . . to be expunged from the divine essence as anthropomorphisms in favour of a higher third thing which as such is neither real knowledge nor real will" (II/1, p. 551).

[15]Davaney, p. 39.

[16]Davaney, p. 48.

[17]It is essential to the very definition of deity that God's power not be limited/conditioned by anything outside itself and that it be absolutely efficacious. "The power with which He wills is omnipotent or unlimited power over everything" (II/1, p. 601).

[18]In Barth's definition we have an echo of the meaning for omnipotence that we found in Calvin's definition.

This necessity by which everything that happens must do so in accordance with the divine will and decree is not a *necessitas coactionis*. It is a *necessitas immutabilitatis,* the necessity in virtue of which everything in its final result must correspond in all circumstances to the one unalterable divine will. . . . A sovereign power is put forth which everything obeys and nothing can withstand (II/1, pp. 519, 601).

Barth rejects any distinction between *voluntas efficax* and *voluntas inefficax.*

On the contrary, whatever God wills also comes about. . . . In whatever happens, it is always His will that is active, and never finally and properly another will independent of His, effectively resisting it and capable of opposition to it. Always and everywhere His will is operative, and it is only conditioned and limited by itself, and in this sovereignty it is the determination and delimitation of all things and all occurrence (II/1, p. 596).

Barth holds a strong conviction of the centrality of omnipotence to our concept of God. He observes that the earliest creeds thought it sufficient to ascribe only this one attribute to God. "*Credo in Deum patrem omnipotentem.* . . . Clearly they saw in this attribute that which embraced all the others; what might be called a compendium of them" (II/1, p. 522).

The Operation of Divine Power: Barth's Doctrine of Providence

Barth's discussion of providence includes a helpful explication of the way in which divine power operates.[19] He sees creaturely happenings as completely subject to the direction of God which is personal, conscious, and purposive. Divine power is universal in its scope and particular in its operation.[20]

Barth discusses three aspects of providence: divine preserving, accompanying, and ruling of creaturely reality.[21] Divine *preservation* is necessary because God has not created a reality distinct from God and now self-sufficient. Without God's

---

[19]In his doctrine of providence as well we see that Barth has close kinship with Calvin.

[20]"Whatever occurs . . . will take place not only . . . under a kind of oversight and final disposal of God, and not only generally in His direct presence, but concretely, in virtue of His directly effective will" (III/3, p. 13).

[21]This brief treatment is aided by the helpful summary of Barth's doctrine of providence found in Davaney, pp. 85–90.

preservation, nothingness (*das Nichtige*) would quickly overwhelm and destroy all creaturely reality. In a sense, *das Nichtige*, the rejected possibility, is coeternal with God. This explains why God must exercise power in creation and then must constantly do so. This preservation is not owed to the creature but has its basis in God's gracious determination to be faithful to and stand by God's decision for the creature.

Divine *accompanying* is God's action that precedes, goes along with, and follows after human activity. Divine "preceding" is not merely a setting of parameters or envisioning of possibilities among which the creature will then choose. It is not merely ability to predict choices of free creatures; it is, rather, absolute determination (III/3, p. 120). The divine action "goes along with" human acts, not as a catalyst eliciting response, but as first cause. Divine and human action coincide; they are "a single action" (III/3, p. 136). But in that coincidence there is always a definite order (superior/inferior) which can never be reversed.[22]

In discussing the divine *ruling*, Barth speaks of the "fatherly lordship of God over all His creatures" (III/3, p. 154).[23] This discussion presupposes preserving and accompanying activity but emphasizes the purposeful nature of divine determination. Providence is manifest as divine world governance controlling and ordering world occurrence in accord with the divine will. God is sovereign. God's "power is royal power. God does not merely control. He rules, rules as a King rules, rules as He alone, the true King, rules and can rule" (III/3, p. 157).

Barth's doctrine of providence in its three forms of preserving, accompanying, and ruling emphasizes divine power in a dominating and controlling mode. For Barth, this is its method of operation as well as its essential meaning.

Barth's Response to the Legacy of the Middle Ages

Barth takes an interesting approach to the issues surrounding what we earlier identified as Calvin's two "negative moves," in which Calvin rejected the settlement achieved by the medieval theologians on the problem of omnipotence.[24] While Barth's

---

[22]In this it would seem that creaturely activity is robbed of any lasting significance.

[23]Here Barth is employing the metaphors that Calvin used and with much the same meaning.

[24]In their struggles to achieve a more coherent and religiously viable doctrine of omnipotence, they had limited the scope of omnipotence in two ways: (1) by limiting

position is not a wholehearted endorsement of the medieval resolution, his response to its proposals diverges significantly from Calvin's.

Barth seems at first to be accepting the Thomist definition of omnipotence, in which God can do everything that is logically possible and not self-contradictory. However, Barth goes on to insist that God is the substance and determiner of what is possible.[25]

Barth does in fact accept the medieval distinction between absolute and ordained power.[26] He makes use of the distinction as he finds it in Thomas, where

> *potentia absoluta* is the power of God to do that which he can choose to do, but does not have to, and does not actually choose and do. *Potentia ordinata* on the other hand is the power of God which God does actually use and exercise.[27]

For Barth, to abandon the distinction between what God can do and what God does do denies God's freedom in acting. God's power is thereby reduced to omnicausality and identified with worldly reality. Barth insists that God's power is not to be seen as "dissolved and disappearing" in God's actual willing and acting. There is a divine Subject behind the action and apart from any activity in the world.[28]

---

the range of activities possible for omnipotence to the set of those things which are *logically* possible, and (2) by drawing a distinction between God's "absolute" power and "ordained" power. Calvin refused both of these moves.

[25]"God is able, able to do everything; everything, that is, which as His possibility is real possibility" (II/1, p. 522). "It is He and He alone who controls and decides what manifests Him and is therefore possible, and what contradicts Him and is therefore impossible. . . . The limit of the possible is not, therefore, self-contradiction, but contradiction of God. It is not the impossible by definition, but that which has no basis in God and therefore no basis at all" (II/1, pp. 535–536).

[26]Calvin had rejected this distinction in order to protect divine power from being conceived in the abstract in separation from divine justice. Barth provides this protection by other means and makes use of the distinction between absolute and ordained power.

[27]Thomas Aquinas, *Summa* I, q. 25, art. 5, ad I.

[28]It is interesting that Barth accepts another distinction that Calvin refuses—the distinction between *voluntas efficiens* and *voluntas permittens*. The permissive will provides a way of speaking about how it is that evil exists (and yet is not another principle alongside God) and therefore must exist by the will of God or at least not without it. Barth is unwilling to say that evil escapes God's "lordship and control," nor does he want to say that it is positively willed by God. Though it is not in God's "creative will," it is still under God's "controlling will." This is not a merely figurative distinction for Barth. The permissive will is provisional, subordinate, and revocable (II/1, p. 594).

Barth's Modifications in the Scope of Power Attributed to God

Of the modifications in the scope of power that Barth introduces, two seem most far-reaching. Stated briefly, they are Barth's allowance for divine self-limitation and his insistence upon a christological point of reference in defining omnipotence. Barth will contend that though God's power is not an imperfect power, neither is it an unlimited power (II/1, p. 538). It is proper to delineate certain limitations in the scope of divine power.

Divine Self-Limitation

Barth continues and intensifies the personal model we find in Calvin. For Barth, "God is not merely personal but the supreme instance of personality."[29] The metaphors "Father" and "Lord" that Calvin employed become literalized in Barth's usage.[30] The effect of this alteration is a narrowing of the scope of divine power from a larger, abstract concept to one with greater specificity and concreteness. The predicate omnipotence is defined by this Subject and its scope is thereby limited.[31] "This power is God's power, and not merely any kind of power" (II/1, p. 526). Nevertheless divine nature is not simply a given, for God as personal is self-determining, self-limiting.

The primal decision to create is an expression of divine freedom in that: (1) God was free to become other than God in Godself and became "God for us" and (2) God was not under any necessity internal or external (II/1, p. 518) in the act of creating (i.e., God did not have to create in order to be "love," for God was already this in intertrinitarian relation).[32] In the act of creation, God acted in a self-determining and

---

[29]Gunton, p. 191. "The real person is not man but God. It is not God who is a person by extension, but we . . . " (II/1, p. 272). The doubtful thing is not whether God is person, but whether we are.

[30]"God alone . . . is properly and adequately to be called Father" (I/1, p. 393).

[31]"We are not dealing with any kind of power, or power in itself, or even omnipotence in itself and in general. On the contrary, we have to do with the power of God, and in this way and to this extent with omnipotence, with real power. Here, too, the forgetfulness which would lead us to define the subject by the predicate instead of the predicate by the subject would lead to disastrous consequences. . . . To define Him in terms of power in itself has as its consequence, not merely the neutralisation of the concept of God, but its perversion into its opposite. Power in itself is not merely neutral. Power in itself is evil" (II/1, p. 524).

[32]A real but free relation to creation is thereby established.

self-limiting act, electing not to be God alone but to be God with and for the human being (II/2, p. 169). Entailed in this is a decision for God to "be God" in a particular way (i.e., to be "God for us" and "God with us").[33] Therefore God is affected in relation to the world in that if God had never known or willed the world, God would have been different, though no less God.[34]

Now that this decision to create has been accomplished, God is still free, but no longer free in the same sense. Since God is self-determined by the decision to create, God's freedom lies in being Godself (as God has chosen to be). "The real and effective limit of the possible is the one which God has imposed on Himself and therefore on the world and on us" (II/1, p. 538). What this illustrates is that omnipotence, for Barth, does not exclude the possibility of a *voluntary self-limitation of power.* Barth does not see this as a diminishment but as a higher perfection of power.[35]

There are two serious difficulties with this approach. One relates to the literalizing of metaphors. Aside from the larger question of whether language about God can ever be literal, there are problems that Barth gets himself into by this literal way of speaking. Barth has insisted elsewhere that, because God is ontologically independent, terms such as "past," "present," and "future" do not apply. Yet he speaks here as if at some point before or beyond time, God made a decision to be God in relation to creation rather than God alone. This introduces a before and after in God. Presumably there was a time before such a decision and now is the time after it. We are led to wonder what God was like *before* this decision. *Who*, in fact, *was there* making the choice to be "with and for" the human being? Such choice would have to have been made by some *other* nature not characterized by this limitation.[36] Yet, Barth insists, it is "forbidden to reckon an essentially different omnipotence from that which God has manifested in His actual choice and action" (II/1, p. 542). He will allow that we can count upon God's having a *greater* omnipotence but not a *different* one.

---

[33]"God has limited Himself to be this God and no other" (II/1, p. 518).

[34]Davaney, p. 43.

[35]"God's will is different from ours in that it fixes a sphere which it does not overstep" (II/1, p. 555).

[36]This line of thinking would go against Barth's insistence that there is no "God behind God." God in Godself and God as revealed to us in Jesus Christ are the same God. Barth is unwilling to make a separation between *Deus absconditus* and *Deus revelatus.*

A second serious difficulty regards the usefulness of such a proposal for eliminating the difficulties that attend the traditional doctrine of omnipotence. The prospect of divine self-limitation, as Barth presents and expounds it, does provide a means for reducing the scope of divine power. It may be argued, however, that for the purposes of constructing a theodicy, self-limitation is as good as no limitation at all. Limitations that are a function of the will (moral limitations as opposed to metaphysical limitations) may ordinarily be willfully withdrawn at any moment.[37] Even if the decision cannot be reversed—and Barth implies that it cannot—one is still held accountable for the limitations one imposes on oneself and for the outcome—especially when one has perfect foreknowledge. If, for example, because of the divine self-limitation, God is unable to intervene to eradicate evil—whereas without that self-limitation God *could* do so—then God is indictable for having chosen this self-imposed limitation. Unless something else imposed this self-limitation, God is to be held responsible. On the other hand, if something else imposed this self-limitation, it cannot properly be called *self*-limitation.[38] The theodicy problem is not really ameliorated by this proposed reduction of the scope of divine power which has its origin in divine decision.

Christological Orientation

Barth's christological orientation also modifies the scope of divine power.[39] In principle, Barth understands Jesus Christ to

---

[37]There is some question whether, in Barth's system, the divine self-limitation once chosen can in fact be withdrawn. Barth does imply that after the decision to be with and for human being, God stays within the parameters set. God's power now consists in the capacity to be Godself as God determined to be in that act of creation. Even so, the difficulty remains.

[38]In the case of God, there is clearly no such imposition. "His will is pure will, determined exclusively by Himself. . . . In this self-determination it has no law over it. It does not have an external law in which one of its objects is necessarily in its existence or nature a motive either as a goal or as a means to other goals. Nor does it have an internal law, because it is itself God, and therefore the standard of everything divinely necessary and the substance of everything holy and just and good, so that there can be nothing divine which must first be its motive or norm, or which it needs as a motive or rule, in order to be the divine will" (II/1, p. 560).

[39]In spite of Barth's heavy dependence upon Calvin, he faults Calvin and all the older Protestant theology for not interpreting the doctrine of providence christologically—thereby failing to give it a distinctly Christian content. The outcome is that the content can be filled out in a way that is far from Christian. He notes that "providence" was one of Hitler's favorite words.

be the embodiment of divine power and our only guide to
what power means in relation to God.[40] He insists that how we
understand God's omnipotence must be circumscribed and
determined for us by the God who is and has this power—
namely, the God who is revealed to us in Jesus Christ—and
not by any preconceived notions of what power means. It is
from Jesus Christ that we will learn the meaning and scope of
operation of true omnipotence.[41]

There is no question that such a starting point could significantly alter the doctrine of omnipotence derived. In Jesus
Christ, what we most obviously see is divine suffering love,
vulnerability, humility, and weakness. If followed through
consistently, such a point of orientation could transform not
only the *scope* but also the *meaning* of power attributed to
God. However, because Barth does not allow the christological principle to have its full force, this does not occur.

The christological orientation *does* provide clues as to how
(and to what purpose) we might reasonably expect God to
exercise power. It makes clear that the operation of divine
power will always be within the scope of that which is loving
and gracious and for our good. Thus it does, in a sense, narrow
what may properly be thought of as within the scope of divine
power. But, the christological center is not allowed to redefine the meaning for power underlying the doctrine of omnipotence. Barth's presupposed meaning for power remains
intact.

Barth seems on the surface to be open to a more radical
reassessment. He insists that if our prevailing understandings
about God are clearly contradicted by what we see in Jesus
Christ, then they must be abandoned.[42] Nonetheless, Barth's
christological orientation does not take him to any redefinition of divine power. What he concludes from the incarnation
is that God's power is of such magnitude that it can assume
the form of weakness and impotence and do so as omnipo-

---

[40]"We cannot and should not form any conception of God in abstraction from what
He has effected, His reality in Jesus Christ" (II/1, p. 518).

[41]Davaney, p. 31.

[42]"We may believe that God can and must be only absolute in contrast to all that is
relative, exalted in contrast to all that is lowly, active in contrast to all suffering,
inviolable in contrast to all temptation, transcendent in contrast to all immanence,
and therefore divine in contrast to everything human, in short that he can and must
be only the 'Wholly Other.' But such beliefs are shown to be quite untenable, and
corrupt, and pagan, by the fact that God does in fact be and do this in Jesus Christ"
(IV/1, p. 186).

tence, "triumphing" in this form.[43] This does not seem to be a reconception of omnipotence in the light of the Christ event but rather persistence in a preconceived notion of omnipotence while adding to it a contradictory set of features.[44] Barth, however, would deny any contradiction, maintaining that these features may be combined, for we see the combination as "actual" in Jesus Christ (II/1, p. 187). What the Christ event reveals is that God is free and powerful enough to have the capacity to enter into relationship with the human being. God can be what God wills to be. This event is a further demonstration of divine self-determination and world-determination. Thus, condescension and humiliation are not alien to God in Godself—and, in fact, they are part of the intertrinitarian life. Between the "Father" and the "Son" there is a relationship of superiority and inferiority, a *prius* and a *posterius* (IV/1, p. 195). There is within the trinity a hierarchy, a relation of domination and submission.

"Humanity of God," for Barth, essentially means God's decision and act in Jesus Christ to be with and for humanity. God has taken the human condition to heart (HOG, p. 51).[45] The condescension we see here is an act of power, a sovereign decision. "Stooping down to us He does not cease to be the Lord, but actually stoops to us from on high where He is always Lord" (II/1, p. 527).

In the incarnation, nothing is being laid down or given up or surrendered, and no genuine weakness or vulnerability is implied. There is in no sense a relinquishing of power in the sense of control. Consistent with this position, Barth argues against kenotic Christology.[46] It almost seems that Barth's

---

[43]This is similar to Barth's claim that God can be eternal in time.

[44]Simply put, Barth seems to be saying that the God thought to be white can be white as black, rather than entertaining the notion that the God thought to be white might really be black.

[45]What we learn from the "humanity of God" in Jesus is the largeness of deity. "It is when we look at Jesus Christ that we know decisively that God's deity does not exclude, but includes His humanity. . . . In His deity there is enough room for communion with man. Moreover God has and retains in His relation to this other one the unconditioned priority. It is His act. *His* is and remains the first and decisive Word, *His* the initiative, *His* the leadership. . . . His deity *encloses humanity in itself*" (HOG, pp. 49–50).

[46]"The self-emptying does not refer to His divine being. . . . Positively His self-emptying refers to the fact that, without detracting from His being in the form of God, He was able and willing to assume the form of a servant and go about in the likeness of man, so that the creature could know Him only as a creature, and He alone could know Himself as God. . . . His divine glory was concealed from the world. . . . The divine form hidden under the form of a servant" (II/1, pp. 516–517).

Christology takes on a docetic cast. Where the matter of power is concerned, the incarnation turns out to be a divine deception in which God appeared to be weak and vulnerable when in fact God was not. God put on weakness as one would put on a garment. Weakness, as God "assumes" it, is no longer weakness. We find Barth implying that divine power in its true form is concealed as opposed to being fully revealed when God takes on the "form of a servant." This outcome is, of course, contrary to Barth's expressed intention of finding in Jesus Christ—not elsewhere—the clue to the divine nature.

The cross is, for Barth, "the epistemological principle for understanding divine power."[47] Love and power entail each other in Barth's schema, and the cross is the moment of the ultimate manifestation of both—of a love that is always efficacious and of an omnipotence that is ever gracious.[48] But it is power in the mode of domination and control that is allowed to interpret the power revealed in the cross event. This is most evident in Barth's explanation of the divine "weakness" that is apparent in the cross. Barth has already set forth his meaning for omnipotence as independent knowing and willing; power that is unconditioned externally or internally, nonpassive, and nonreceptive. In the cross we see God *seeming* to give Godself up to be conditioned and determined by human action and in fact undergoing suffering and humiliation in a passive and receptive manner.[49] Not so, Barth says. Even in the cross God's power is completely active because the cross is freely chosen; it is in fact an event of divine self-determination. God is not, as it would appear, being determined by the world. God has not relinquished control in any sense. If God appears to be conditioned by the world in these events, it is because God determined to be conditioned in this way or determined to appear to be conditioned in this way. Barth cannot permit any tension between divine power as such and divine power as expressed on the cross. In this he is consistent. Thus the cross is not really permitted to reshape the overarching definition of power. The definition is taken from elsewhere and then applied to the cross.

Barth defends his position, arguing that just as "power in

---

[47]Berkouwer, p. 312. "It is . . . the knowledge of Jesus Christ the Crucified which is the knowledge of the omnipotent knowing and willing of God. It is in Jesus Christ the Crucified that that is loosed which is to be loosed here, and that is bound which is to be bound here. Therefore it is the knowledge of Him and this alone which is the real and incontrovertible knowledge of the omnipotence of God" (II/1, p. 607).

[48]Davaney, p. 62.

[49]Davaney, p. 52.

itself" and "power as we know it" were rejected as not appropriately attributed to God, neither is "weakness in itself" or "weakness as we know it" properly to be attributed to God. Nevertheless it must be observed that what we find Barth attributing to God in the cross event is much more like "power as we know it" than it is like "weakness as we know it"—even though what we see in that event appears to be more like the latter than the former.

What I propose is happening in Barth's discussion of both the incarnation and the crucifixion is that a preconceived meaning for power—the same meaning presupposed by the tradition—is being allowed to determine what Barth finds revealed about divine power in Jesus Christ. Barth's methodology might have lent itself to a more radical reassessment of the meaning of the traditional doctrine,[50] but because he does not follow through consistently, only modifications related to the scope of divine power are gained and even these turn out to be minor modifications. The apparent vulnerability we see in the incarnation and the cross—which might have pointed Barth to a new meaning for power—is swallowed up in and interpreted by the larger picture of divine power in the mode of domination and control.

The Tests of Coherency and Religious Viability

Lack of coherency would not be taken by Barth as a very damaging criticism. He is far more concerned to make statements that correspond with and reflect the divine self-revelation. If, in doing so, he says some things that seem mutually contradictory, then it is human judgment and not divine revelation that is in error. Revelation constitutes an unchallengeable frame of reference for Barth. He thus repudiates the ordinary criteria for coherency. The question remains whether in doing so he runs the risk of being vacuous.

In Barth's doctrine of omnipotence, some things he wants to affirm seem to contradict directly other things he also wants to affirm. We will examine two such issues that are also the very

---

[50]We see a sample of the possibilities that christological orientation opens up in the work of Jürgen Moltmann. In his book *The Crucified God* (New York: Harper & Row, 1974), Moltmann has followed through more consistently upon Barth's proposal and with more far-reaching results. In his interpretation of the cross, he is willing to admit divine vulnerability. In some other Christologies, notably kenotic Christology, powerlessness is allowed to become a genuine episode—though only an episode and not a divine characteristic—in the life of God. The king becomes servant for a time and then returns to glory. In Barth there is not even a brief episode of vulnerability.

issues that make Barth's doctrine of omnipotence questionable from the standpoint of religious viability: (1) Barth wants
to affirm complete divine determination of creaturely reality
on the one hand and creaturely freedom on the other. (2)
Barth wants to affirm the goodness and omnipotence (as he
has defined it) of God in the face of genuine evil.[51] The crucial
point of difficulty in both instances is, in fact, the meaning for
power which is operative in Barth's theology.

Divine Determination and Creaturely Freedom

The charge of incoherence may be leveled where Barth
tries to reconcile his assertion that divine power is all-controlling with his assertion that creatures are free beings. He affirms both in a compatibilist framework, but the two are never
convincingly made compatible. Creaturely reality is said to be
distinct from but upheld by divine reality whose control it
never escapes (II/1, p. 503). In taking this stance, Barth is
rejecting dualism (the creature is not separate from divine
reality), monism (the creature is not commingled with divine
reality), and synergism (God's activity has absolute priority
over creaturely activity).[52] As it was in the compatibilism of
Calvin, so it is in Barth's compatibilism: Barth is seeking to
exclude both indeterminism and determinism. Each position is
unacceptable by virtue of its presenting the *creature* as in
some way conditioning and limiting the work of God: either
by its contingency or by its relative necessity as it obeys the
law of its being.

Perhaps Barth's strongest statement *affirming* creaturely
freedom is as follows:

> The creature does not belong and is not subject to [God] like a
> puppet or a tool or dead matter—that would certainly not be
> the lordship of the living God—but in the autonomy in which it
> was created, in the activity which God made possible for it and
> permitted to it. . . . God rules in and over a world of freedom
> (III/3, p. 93).

It is when Barth sets about interpreting what he means by

---

[51]Barth is fully familiar with these issues. He himself asks the questions: "How can
a will that is moved by the divine will be a free will? And if we assume that God's will
moves the human will in all circumstances, do we not inevitably interpret and understand God as the author of sin too?" (II/1, p. 571). Barth intends his proposals as
answers to these questions. We will be considering whether or not he succeeds in his
intent.

[52]Davaney, p. 90.

freedom that we see the direction in which he has moved in order to make "creaturely freedom" conform to "divine determination."

Like Calvin, Barth redefines freedom. Freedom consists in obedience to God and thus does not stand in conflict with our being totally ruled and determined by God. Freedom does not mean self-determination except, notably, in God's case. Self-determination is ruled out by creaturely status. It is not a created will if it is free in this absolute sense.[53]

Barth interprets creaturely freedom by means of primary and secondary causes. God is seen as primary cause, who posits and absolutely conditions all other causes (III/3, p. 98). There is no real analogy between God's self-positing causation and our causation which is grounded wholly outside ourselves.[54] Barth claims that we are "causes" in our own realm, though only in this derived and secondary sense.

All creaturely activity is primarily and simultaneously God's own activity (III/3, p. 105). Two agents are at work in every act. Because these agents are of different orders, no conflict is involved in their double agency. Barth employs the analogy of writing and in doing so shows the restricted sense in which he is applying the term "agency" to creaturely being. "The hand guides and the pen is guided, so the divine activity overrules in its conjunction with the creaturely, and on the part of the creature there can only be submission" (III/3, p. 134). Here it becomes clear that the creature is an agent only in an instrumental sense, as a tool and not an agent in the usual sense. The creature's agency is completely controlled. What, then, is the meaning of "agency"?

Barth makes a defense of his position by insisting that while we are controlled, we are not coerced or under compulsion; we are not used as instruments *against our will*. But he then presents an account of the "twofold working" of God that renders this kind of disclaimer of little use as a defense. It calls into question whether, in Barth's schema, we may even be said to *have a will of our own*. God's work in the creature is twofold: external/internal, objective/subjective, Word/Spirit. By the divine Word, God works objectively, confronting the creature with a command; by the divine Spirit, God works subjectively in the creature effecting the response (III/3, pp. 141–143). But if both the confrontation and the response are

---

[53]"The creature which conditions God is no longer God's creature, and the God who is conditioned by the creature is no longer God" (II/1, p. 580).

[54]Griffin, p. 152.

God's, what part is our own? How are our wills "other" than parts of God's will?[55]

When Barth seeks to reconcile the contradictory assertions of complete divine determination and human freedom, he does so, I submit, by equivocating on the central terms discussed above: *freedom, agency,* and *will.* There are two more responses Barth offers to those who would accuse him of being incoherent in trying to hold to both assertions. On the one hand, he claims we know that this seeming contradiction is possible because we know it is actual. This response seems to beg the question. On the other hand, he makes the claim that we know that both things are true because in the Bible we find both things said. There is some question whether the biblical record confirms Barth's interpretation of the matter. Even if it did, that would not settle the question for all of us.

The extreme to which Barth goes in denying freedom (as the term is ordinarily used) cannot be overlooked. It seems to stem from his zeal to protect divine power from any compromise with other powers. When power means ability to dominate and control, independent powers can only be viewed as a threat. For this reason, in Barth's system, God must have a monopoly on power.[56] All other beings have power only in a derivative sense, and in the exercise of "their" power, God is "controlling or permitting, and really controlling even in His permission" (II/1, p. 561). "The created world . . . never escapes His control by reason of its own reality or autonomy, but it is wholly and utterly under His dominion and in His hand" (II/1, p. 503). God rules unconditionally "with the absoluteness which is possible only for the Creator ruling over the creature" (III/3, p. 93). The upshot of this is that we are no more than clay in the hands of the potter. God's power is that of "the One to whom the clay belongs" (II/1, p. 526).[57]

---

[55]"There is no being not subject to the will of God. There is also no other will outside or beyond God. There is no will which conditions or hinders God's will" (II/1, p. 555).

[56]"God and God alone has real power, all the real power" (II/1, p. 531). Barth seems unwilling to grant the creature any power of genuine freedom for fear that this would compete with or threaten divine power. "The doctrine of creaturely freedom as a limitation of God's omnicausality and omnipotence [is] a denial of His sovereignty [and] involves an attack on His deity" (II/1, p. 578). "The creature who conditions God is no longer God's creature, and the God who is conditioned by the creature is no longer God" (II/1, p. 580).

[57]To Barth's way of thinking, it seems absurd that we should want it any other way. "To be thankful of our own free will it is necessary that we should have unconditionally acknowledged the divine foreordination of our free will. It is in this acknowledgement that our gratitude exists. . . . If we want to play off our self-determination

Barth has insisted that "between the sovereignty of God and the freedom of the creature there is no contradiction. The freedom of its activity does not exclude but includes the fact that it is controlled by God" (III/3, p. 166). The argument of the preceding pages has been that while he makes this assertion, he is unable to argue convincingly enough for it to make his compatibilism persuasive. What he ends up doing is equivocating on the central terms ingredient to one of the assertions. It may be argued that Barth has sacrificed any plausible notion of creaturely freedom. His severely altered account of freedom is, however, the only account that may conceivably accompany a doctrine of omnipotence in which divine power is conceived as the ability to dominate and control.

A troublesome set of problems arises from Barth's stance regarding divine determination and creaturely freedom, and, taken together, I would propose that they add up to the nonviability of Barth's doctrine of divine omnipotence for religious purposes. If we are not free, we are not responsible. All our willing and acting have no lasting significance. In the final analysis, they are not *our* willing and acting. If God is the only one with real freedom/power, then God is the one responsible for all that is—including evil. Furthermore, the reality of our experience is denied by this presentation. We experience ourselves as free and responsible. Are we self-deceived?

Perhaps the most serious problem is this: the conditions necessary to divine-human relationship are removed by Barth's strictures. It seems there is no genuine "other" there for God to love. There can be only a kind of self-love if the human being is no more than an extension of the divine will and action. A relationship, in ordinary usage, includes a social element[58] with some degree of reciprocity and mutuality. It is difficult to see how this can exist in the framework Barth proposes. Furthermore, if we are not free, we cannot love God. Barth himself has said that love must be free if it is to be love.

Given the above criticisms, we may conclude that Barth's doctrine of omnipotence, with its presupposed understanding

---

against His foreordination and assert it, this simply means a despair that is self-chosen, a defiance that is superfluous, and a recklessness that is out of place. The doctrine of the autonomy of the free creature over against God is simply a theological form of human enmity against God's grace, the theological actualisation of a repetition of the fall" (II/1, p. 586).

[58]Davaney has noted that Barth seeks to maintain a social notion of love alongside a nonsocial notion of power and that this is unworkable (p. 60).

of power, is open to charges of incoherence and nonviability
for religious purposes. He is unable to substantiate his conflicting claims for divine power expressed as all-determining
on the one hand and for created existents as genuinely free on
the other.

The Problem of Evil

We run into yet another set of problems when we closely
examine Barth's claim that God is both good and omnipotent
(in the sense Barth has assumed) and yet not responsible for
evil. Although Barth treats the theodicy problem in a fresh
and original way, he is unable, in the final analysis, to bring it
to resolution, since he finds it impossible to give a coherent
account of divine goodness and omnipotence on the one hand
and the reality of evil on the other. Barth is forced to begin
with the assumption of the absurdity of evil and to end with
explanations that create their own problems.

Barth's intent is to avoid dualism while at the same time
taking evil seriously.[59] In an extended analysis of Leibnitz and
Schleiermacher, Barth argues against the efforts of traditional
Western philosophy to domesticate evil and incorporate it
into the created harmony (III/3, p. 348). This has the effect of
confusing radical evil with God's good creation so that true
evil is never recognized as such or at all.[60]

The origin of evil cannot be lodged in the creation which, as
the sphere of God's positive will, is good by definition. The
presence of evil in the world does not really count against
the goodness of creation, for it does not prohibit creation's
serving its God-given purpose as the external basis of the
covenant.[61]

Barth will also refuse to locate the entry point for evil in the
freedom of the human will. Freedom, for Barth, cannot mean
freedom to choose between good and evil but will always
mean "freedom for God"—freedom to respond in obedience

---

[59]"Barth tries to walk a razor-edged path which cuts between the view that would
see chaos as preexisting creation and hence as a once autonomous reality, and the
view which incorporates chaos into creation as a part of God's plan. Barth intends
firmly and completely to exclude both of these alternatives. Chaos is not autonomous.
It is not a self-grounded reality which exists outside of and independently of God's
will. At the same time it is absolutely no creature of God and no part of His plan."
Ruether, "The Left Hand of God in the Theology of Karl Barth," p. 4.

[60]Ruether, "The Left Hand of God," p. 4.

[61]The perfection of the creation is judged by its serviceability to God (III/1, p.
370), and this is a thing to be judged from God's standpoint and not ours.

to God's word. Our proper nature has no capacity for sin whatsoever.[62] Our nondivinity makes us vulnerable to chaos, but our nondivinity is itself "good" and cannot be thought of as the beginning point for evil.

Neither is Barth willing to find a basis for evil in God. There can be no grounding in God for evil, since evil is, by definition, *that which God does not will.*[63]

Because evil is inexplicable either from God's side or from the side of creation, it is truly inexplicable. Barth will maintain the inexplicability/absurdity of evil and will cast away the aid of any of the traditional explanations: the freewill defense,[64] aesthetic arguments, *felix culpa*, the *privatio boni* theory, and so forth.[65]

Barth refuses the traditional theoretical statement of the problem and does not feel a need to make a coherent combination of the three propositions.[66] He finds it to be a "meaningless abstraction," for it is taken out of the context of the covenant, grace, and salvation. For Barth, this context must be the starting point and goal of a Christian theology. He insists that we must not work philosophically "from without" but theologically "from within." If we stay within the parameters Barth has set for the discussion of the problem of evil, we

---

[62]Sin, the concrete form of *das Nichtige*, is not an unfortunate but necessary by-product of freedom. Sin exists not only in contradiction to God and to divine purposes but also in contradiction to true human nature. The decision to sin is an absurd choice against God and against oneself. From Davaney's summary, pp. 78–80.

[63]Kant's analysis of the relation of evil to God's will is useful in this regard. He observes that possible positions fall into one of three categories: (1) Evil is willed by God as part of God's plan. (2) Evil is not willed by God but is necessary to God's plan. (3) Evil is not willed by God and is contrary to God's plan. The Irenaean theodicies tend to fall in the first category and the Augustinian theodicies in the second category. Barth's theodicy is clearly of the third type.

[64]It is just as well that Barth did not have to base his theodicy upon a freewill defense, since, as we have shown in the section above, he has a difficult time making a plausible case for free will in the face of his particular understanding of divine power.

[65]For a good presentation of each of these theodicies, see John Hick, *Evil and the God of Love*. The ones not fully described in this book are very briefly sketched here. The "aesthetic" approach to theodicy argues that evil is a matter of our perception from a limited perspective. It is as if we were looking only at the dark shades in a painting and saying that the painting is ugly; if we could but see the "whole," as God—the artist—does, we would agree that these shades are necessary and the painting is beautiful. *Felix culpa*, as an answer to the theodicy question, declares that the fall is a "happy fall." Our present state is better than our former state, or at least it makes possible good things that would not have been possible apart from it. The *privatio boni* theory insists that evil in itself has no being. It exists only as the absence of the good, as blindness is the absence of sight.

[66]III/3, pp. 293ff. He sees the theodicy problem as "an extraordinarily clear demonstration of the necessary brokenness of all theological thought and utterance."

cannot really "play for keeps." We cannot really call God's existence or goodness or power into question (in the face of evil), because they are already established on other grounds. Unless the question is asked from within the context of Christian faith, Barth will not admit it. Once it is asked within that context, for Barth, it is already answered. This amounts, in my view, to a refusal of the problem. Barth questions whether there is any *need* to unify God's holiness and omnipotence in the face of nothingness (III/3, p. 294). The refusal seems a forced option for him: if he admits the problem, his definition of omnipotence will require that he deny either the goodness of God or the reality of evil. Rejection of the problem is the price that must be paid in order for Barth to maintain all he wants to maintain. John Hick sums up Barth's position well:

> All that we can properly do, he suggests, is to affirm the apparently contradictory truths that we learn from Scripture—the utterly malignant character of evil as God's enemy, and yet its subjection to His control—without professing to weave these together into an intelligible unity.[67]

Barth has set aside the idea of "systematic theology," rejecting with it the ideal of internal consistency. The problem of evil is one of his best reasons for doing so.

Perhaps Barth's most significant contribution to the discussion of the problem of evil lies in the distinction he draws between "the shadow side of creation" (*Schattenseite*) and evil in the much stronger sense of "nothingness" (*das Nichtige*). This distinction is used in the place of the traditional distinction between moral and metaphysical evil.[68] "Shadow side" corresponds roughly to the traditional definition of metaphysical evil as the conditions that attend our finitude. But *das Nichtige* is a concept not exhausted in the traditional notion of "moral evil." While shadow side is only evil *prima facie*, nothingness is genuine evil.[69]

---

[67]In spite of this stance, we will find that Barth steps outside his own self-imposed bounds in developing his concept of *das Nichtige* which is neither "part of nor is it an unproblematic deduction from, the biblical revelation." Hick, pp. 138, 143.

[68]For a discussion of the distinction between moral and metaphysical evil, see footnote 9 in Barth, DO, chapter 3.

[69]The distinction between these two is an important one. For purposes of this discussion we will mean by "genuine evil" anything—all things considered—without which the universe would have been better. "*Prima facie* evil" will mean anything that appears at first consideration, from a partial perspective, to be evil but turns out upon reflection or upon consideration of a larger context, not to be. *Prima facie* evil is compensated for by the goodness to which it contributes. Depending upon which

The shadow side of creation lies in characteristics of created existence generally such as finitude, imperfection, impermanence, and the fact of our having been created *ex nihilo* and ever being on the verge of collapsing back into nothingness. Barth is in agreement with the traditional perspective that these things are not evil in themselves. Aging, suffering, and even death are within the sphere of the natural and are therefore good. The metaphysical evil that attends creation is not evil in the real sense of the term and does not qualify the goodness of creation. It is well, in fact, that God's good creation should have this twofold (positive and negative) character. Neediness and dependence are not evil but are the proper stance of the creature (III/3, pp. 375–376). The presence of the shadow side points to our need for the Creator by showing that though the creature is something, it is something on the edge of nothing, bordering it and menaced by it and having no power of itself to overcome the danger (III/3, p. 296).[70]

With regard to "nothingness,"[71] we have in hand a matter that is altogether different from the shadow side of God's good creation. Here we are dealing with that which is unqualifiedly evil as *that which God does not will*. There is no common ground between the shadow side and nothingness—"the power inimical to the will of the Creator and therefore to the nature of His good creation, the threat to world-occurrence and its corruption" (III/3, p. 296). To confuse shadow side and nothingness is to slander creation and the Creator. Real evil is concealed; it becomes incorporated into one's philosophical outlook and finally justified as an essential, innocuous, and even salutary aspect of creation (III/3, p. 299).

---

understanding of evil is being used, the theodicy problem tends to be approached differently. Some will argue that God's moral perfection requires that God would want to prevent evil (meaning genuine evil), while others will say it does not (meaning *prima facie* evil).

[70]"For all we can tell, may not we ourselves praise Him more mightily in humility than in exaltation, in need than in plenty, in fear than in joy, on the frontier of nothingness than when wholly orientated on God? For all we can tell, may not we ourselves praise Him more purely on the bad days than on good, more surely in sorrow than in rejoicing, more truly in adversity than in progress?" (III/3, p. 297). We may well be moved to ask whether in the face of all our suffering from the shadow side of existence, the increased praise we might render to God is the only consideration. Is it God's only consideration?

[71]There is no adequate translation for *das Nichtige*. "Nothingness" is one of the more common renderings and will be used in this discussion except where Barth's own term is simply repeated.

It is here, in the discussion of *das Nichtige,* that we see the full implications of Barth's understanding of divine power for the theodicy problem. Barth claims that God's power, being omnipotent, is such that even God's nonwilling is "effective." With the divine decision to create, nothingness gained an entree as that which God did not will but "passed over" and rejected. It has a kind of "parasitic" existence and cannot exist in itself independently; and yet *nothingness is not nothing.*

> [Nothingness] "is" problematically because it is only on the left hand of God, under His No, the object of His jealousy, wrath and judgment. . . . It "is," not as God and His creation are, but only in its own improper way, as inherent contradiction, as impossible possibility (III/3, p. 351).

Das Nichtige does not exist in either the primary essential sense that God does, as the one self-determining actuality, or in the secondary derivative sense the creature does, as posited and grounded in divine willing.[72] *Das Nichtige* is a *tertium quid* existing in a contradictory mode. How can nothingness exist? It cannot. Only that which God wills can exist. Nothingness is—by definition—that which God does not will. Hence it cannot exist; and yet it does. Its existence is absolutely inexplicable. It has no ground and no future either from the side of the Creator or from that of the creature. Yet all things are affected by nothingness, enmeshed in and bound up with it.

Barth's proposal, in its originality and profundity, makes an interesting and suggestive contribution to the discussion of the problem of evil. Nevertheless it is finally unsuccessful in bringing resolution to the theodicy problem and, in fact, creates for itself additional perplexities. A case can be made that as Barth pursues his line of argumentation, what he ends up doing is holding in suspension each one of the three propositions of the traditional statement of the problem of evil[73] in turn. This is not his intention, of course, but it is a direct result—it will be argued—of the particular understanding of divine power he has adopted.

Barth accounts for the origin of *das Nichtige* by appealing to God's omnipotent "nonwilling" (III/3, p. 164). This is said to be God's *opus alienum* and the work of God's "left hand." "God is the *Grund* and *Herr* of *das Nichtige,* which is there not by accident (*nicht von ungefähr*) but is from God (*von Gott*)"

---

[72]Davaney, p. 69.
[73]God is good, God is omnipotent, and there is genuine evil in the world.

(III/3, pp. 304–305).[74] In taking this stance, Barth becomes vulnerable to the charge of, in Barth's own words, "speaking, with Manichaeans . . . , of a *causalitas mali in Deo* and thus violating the holiness of God" (III/3, p. 292). Whether one says that nothingness was "created" or "rejected" by God, it is still God's activity that caused it to "be" in its own peculiar way. Thus God is responsible for evil. Even though evil is that which is *not willed,* divine omniscience—which, for Barth, includes both foreknowledge and predetermination—would entail God's knowing beforehand that nothingness would be a by-product of the creative act. God created in full cognizance of this outcome. Thus God is *indictable,* as well as responsible for evil. In this regard, Barth's proposal does not work as a theodicy.

An additional perplexity is created by Barth's proposal that the origin of evil is to be lodged in "omnipotent nonwilling." It seems to run counter to claims Barth makes elsewhere concerning the nature of divine power. Divine power is said to include the power of complete *self-determination.* If that is the case, then the fact that God's nonwilling operates in the way it does is a function of divine decision and not a function of any internal or external necessity.[75] Yet Barth seems to be claiming that God could not prevent the divine nonwilling from functioning in the way it did in the act of creating. This would seem to imply that God is subordinate to some external or internal necessity. Barth cannot have it both ways. Either God is subject to necessity and therefore could not prevent evil and is not omnipotent (in the way that Barth has defined omnipotence) or God is not subject to necessity and therefore *could* have prevented evil and is therefore indictable for evil. In the first case, God's omnipotence is suspended; in the second case, God's goodness is suspended.

Barth seems to show here an uneven handling of God's power in its two expressions of self-determination and world-determination. Divine self-determination—even though it involves distinguishing between what God wills to be and what God does not will to be—does not result in the coming to "be"[76] of the rejected possibility. We do not have "God" and "not-God." Divine nonwilling does not have the same kind of

---

[74]Nothingness, however alien, "cannot be envisaged and apprehended as outside the jurisdiction of the fatherly rule of God" (III/3, p. 365).

[75]Davaney, pp. 73ff.

[76]That is, of coming to "be" in the peculiar sense in which *das Nichtige* "is."

"effectiveness" when it comes to God's self-determination as it does with reference to God's world-determination.

The outcome of Barth's locating the origin of evil in the peculiar power of omnipotent nonwilling is that the difference between God's willing and nonwilling becomes a merely verbal distinction.[77] One wonders whether the results would have been any different if God had positively willed *das Nichtige*. Presumably the "allness" of creation would still have come to be by God's "not willing" it.[78] What kind of power is this, where precisely what one *does not will* comes to be? This would seem to be more a form of impotence than a form of desirable power.

If the distinction between divine willing and nonwilling is merely a verbal one, Barth's affirmation of divine omnipotence is in jeopardy. This is the case because of the extent to which Barth has interpreted the positive content of omnipotence in terms of divine *willing*. Along with divine knowing, divine willing is central to Barth's definition of omnipotence. In lodging the origin of evil in "omnipotent nonwilling," Barth may have in effect—though without intending to do so—sacrificed divine omnipotence in his attempt to account for evil.

Barth may also be seen to be equivocating on the reality of evil. This is especially evident in the relationship between "the shadow side" and *das Nichtige*. Barth has viewed the shadow side as a kind of frontier between the sphere of God's good creation and nothingness. The problem is that the frontier has a way of becoming blurred. It becomes increasingly difficult to draw the border and "to distinguish between natural tragedies which can be borne and tragedies which are the expression of a disorder to be combated."[79] Disease and pain and death, which in theory belong only to the innocent shadow side of creation, concretely, as they occur within our sinful human experience, become manifestations of *das Nichtige*.[80]

---

[77]Both Hick (pp. 166–167) and Griffin (p. 148) concur with this assessment that God's nonwilling is really a powerful willing, which fixes limits and therefore directs and governs.

[78]Curiously, Barth has elsewhere observed that God's power is qualitatively different from ours precisely in the fact that, while we are not able to do what we will and we are able to do what we do not will, it is not so with God. What becomes of this distinguishing mark of divine power if divine nonwilling has the peculiar effectiveness that Barth attributes to it here?

[79]Ruether, "The Left Hand of God," p. 15.

[80]Hick, p. 132.

Barth makes three other claims about *das Nichtige* that in fact serve to blur the boundary between *prima facie* and genuine evil: (1) *Das Nichtige* is transient; it is deprived of perpetuity.[81] (2) God has already defeated it in Jesus Christ.[82] What remains is only a "dangerous semblance" of evil. (3) God is using divine power to restrain and control even this semblance of evil and to make it serve divine purposes.

With respect to the first of Barth's claims, questions arise. If nothingness was a necessary accompaniment to what God positively willed in the creation, how can it ever be otherwise (as long as the creation continues to exist)? If nothingness will at some future point no longer be a necessary accompaniment, why was it ever so? Evil, by definition, is what God does not will. How can there come a time when the things God does not will, will no longer be rejected? What could account for such a change?

The second of Barth's claims is difficult to understand, given the fact that the christological victory happens from eternity. This being the case, *das Nichtige* has never been more than a dangerous semblance.[83] If evil has always been only this, its seriousness is severely undercut. In pursuing this line of argumentation, Barth moves in the direction of a denial of the reality of evil.

The christological victory, as Ruether has observed, has a "hollow note." "It appears to be more of a juridical than a real victory. . . . Nothingness, though defeated, and only apparently still powerful, still continues to look as though it were powerful."[84] We tend to doubt the veracity of this sort of claim, we look for triumph over evil to be *real* triumph. If evil is indeed defeated, then why is the world not transformed?[85] In this claim it would seem that Barth is denying either the reality of evil or the reality of the triumph over evil.

---

[81]The *opus alienum* is not equal in status to God's *opus proprium* (III/3, p. 360).

[82]In Jesus Christ we know both that God is opposed to *das Nichtige* and that God has overcome it. God "comprehends, envisages and controls it. . . . For God is Master of this antithesis. He overcomes and has already overcome it" (III/3, p. 302).

[83]"His conception leaves the impression that everything has already been done, all decisions have been taken, so that one can hardly say that the historical reconciliation is at issue, but only the revelation of redemption in history and the revelation of the definitive Yes of God's grace." Berkouwer, p. 250.

[84]Ruether, "The Left Hand of God," p. 21.

[85]Barth has anticipated the question and offers three answers: (1) The world is transformed, but we do not see it. (2) This is only the first and not the final stage. (3) The delay provides us time to share and witness. None of these answers seems altogether satisfying. With regard to Barth's first response—that we are blind to the transformation that has occurred—Barth goes on to say that our blindness to the

In Barth's third claim, the dangerous semblance that "masquerades as reality" is said to be fully under God's control and serving God's purposes. Evil lies under God's power in the same way a criminal in jail awaiting execution is under the power of the jailer even while remaining completely contrary to the will of and antagonistic to the jailer.[86] From this we might infer that we have nothing really to fear from evil and no need to work to resist it. In fact, the dangerous semblance of evil is instrumentally *good.* It serves God's purposes in that our living on the edge of nothingness makes us aware of our utter powerlessness and complete dependence upon God.

In summary, it appears that Barth is putting forward a view that *there is now no genuine evil in the world.* All apparent evil is either to be attributed to the shadow side of creation, which is not really evil, or to the dangerous semblance of an evil that no longer really exists. Since Jesus Christ, all evil is *prima facie* evil. There once was genuine evil, but there is no longer. Barth's working out of his proposal has the effect, at the very least, of undercutting the seriousness with which "evil" is to be taken and, at the very worst, denying that there *is* genuine evil.[87] In this respect, Barth's proposal falls short of being a workable resolution of the theodicy problem.

I would submit that the traditional doctrine of omnipotence that Barth adopts forces him into the difficulties explicated above. The elements in Barth's position that seemed most promising as a way of ameliorating the problems created by the traditional understanding of divine power, namely, his concept of divine "self-limitation" and his christological orientation, are not allowed to significantly modify the even scope of divine power.

---

defeat of evil is not an innocent blindness but a culpable blindness reflecting faithlessness. If so, would this not be an admission of some *continued real power of evil?* Barth's second answer causes us to wonder if there can *ever* be a final stage. Evil is by definition the "not-willed" by God. How then, given the peculiar power of omnipotent nonwilling, can evil ever cease to "be" in its own curious way? Third, if there *can* be a final stage, why the delay? After two thousand years of "sharing and witnessing" it is not self-evident that the world is much better off. Considerable evil has been perpetrated in the interim. Is the wait worth the cost?

[86]Ruether, "The Left Hand of God," p. 21.

[87]This would be very much contrary to Barth's own intentions. He criticized others for incorporating evil into the "created harmony" in such a way that it seemed innocuous. This amounts to calling evil "good."

PART THREE

Alternatives: Process Theology and Feminist Perspectives

4

Hartshorne

The proposed alternative model for understanding divine power to be presented here differs fundamentally from the classical model and its modifications. The difference is not a matter of further limitation of the *scope* of power but of a substantially different understanding of the *meaning* of power. The difference can be summarized as follows. While the other models tend to be monopolistic and define power in terms of active/causative determination of all reality, the alternative model offered by Charles Hartshorne[1] will refer to shared power and will admit passive/receptive dimensions to divine power. Instead of lodging all power in divine agency and conceiving all other "powers" as being derivative, nonagential, and instrumental, Hartshorne proposes that there are a multiplicity of agencies and a multiplicity of powers that influence and are influenced by one another. Calvin and Barth understood omnipotence to mean that world process—in general and in all its particulars—is actively and effectively brought into conformity with divine willing in a kind of unilateral determination. For Hartshorne, omnipotence does not entail unilateral divine determination. God is seen as influencing world process but not as controlling it in such a way that it is made to conform to divine willing.

This chapter will explore Hartshorne's thoroughgoing critique of the traditional doctrine of omnipotence. It will then present Hartshorne's constructive proposal, showing what his

---

[1]Many other process philosophers and theologians, following the insights of Whitehead, could be used to illustrate an alternative understanding of divine power. Hartshorne is one who has given considerable attention to a reassessment of the doctrine of omnipotence. For this reason and for reasons of brevity, only Hartshorne's contributions will be presented here. Occasional references to Whitehead will be used to illumine Hartshorne's thought.

basic principles yield in the way of a new understanding of divine power.

Hartshorne's Critique of the Traditional Understanding of Divine Power

Hartshorne is extremely critical of what he typifies as the traditional view of omnipotence. He considers that perspective to be "the chief source of the metaphysico-theological paradoxes," a "false report upon experience" (DR, p. 50)—repugnant to both logic and true religion. The God of classical theism, an absolute Being of changeless perfection, is, in his opinion, a result of the mistaken attempt to wed Greek philosophy to biblical faith—a decided mismatch.[2] In his critique, Hartshorne not only appeals to the canons of logic but also makes appeal to scripture and to religious sensibilities. "For it is our contention that the 'theological mistakes' in question give the word *God* a meaning which is not true to its import in sacred writings or in concrete religious piety" (OOTM, p. 1). He is committed to the task of reconceiving the meaning of God and implores, "The fate of theism depends . . . upon the possibility of an alternative idea of divinity" (LP, p. 34). The alternative idea that he presents contains within it a very different notion of divine power.

Hartshorne argues, on the one hand, that the traditional concept of omnipotence lacks coherency. On the other hand, he argues that the conclusions drawn by the tradition are not the necessary conclusions of religious consciousness.

The first argument is from the nature of actuality. Hartshorne proposes that actuality, by its very nature as actual, entails power. ("Being is power," said Plato.) By "power" Hartshorne means some capacity for self-creation and other-creation.[3] If there exists any world that is *actual*, that in itself will make nonsense of a concept of omnipotence as "possessing all the power that is" or as "the ability to control/determine all events." The incoherency[4] of the traditional

---

[2]"Not the Gospels and the Old Testament, but Greek philosophy was the decisive source for the classical idea of divine perfection" (LP, p. 34).

[3]"Self-determination" and "other-determination" are terms used more commonly for the properties Hartshorne has in mind. "Creation," however, is a term more central to Hartshorne's larger system than the term "determination," and the former will be used in preference to the latter.

[4]A brief word may be offered here concerning Hartshorne's methodological presuppositions. His is a rationalist approach. He assumes that reality has an intelligible structure which human reason has the capacity to understand. There is a con-

definition of omnipotence is a key ingredient in Hartshorne's argument for a reconceiving of the meaning of omnipotence. His proposal is not simply one more among many proposals that limit the scope of the present concept; rather, the concept itself is reexamined. In his own words,

> It has become customary to say that we must limit divine power to save human freedom and to avoid making deity responsible for evil. But to speak of limiting a concept seems to imply that the concept, without the limitation, makes sense. The notion of a cosmic power that determines all decisions fails to make sense (DR, p. 138).

Thus Hartshorne begins a search for a meaning that will "make sense" in relation to a world that is "actual."

The second of Hartshorne's two arguments explores Anselm's proposition that God is "that than which nothing greater can be conceived." Hartshorne agrees with Anselm's formal definition of God but thinks its use is spoiled by certain assumptions that were at work in the understanding of "perfection"—such as *immutability, independence,* and *pure activity.* These presuppositions predetermined what could be imagined as the "greatest conceivable." Hartshorne's approach is to invite a reevaluation of those elements which were presupposed to characterize divine perfection. He maintains that it is not self-evident that perfection entails these elements.[5] We will briefly note his reservations.

Hartshorne is critical of the assumption that perfection excludes changeability. This has been argued from the perspective that change must be either for the better or for the worse. Either kind of change admits imperfection (Plato, *The Republic*). But ordinary meanings of perfection do not exclude change. God might be absolutely unchangeable in righteous-

---

gruence expected between experience and reality. One can therefore begin with experience as the grounding for all ideas, metaphysical or empirical. Hartshorne's method is to begin from what we know best—human experience—and to extrapolate from those particulars to the nature of reality in general. He is presupposing that what is can be known, though perhaps not in all aspects by all parties. The knower contains and includes the known. (God does so without distortion and without remainder.) Davaney, pp. 130ff.

[5]Hartshorne finds in Anselm's definition a certain open-endedness. It permits or perhaps mandates evaluation of any attribute in terms of whether it genuinely constitutes a "perfection." "One of the beauties of Anselm's formula is that it frees us (far more than he realized!) from automatic commitment to traditional views about God. It may very well not be 'best' to be 'omnipotent,' in the sense which generates the problem of evil in its classic form" (AD, p. 202).

ness but changeable in ways compatible with, neutral to, *or even required by* this unswerving constancy of righteousness in relation to a changing world (OOTM, p. 15).

The notion that total independence is admirable seems, to Hartshorne, also to be without foundation in experience. We do not respect or admire those who are unaffected by the weal or woe of others. Why admire it in God?

> What is the ideal of the tyrant? Is it not that, while the fortunes of all should depend upon the tyrant's will, he should depend as little as possible, ideally not at all, upon the wills and fortunes of others? This one-sided independence, in ideally complete or "absolute" form, was held the crowning glory of deity! (DR, pp. 42–43).

In some senses *independence* is admirable (i.e., in ethical character) (DR, p. 45), but when it comes to concern regarding the well-being of others, *dependence* is more to be admired.

Nor is it self-evident, to Hartshorne, that perfection implies "a purely one-way causal action, an action without reaction or interaction" (MVG, p. 26). "Perhaps the supreme action is also, necessarily, the supreme interaction" (MVG, p. 26). Hartshorne's contention with the tradition regarding the attributes of God is particularly well illustrated as he pursues the discussion of active and passive power. He grants that divine power, being the highest conceivable, must excel all others, but he reconsiders what that would in fact mean. In classical theism, perfect power was decidedly active power, causally determining all things.

> This question was scarcely put seriously at all, the answer was felt to be so obvious: it must be the power to determine every detail of what happens in the world. . . . The founders of the theological tradition were accepting and applying to deity the tyrant ideal of power (OOTM, pp. 10–11).

Hartshorne contends that the traditional doctrine of omnipotence, with its one-sided concentration upon active, determining power, boils down to an idealization of the tyrant/subject relationship. He finds no stimulus to admiration or respect—much less love—in this doctrine. Since we do not admire this figure in human relations, why do we admire it in God?[6]

---

[6]"Worship of mere absoluteness, independence, and one-sided activity or power, this transcendentalized admiration of politico-ecclesiastical tyranny, the ideal of which is to act on all while avoiding reaction from them, this spiritual blindness and false report upon experience is, as we are about to see, the chief source of the

Hartshorne refers to the analogy as "perhaps the most shockingly bad of all theological analogies, or at least the one open to the most dangerous abuses"(MVG, p. 203). Yet it is the analogy upon which the doctrine of omnipotence has been based. Quoting Whitehead, Hartshorne notes that in the formula of the Christian doctrine of omnipotence "the deeper idolatry, the fashioning of God in the image of the Egyptian, Persian, and Roman imperial rulers was retained. They gave unto God the properties that belonged to Caesar."[7] Hartshorne then observes that our diminished awe of kings and emperors makes it easier for us than for our ancestors to look elsewhere for our model for the divine nature. " 'Divine sovereignty' sounds to some of us like a confession, an admission that it is sheer power, not unstinted love that one most admires" (OOTM, p. 14).

Hartshorne's Approach to the Doctrine of God

Hartshorne takes a decidedly different approach to the derivation of divine attributes and it leads him to a genuinely different understanding of divine power. Instead of beginning with the elements that composed the traditional understanding of perfection—immutability, independence, and pure activity—Hartshorne recommends beginning with the "religious meaning of perfection," which he designates "worshipfulness" (DR, p. 41). "In theistic religions, God is the One Who is Worshipped. This is, in some sort, a definition. We have therefore, only to find out what worship is to know the proper use of the name 'God.' "[8] A God worthy of worship must be worthy of admiration, respect, and love without limit[9]—an ideal for human imitation. Such cannot be said of a God whose power is active, never passive, and who is completely immutable and independent. Thus the God of classical theism does not meet Hartshorne's qualification of being "worthy of worship."

The tyrant/subject model for understanding divine power is not by any means deducible from the idea that God is the "all-

---

metaphysico-theological paradoxes of which so much has been heard. . . . Upon the unjustified prejudice, the rotten foundation, of the worship of mere power or absoluteness, we ought to build no edifice, sacred or profane" (DR, pp. 50, 52).

[7]Whitehead, *Process and Reality*, p. 520.

[8]Hartshorne, "Philosophical and Religious Uses of 'God,' " p. 103.

[9]"But what is worship? It has been very accurately defined. To worship X is to 'love' X with all one's heart and all one's mind and all one's soul and all one's strength. Perfection is the character which X must have to make sense out of this" (LP, p. 40).

worshipful One." Hartshorne says that " 'brute power' is . . . practically efficacious, for good or ill, and has to be reckoned with. The one thing we need not and ought not to do is—to worship it!" (DR, p. 155).[10] He states his objection strongly: "No worse falsehood was ever perpetrated than the traditional concept of omnipotence. It is a piece of unconscious blasphemy" (OOTM, p. 18).

As to what *is* deducible from a definition of God as the "all-worshipful One," Hartshorne points to a Being that is "all-surpassing and all-inclusive" (OOTM, p. 44). Each term bears consideration.

In order to be worthy of worship, a being must be unsurpassable *by another*, exalted beyond all possible rivals.[11] God might be either absolutely unsurpassable or unsurpassable except by Godself. Hartshorne proposes that either can be said of God depending upon the values to which we are referring. He notes that some values are capable of absolute maximum while others are not[12] and proposes that the former are held by God in their absolute maximum state, whereas the latter are capable of increase in the divine life.[13] In addition, since not all values are compossible (they sometimes conflict with one another), a purely final or static perfection, possessing all possible values, is not possible. Divine perfection, then, must be conceived dynamically.[14]

Divine all-inclusiveness is another implication of the definition of God as "the worshipful One." According to Hartshorne, it is

> fragmentariness, not finitude that sets the problem of worship. . . . Cosmic wholeness, not infinity, is the essential concept. . . . Not static, unchanging completeness, but all-inclusiveness is what is required.[15]

---

[10]Hartshorne is in agreement with Whitehead, who said that "this worship of glory arising from power" could only be based upon a "barbaric conception of God." Whitehead, *Religion in the Making*, p. 55.

[11]If any rival could surpass God, then it is the rival who would be the one "worthy of worship." Hartshorne, "The Formally Possible Doctrines of God," p. 200.

[12]Divine happiness, for example, cannot be thought of as being at an absolute maximum, for it could be increased if human sinfulness were decreased.

[13]"There is indeed unsurpassable, unchangeable divine perfection, but it is only an abstract aspect of deity, which concretely is self-surpassable yet not surpassable by others, and changeable only for the better" (OOTM, p. 38). Hartshorne quotes Gustav Fechner approvingly: "The perfection of God generally is not in reaching a limited maximum but in seeking an unlimited progress" (OOTM, p. v).

[14]Hartshorne, "The Formally Possible Doctrines of God," p. 200.

[15]Hartshorne, "Philosophical and Religious Uses of 'God,' " p. 105.

Moreover, if there were anything outside God, then the injunction to "love our neighbor" might be said to conflict with the injunction to love God wholeheartedly (LP, p. 40).

Unsurpassability and all-inclusiveness are not merely differences of degree but differences in kind. We have here a categorical superiority, a superiority in principle for which "perfection" is an appropriate designation. Hartshorne's thought leads toward a genuinely different approach to the divine attributes and consequently to an alternative definition of divine power.

This new method of derivation of the attributes is fleshed out in Hartshorne's application of what he refers to as the "principle of eminence." In applying this principle, Hartshorne opens up his God concept to "include" in "unsurpassable" form positive creaturely properties.[16]

> Whatever is good in the creation is, in superior or eminent fashion, "analogically not univocally," the property of God. Thus knowledge, purpose, life, love, joy, are deficiently present in us, eminently and analogically present in God. It is only in this manner that the idea of God acquires any positive meaning controllable by analysis, and yet free from anthropomorphic crudities (DR, p. 77).

Thus, if God is *relative,* God is relative eminently or supremely. Hartshorne uses the term "surrelative." Human beings love, but not literally, rather in an attenuated and qualified sense. Only God *literally* is love. God is literally, not metaphorically, *personal* (DR, p. 28).[17] Similarly, if God has power, God possesses it eminently, but that need not mean that human beings do not also possess power in an attenuated and qualified sense. God need not be—in order to be worshipful—the One possessing all power over against a world that has only derivative, nonagential, instrumental power.[18]

---

[16]This principle seems to parallel Whitehead's insistence that God need not be thought of as the single exception to whatever characterizes the rest of reality but as the "chief exemplification" of those characteristics.

[17]Like Calvin and Barth, Hartshorne maintains and underscores the personal nature of God.

[18]Thus Hartshorne carries through with his conviction that the divine nature should not be set over against all other natures as the exception to all their qualities but should rather be seen as the chief exemplification of *all* qualities exhibited by other natures. Yet the difference between these natures and God's is not a merely quantitative one but rather a qualitative one. While other natures partake of the categories, God is the only "literal instance" of them.

Hartshorne offers this "principle of eminence" as a corrective to the method employed by classical theism:

> Retreating from popular anthropomorphism classical theology fell backward into an opposite error. Intent on not exaggerating the likeness of the divine and the human, they did away with it altogether. . . . Love . . . became mere beneficence, totally unmoved . . . by the sufferings or joys of the creatures. . . . Scholastic theology utterly failed to express the Biblical idea of God. . . . A well-meaning attempt to purify theology of anthropomorphism purified it of any genuine, consistent meaning at all (OOTM, p. 29).

One result was religious sterility and nonviability. Another result was creation of paradoxes. If positive personal attributes cannot be analogically applied to God, then much of our religious language is turned into nonsense.[19] Hartshorne has little patience with paradoxes: "A theological paradox, it appears, is what a contradiction becomes when it is about God rather than something else, or indulged in by a theologian or a church rather than an unbeliever or a heretic" (DR, p. 1). Decrying the "metaphysical false modesty" of "seeking to honor deity by refusing to apply any of our positive conceptions to him" (DR, p. 35), Hartshorne applies both poles of the metaphysical categories to God to describe a "fuller perfection."[20]

In deriving the divine attributes, Hartshorne builds upon "the religious meaning of perfection"—worshipfulness. As he fills out the content of unsurpassability and all-inclusiveness which worshipfulness entails, Hartshorne does not find it necessary to avoid reference to positive human attributes; rather, these are seen as possessed eminently by God. This method leads to an understanding of divine perfection, genuinely dif-

---

[19]"To say, on the one hand, that God is love, to continue to use popular religious terms like Lord, divine will, obedience to God, and on the other to speak of an absolute, infinite, immutable, simple, impassive deity, is either a gigantic hoax of priestcraft, or it is done with the belief that the social connotations of the popular language are ultimately in harmony with these descriptions. Merely to speak of the 'mysteriousness' of God is not sufficient. If he escapes all the resources of our language and analysis, why be so insistent upon the obviously quite human concepts, absolute, infinite, perfect, immutable?" (DR, p. 26).

[20] "To combine in one's individuality the extremes of abstract and concrete, universal independence or nonrelativity and universal dependence or sensitivity, is to have maximal security and value as an individual" (DR, p. 81). More will be said about this perspective on perfection when Hartshorne's doctrine of dual transcendence is discussed.

ferent from that developed in classical theism. This is well illustrated in the notion of "perfect power," to which we now turn.

The Positive Content of Hartshorne's Understanding of Divine Power

Two metaphysical presuppositions shape the positive content of Hartshorne's understanding of divine power. The first, the *sociality/relativity of all reality*, largely forms the meaning of *"unsurpassable* power" and what it must necessarily include and exclude. The second, the *principle of dual transcendence*, directs toward a definition of omnipotence that is all-inclusive, taking in values expressed at both poles of the metaphysical contraries.

The Effect of Applying the Principle of the Relativity/Sociality of All Things to the Concept of Omnipotence

A central assumption of process theology is the relativity/sociality of all things. Hartshorne works within this framework and offers a thoroughgoing description of the implications of this assumption for the nature of divine power. In brief, the argument goes as follows: If reality is social/relative, then the highest conceivable power—unsurpassable power—will not be "a monopoly of power,[21] unilaterally determining all things, but . . . an ideal form of give and take" (LP, p. 44).[22]

Thus, God is necessarily one power among and related to[23] other powers. "Power," in Hartshorne's usage, connotes capacity for self-creation as well as other-creation. Every actual-

---

[21]"A monopoly of power is no ideal but . . . a nightmare, a ghastly semblance of meaning, which, looked at soberly and analytically, exhibits its inherent absurdity" (NTOT, p. 122).

[22]The ideal or perfect agent will enjoy the "optimal concentration of efficacy which is compatible with there being other efficacious agents." Hartshorne, "Omnipotence," p. 545.

[23]Both Barth and Hartshorne believe that God is such that relationship is primary and both seek to develop consistently relational interpretations of divine reality. But for Barth, while the intertrinitarian relationship is necessary, the God-world relationship is gratuitous. For Hartshorne, a general other (some world) is necessary. Similarly, while, for Barth, God is known only as a result of divine free decision, for Hartshorne, knowledge of God is a universal possibility. Davaney, p. 137.

Hartshorne also manifests a certain kinship with Calvin despite obvious differences. This can be seen in such comments as, "Self-knowledge and knowledge of God are apparently inseparable." Hartshorne, "The Idea of God: Literal or Analogical?" p. 136.

ity possesses power of this sort. If this is so, then God cannot
be conceived as a being possessing *all* power set over against a
world of purely derivative, nonagential, instrumental powers.

Traditional ways of describing omnipotence, such as the
"power to do anything that can be done," lose their meaning in
such a metaphysical framework. "There could not be a power to
'do anything that could be done.' Some things could only be
done by local powers; some only by cosmic power" (DR, p.
134).[24] Nor could there be a power that is "all-controlling."
Hartshorne is resolutely refusing to identify the unsurpassability
and all-inclusiveness of divine power with sheer "monopoly of
control," a concept he finds neither worshipful nor plausible,
given the nature of reality as he understands it.

The sociality/relativity principle is being applied to God
just as it is to all of reality. The difference between creaturely
relativity and divine relativity is that creaturely relativity only
applies to some aspects of a few things under certain circumstances, whereas God's relativity applies to all things and all
their aspects regardless of circumstances. Creaturely relativity is a "relative" matter, whereas God is *supremely* relative
or "surrelative."[25] Only God is literally and adequately related to all things.

Included in all instances of relativity is the condition of being
dependent upon and constituted by other realities. The attribute
of complete *independence,* so emphasized by the traditional concept of God, is being relinquished here. In its place a consistently conceivable notion of a "personal" God with the capacity
for genuine relations is gained.[26] The relations are internal; there
is no unchanging substance[27] (behind the process) having only
external relationships. Complete *immutability* is thereby also relinquished.[28] By virtue of these internal relations, God is consti-

---

[24]Hartshorne carries the principle of relativity to its logical conclusions with respect to
divine omniscience as well as omnipotence. Instead of being determinative of what is (as it
was for Calvin and Barth), divine knowledge is seen as being relative to its objects. As a
result, God knows the actual as actual and the possible as possible (OOTM, p. 27).

[25]"Deity is the supreme case of the social principle, rather than an exception to it"
(DR, p. 29).

[26]"A personal God is one who has social relations, really has them, and thus is constituted by relationships and hence is relative—in a sense not provided for by the traditional
doctrine of a divine Substance wholly nonrelative toward the world, though allegedly
containing loving relations between the 'persons' of the Trinity" (DR, p. x).

[27]In contrast to substance metaphysics, there is here no changeless substance behind
the process. Concrete reality is not substance or being but synthesis and becoming.
Davaney, p. 115.

[28]In fact, if God always relates to the world in an adequate manner, the content of that

tuted by and dependent upon those realities and therefore subject to the influence of creatures. Also relinquished is the assumption of divine *atemporality*.[29] Social experience is irrevocably temporal. The influence of one reality upon another is the influence of the past upon the present and the present upon the future. The past does not completely determine the present. In each moment of experience an entity creatively synthesizes the multiple data or stimuli presented by the past into a new emergent whole in an act of self-creation.[30] Both freedom and determination are in this manner accounted for.

Hartshorne argues that such a reassessment of omnipotence is not, as some would claim, a matter of allowing the world to "limit" the power of God. The reassessment, rather, points out that since reality is social, there is a social element in the very idea of power[31] that must be retained in forming *any* concept of maximal power.[32]

---

relationship must necessarily change as the world changes. A certain changeableness, then, is *required* as an accompaniment to relational adequacy. Davaney, p. 128.

[29]In this step all the questions concerning God's relation to the temporal world that trouble the tradition receive an answer. If temporality is admitted into the divine life, then the past is genuinely past for God and the future is genuinely future. There is no longer any assumption that God's omnipotence and omniscience bear the same relation to past, present, and future. Thus it no longer makes sense to ask whether God can change the past by virtue of divine omnipotence or know the future (as actual) by virtue of divine omniscience.

[30]"Each momentary unit of process comes into being by taking account of, appropriating, and integrating its past world into a unified integrity, and having reached this unity, it thereby ceases to be an active, experiencing subject; upon achieving this integrated determinateness, the unit becomes available as a stimulus, object, or datum for future experiencing subjects. Once it has reached this point, it cannot change, be affected, nor influenced." This is the settled facticity of the past. In this manner, God becomes datum for all and all things are datum for God. Davaney, p. 116.

[31]Sheila Greeve Davaney, in her comparison of the ideas of divine power held by Barth and Hartshorne, sees Hartshorne's social notion of power as the fundamental difference. Barth maintains a nonsocial notion of power. God keeps a monopoly on power, which is of the all-determining sort, even on the cross. Both Barth and Hartshorne seek to free the notion of omnipotence from its connotations of despotism or brute force, but Barth does so by emphasizing the gracious and benevolent character of divine ruling; he does not call into question its absolute nature. Hartshorne does exactly that. He is arguing that "monopoly of power" contradicts ethical, philosophical, and religious ideals of perfection. Even if concentrated in a benevolent deity, it amounts to tyranny which is to be resisted (AD, p. 201; CSPM, p. 292). While Barth may be said to be attaching a *nonsocial* understanding of divine power to an intentionally *social* doctrine of God, Hartshorne, on the other hand, follows through with a consistently social interpretation. Davaney, p. 144.

[32]Hartshorne, "Is Whitehead's God the God of Religion?" p. 220. Although Hartshorne does not draw the distinction between *scope* and *meaning* that I have been making, it seems to me that this is the issue which underlies this particular argument. A critique has been leveled that Hartshorne is limiting the *scope* of divine power. Harts-

Hartshorne insists that the kind of power that remains to be ascribed to God after the reassessment is not an inferior but a superior power to the one that the tradition offers. He remarks that the only form of power philosophically intelligible for a being that has *all* the power would be power exercised over nothing at all or over powerless things (which are really themselves nothing if it be true that "being is power"). The most perfect power conceivable (maximal power, unsurpassable power) is power over something that has power. "Omnipotence, in the only religiously sensible meaning, is *the ideal case of power assuming a division of power*, the maximal concentration of power that permits distribution of powers among a plurality of beings."[33]

An important point to note is that this principle of the relativity/sociality of all things is intended as a *metaphysical principle* that lies in the nature of things. Hartshorne does not see it as a contingent feature of reality or a matter of divine decision; it is a given even for God. Thus the presence of other powers is not a matter of divine volition that God could revoke at any time. Here Hartshorne parts company with thinkers who agree that God exercises power persuasively in a world of free creatures but insist that this is a matter of divine choosing, a moral limitation rather than a metaphysical one.

In conclusion, Hartshorne presents us with the import of the choice of whether or not to admit the metaphysical principle of the relativity/sociality of all things. "The dilemma appears final: either value is social and its perfection cannot be wholly within the power of any one being, even God; or it is not social at all, and the saying, 'God is love,' is an error" ("The Formally Possible Doctrines of God," p. 210). The tradition has gone too long without making this choice being made.

The Consequences of Hartshorne's Principle of Dual Transcendence for the Meaning of Omnipotence

Hartshorne, along with the classical tradition, affirms that God is the one perfect Being. He differs with the tradition fundamentally, however, in his understanding of what constitutes perfection. The view he develops, which he names "di-

horne claims that this is not so. Rather, the term "power" has been ill-defined as to *meaning* because of the failure to regard the relative/social nature of all reality.

[33]Hartshorne, "Is Whitehead's God the God of Religion?" p. 220.

polar theism" or "the principle of dual transcendence," constitutes a major insight that may prove useful for purposes of reshaping the doctrine of omnipotence.

Hartshorne observes that all basic metaphysical ideas come in pairs of contraries that are inseparable and that mutually imply one another. He criticizes the tradition for its "one-sidedness" in associating perfection with only one side of the metaphysical contrasts and denying the other (e.g., being is real, becoming is illusion).[34] He proposes that a primary "mistake" of classical theism is in distinguishing

> God from all else by putting God on one side of a long list of contraries: finite-infinite, temporal-eternal, relative-absolute, contingent-necessary, physical-spiritual. . . . This is a species of idolatry, implying that what we worship is infinity, eternity, absoluteness, necessity. . . . But these are empty abstractions. . . . God contrasts with creatures, not as infinite with finite, but as infinite-and-finite (both in uniquely excellent ways, beyond all possible rivalry or relevant criticism) (OOTM, p. 44).

Hartshorne's principle of dual transcendence offers a more inclusive notion of perfection entailing both metaphysical poles. God is not limited to one side only of the categorical contrasts but expresses each in supremely excellent ways.[35]

It has been noted that Hartshorne's proposal is in danger of the same kinds of contradictions he ascribes to classical theism.[36] He is in fact applying both a predicate and its negation to God. He avoids contradiction, however, by applying the two terms to different aspects or poles—abstract and concrete.[37] We might, for example, say that a certain person is unchangeably kind, yet the concrete instances of kindness will be changeable in response to changing circumstance (OOTM,

---

[34]Davaney, p. 111.

[35]"God is not on one side only of categorial contrasts: he is not merely infinite or merely finite, merely absolute or merely relative, merely cause or merely effect, merely agent or merely patient, merely actual or merely potential, but in all cases both, each in suitable respects or aspects of his living reality, and in such a manner as to make him unsurpassable by another" (NTOT, pp. 74–75).

[36]Farley, p. 138.

[37]Here Hartshorne's thinking is somewhat parallel to Whitehead's, following the distinction he makes between God's Primordial and Consequent Nature. Whitehead in turn was following, to some extent, Plato's "two Gods" thinking, with the purely eternal Demiurge corresponding to the abstract (Primordial) nature of God and the World Soul corresponding to the concrete (Consequent) nature of God. Hartshorne views the twentieth-century process position as in some respects "a return to Plato, after a very long detour" (OOTM, p. 53).

p. 45). Similarly, God may be absolute in the property of having adequate awareness *abstracted from* any determinate content and, at the same time, surrelative in actual adequate
awareness *with* determined content.

Hartshorne points to the religious value and importance of
affirming both the abstract and the concrete poles. It is important that divine immutability, for example, be in some sense
retained, for it is requisite for "reliability." If God were only
"mutable," God might fail us when the conditions were unfa-
vorable. But, on the other hand, "reliability" does not require
that one will be unaffected by changing conditions; in fact, a
certain "mutability" is required for adequate responsiveness
to our changing circumstances. Hartshorne's recommendation
is that,

> instead of allowing a foolish overestimation of independence or
> immutability to limit the possibility that God is love, we can say
> that God is absolute and immutable in just those respects that
> love permits and requires. Then we can be intellectually honest
> without repudiating the highest intuitions of our religious
> heritage.[38]

The abstract corresponds to the enduring identity that characterizes God in all successive states. This pole is not dependent upon but is indifferent to any particular conditions of the
world. It pertains to God's existence[39] and character and is the
unvarying dimension of divine perfection. The concrete "includes and exceeds the abstract" (DR, p. vii).[40] "The absolute
is . . . an abstract feature of the inclusive and supreme reality
which is precisely the personal God. . . . The absolute is not
more, but less, than God—in the obvious sense in which the
abstract is less than the concrete" (DR p. 83).

Of particular importance for the matter at hand is the application of the principle of dual transcendence to the metaphysical contraries "active" and "passive." The tradition, with its
"one-sidedness," sets God over against creatures as the single

---

[38]Hartshorne, "Divine Absoluteness and Divine Relativity," p. 171.

[39]"God is dependent on all things as literally as he is independent of all: the dependence is, every difference makes a divine difference; the independence is, *no* difference makes an *existential* divine difference." Hartshorne, "The Idea of God: Literal
or Analogical?" p. 135.

[40]By the "Law of Inclusive Contrast" one side of each pair can be seen to take
account of and include its polar contrast. There is therefore a certain asymmetry. The
concrete, for example, is the more inclusive of the concrete-abstract pair. It is the
final real thing; the abstract is only real as a constituent of the concrete. Davaney,
p. 112.

possessor of active, agential, determinative, causal power while creatures are by contrast passive/receptive, nonagential, determined, and causal only in an instrumental sense. Hartshorne contends that the assumption of the superiority of the former qualities (attributed to God) to the latter qualities (attributed to creatures) will not hold; it is anything but a report upon experience. The latter qualities do not, he insists, indicate powerlessness but rather additional dimensions of power. He considers openness to influence, for example, not to indicate a deficiency of power. Lack of power lies, not in being influenced, but only in being influenced in the wrong direction or disproportionately (NTOT, p. 134). A superior agent is one who is influenced; one who is open to the conditions of the world and acts with appropriateness and sensitivity (Davaney, p. 146).

Hartshorne, in keeping with his dipolar definition of perfection, insists upon including both sides of the contrast in the definition of power and locating the "literal instance" of each in God. Thus God, as preeminent power, is the "perfection of action-and-passion" (MVG, p. 273). Hartshorne is opposing the traditional notion of divine power as unidirectional determination with a view of divine power as *maximal capacity both to influence and to be influenced.* Both aspects of divine power are universal in scope and efficacy and particular in operation.

There are important repercussions to this step; only four will be explored here: (1) What does this move make possible? (2) How does divine power of this sort "work"? (3) Why is it peculiarly effective and in what sense qualitatively superior? (4) To what end is it directed?

What Does This Move Make Possible?

Perhaps the most important possibility opened up by this move is the possibility for divine *interaction* as opposed to simple action. Instead of being able only to affect, influence, and determine, God is now conceived as able to be affected, influenced, and determined. Genuine interchange with human beings becomes possible. Words like "relationship" and "love" and "service" can be spoken in relation to the divine without indulging in equivocation. The possibility of enriching the divine life is opened up to human endeavor. This is a step of major significance religiously. As Hartshorne has pointed out,

> If God permits us every privilege, but not that of enriching his life by contributing the unique quality of our own experience to

the more inclusive quality of his, by virtue of his sympathetic
interest in us, then he does less for us than the poorest of human creatures. . . . "To love," it has been said, "is to wish to
give rather than to receive"; but in loving God we are, according to Anselm and thousands of other orthodox divines, forbidden to seek to give: for God, they say, is a totally impassive,
nonreceptive, nonrelative being. Such guardians of the divine
majesty in my judgment know not what they do (DR, p. 55).

The possibility of human influence upon divine decisions is
also made available.

To say God is supremely sensitive is to say that in his rule he
allots to us a privilege of participation in governing which goes
infinitely beyond a mere ballot. It means that with every decision, however secret, that takes place in our minds we are cast-
ing a vote which will surely be taken account of and will surely
produce effects in the divine decisions (DR, p. 51).

How Does Divine Power of This Sort "Work"?

Hartshorne maintains consistency between divine power of
influence and human power of influence by using the model of
"knowing" as the mode of operation of both. The mind is
influenced by what it knows. All influence, both divine and
human, takes place by virtue of the one influencing becoming
an object of awareness or experience for the one who is influenced. "The power of God over us consists in his being the
supreme object of our awareness."[41]
Hartshorne's choice of the model of knowing is especially
apropos, given his intent to disestablish understandings of divine power that imply control. Our insight from experience[42]
is that objects of our awareness influence but do not control or
coerce us. This model has the further advantage of presenting
a coherent concept of power that can be applied to both God
and creatures.
Hartshorne has by his description established mutuality and
reciprocity of influence as opposed to unidirectional divine
influence. God manifests passive power in receiving the
world as an object of awareness into the divine life and experience. God's response of integrating that experience is a self-
determination that expresses active power and influences the

---

[41]Hartshorne, "Divine Absoluteness and Divine Relativity," p. 166.
[42]It should be remembered here that experience is a primary source for understanding reality in Hartshorne's system.

world by becoming a datum of experience universally. The creatures then receive this datum and decide how they will integrate it. Their response in turn contributes to the divine life. The degree of divine influence depends entirely upon the response of the one being influenced.

Why Is This Kind of Power Peculiarly Effective and in What Sense Qualitatively Superior?

God as the chief exemplification of power that is present in all reality is supremely powerful in both active and passive senses—capable of influencing and being influenced. There are basically three ways in which divine power expresses itself uniquely, in ways that no other power can: (1) in power to preserve and maintain worldly reality and divine existence in relation to it; (2) in power to order the world by general natural laws (setting limits to creaturely freedom, ensuring against chaos and guaranteeing "optimal conditions" for the attainment of aesthetic value);[43] and (3) in power to provide for every actuality the stimulus ("initial aim" or "ideal aim") to which each actuality must respond.

God's power is said to be peculiarly effective and qualitatively superior not by virtue of ability to ensure that world process will correspond with divine willing but in three other respects. First, God alone is the *universal*—and therefore all-pervasive—object of awareness. At the same time, divine awareness and therefore divine ability *to be influenced* is also universal.

Second, God's "knowing" is unique in ways that enable divine power to be preeminent in both its passivity/receptivity and its activity/responsiveness. God's knowledge is *conformal*. That is, God knows each thing as it is—the past as past, the actual as actual, the possible as possible. Divine knowledge is *all-inclusive* without being completely identified with the things known. God is affected by knowing them, but they are not changed by that act of divine knowing.[44] Divine knowl-

---

[43]The second of these will be shown to create some difficulties for Hartshorne which will be discussed in the closing evaluation of his system.

[44]Both the theory of knowledge in twentieth-century realism and that of medieval thought agree that the knower is relative and dependent with respect to the known and not vice versa. Yet this has traditionally been reversed when the discussion turns to God. Hartshorne is refusing the reversal. The relationship of known and knower in all cases—divine included—is similar to that which exists between the past and the present. The present is internally related to the past, but the past is externally related

edge is *preservative*. In Hartshorne's system, all knowledge is remembering. God's knowledge is perfectly and completely retentive/preservative and therefore stands as an immortal record and standard of truth. God knows and cherishes each experience through all time.

In brief, divine knowledge corresponds perfectly to what is, excludes nothing, and remembers and cherishes everything. God's perfect knowledge makes possible perfect receptivity and responsiveness to the world. Since, for Hartshorne, the very definition of power is capacity to be influenced (receptivity) and to influence (responsiveness), perfect receptivity and responsiveness indicate the qualitative superiority of divine power.

Hartshorne associates this perfection in knowledge with perfection in love. Love is adequate awareness of the value of others, an awareness that God possesses supremely. In the "lovingness" made possible by perfect knowledge, another dimension of the qualitative superiority of divine power is displayed.

A third demonstration of the peculiar effectiveness of divine power and its qualitative superiority is its extreme persuasiveness. "Persuasion" is, in Hartshorne's view, the most adequate way of thinking about the character of divine power. He appropriates this notion from Whitehead: the "divine method of world control is called 'persuasion' by Whitehead and is one of the greatest of all metaphysical discoveries" (DR, p. 142). Hartshorne more often speaks in terms of "influence,"[45] but he everywhere indicates that the power of this influence is in its persuasiveness. God as the supreme object of our awareness can, with changes in Godself,[46] inspire us with novel ideas for novel occasions. The response is entirely up to creatures, but we respond positively because the novel ideas are "fitting" and "attractive."[47] "Power over others consists in this, that one's own reality is rich in value which fits the needs of others and is attractive to them as datum for their awareness" (LP, p. 275). We then "take our cues" by "feel-

---

to—and hence not changed by—the present. There is a becoming, undetermined present and a fixed/determined past.

[45]"Power is influence, perfect power is perfect influence" (MVG, p. xvi).

[46]This is divine self-determination. Changes occur in God in response to world process, and these changes then affect world process as they are received again from God as the primary object of awareness.

[47]"All power is of the nature of appeal, attractiveness, or 'charm,' acting either directly or indirectly." Hartshorne, "Religion in Process Philosophy," p. 262.

ing" that which God desiderates (DR, p. 142). In this sense we are provided with a "lure" and a "vision" that influence our entire activity.[48]

That the divine influence is not only persuasive but extremely persuasive (powerful) is accounted for by Hartshorne in relation to the other two factors mentioned above, namely, receptivity/responsiveness and lovingness.

> The causative power of God is really due to his unique facility in responding as effect to all things as causes, that is to his loving appropriation of all lives. God has power over us because we cannot but love him, at least unconsciously.[49]

This is not the use of coercive force but the lure of value and vision. It is a power of persuasion; influence willingly granted. "The power of God is the worship he inspires" (Whitehead).[50] It is not that the power inspires worship, but that the worshipfulness is the power.

To What End Is This Power Directed?

Divine power lures toward ever-increasing "harmony" and "intensity." Aesthetic terms are used by Hartshorne to describe what is good; "the good" and "the beautiful" coincide for him. God's action is fully informed action, balanced and measured in relation to all who feel its effect[51] and aimed at the above-mentioned goals. In this is the divine righteousness.

There is a coincidence in the interests of the world and God. Divine action in relation to the world is not, as in the tradition, gratuitous and self-sacrificial, for God receives value from the world.[52] The good that God does comes back to God in future enjoyment of a better (richer and more harmonious) world. This is not taken to mean that God has only enlight-

---

[48]"Lure" and "vision" are terms more often used by Whitehead and underscored by Lewis Ford's reading of Whitehead. But Hartshorne's own thought does seem to be consistent with such a reading. God's influence is efficacious because God offers the world the most perfect vision of what it might be. There is a futuring dimension to the exercise of divine power. It operates as a lure. Consequently, to understand the power of God we must focus on how the future can be effective in the present. Ford, *The Lure of God*.

[49]Hartshorne, "Whitehead and Berdyaev: Is There Tragedy in God?" p. 82.

[50]Hartshorne, "Religion in Process Philosophy," p. 184.

[51]Human action is ignorant and insensitive by comparison.

[52]This perspective provides a conceivable "purpose" for creation. In the tradition this has been elusive, since God was complete apart from any world and derived no particular benefit from creation.

ened self-interest in view. In God, egoism and altruism are one. Whereas the ethical task for creatures is often seen as seeking a balance between benefits to the self and to others, there is no such conflict for God. The world's good is God's good. God desires a world where the needs of creatures are maximally met. It is not creaturely needs per se that lead to selfish action but our inability to see our need fulfilled in the good of others (except in relationships of deepest love). This inability is sometimes a function of ignorance and sometimes a function of selfishness (when our needs conflict or seem to conflict with those of others). God's need is in fact the good of others and is accurately perceived by God as such. God seeks to persuade in the direction of the good.

In conclusion, it has been shown that Hartshorne gives a convincing case for his dipolar theism. When his principle of dual transcendence is applied specifically to the metaphysical contraries "active" and "passive," the repercussions for the meaning of divine power are significant. Omnipotence as the ability to control things in such a way that world process comes to correspond with the divine will is denied. In its place is presented a meaning for omnipotence as "maximal capacity to influence and be influenced." This meaning makes possible "interaction" between God and creation rather than unidirectional action. Its operation is modeled on the analogy of knowing, in which the knower is influenced but not coerced by what is known. Its peculiar effectiveness and qualitative superiority consist in its universality, perfect receptivity/responsiveness, lovingness, and persuasiveness. This power is exercised with the well-being (harmony and intensity of experience) of all concerned in view.

5

A Critical Assessment of Hartshorne's Position

This evaluation will be limited to a consideration of the results of Hartshorne's alternative definition for two theological problems: the problem of the relation between freedom and determination and the problem of theodicy. The contribution of his redefinition will be viewed against the backdrop of the tradition's handling of these issues working under the constraints of a different understanding of divine power. The discussion will proceed through the exploration of five questions designed to help evaluate the coherence and religious viability of the proposal that Hartshorne is making. The last of these questions will conclude the chapter with an assessment of the degree to which Hartshorne has succeeded in accomplishing what he set out to do in redefining divine power.

What Is the Relation Between Freedom and Determination in Hartshorne's Position?

Hartshorne's principles of dual transcendence and the relativity/sociality of all things make possible a credible account of the relation between freedom and determination, particularly as it relates to creaturely freedom and divine determination.

Hartshorne insists that "the only livable doctrine of divine power is that it influences all that happens but determines nothing in its concrete particularity" (OOTM, p. 25). This understanding effectively resolves the problem of reconciling divine determination with creaturely freedom. Nevertheless it will be helpful to go into some detail concerning how Hartshorne is conceiving the relation between the two and what he is affirming and denying in his treatment of the matter.

According to Hartshorne, part of the difficulty with the traditional doctrine of omnipotence is that it is formulated apart from a clear vision of the world in which that power is to be exercised.

> The problem is the assumption that the meaning of perfect power or omnipotence can be settled apart from a metaphysical discussion of the nature of the "beings" upon whom this perfect power is to be exercised. This leads writers into arguments that are formally invalid because devoid of necessary premises. . . . Delimitation of the concept of perfect power requires a discussion of the nature of the world.[1]

It is a fundamental assumption of Hartshorne's that the world is an actual world of actual creatures—and actuality entails power. But a creature has no power if it can be totally determined by some being or beings other than itself. Thus real creatures cannot be fully determinable by another.

In fact, he continues, creatures have both the power of self-creation and the power of other-creation.[2] In the language of causality, they have the capacity to exercise final causation in effecting self-creation (concrescence)[3] and efficient causation in effecting other-creation (transition).[4]

Regarding the creatures' freedom/creativity/power, Hartshorne seems to say two things. On the one hand, God has (willingly) created us creators of ourselves; we are God's self-creating creatures (OOTM, p. v). God has chosen to imbue creatures with *real* power for self-creation rather than with only the show of power.[5] On the other hand, Hartshorne seems to say that creating self-creative creatures was *not* a function of divine volition but a metaphysical necessity if there were to be any creatures at all.

> The familiar query "Why did God make free beings, with all the dangers this involved?" is meaningless since it supposes an

---

[1]Griffin, p. 265.

[2]Both of these might seem to fall under Hartshorne's category of power of influence, active power. However, the power *to be influenced*, passive power, is also relevant here. One's self-creation and other-creation are in part informed by the influences of others. This will become more evident in the discussion of universal causality. What one does in the way of self-creation and other-creation takes account of and renders itself appropriate to antecedent causes without being absolutely determined by them (PSG, p. 2).

[3]Griffin, p. 277.

[4]"Its own constitution involves that its own activity in *self*-formation passes into its activity of *other*-formation." Whitehead, *Adventures of Ideas*, p. 248.

[5]Quoting William Ellery Channing approvingly, Hartshorne says, "It is [God's] glory that he creates beings like himself, free beings . . . that he confers on them the reality, not the show, of power" (OOTM, p. v).

alternative where there is none. Possible alternatives are within freedom, not to it.[6]

The freedom of creatures involves a metaphysical necessity because actuality implies power and power is self- and other-creative.[7]

The nature of actuality as powerful and therefore free and creative places a "metaphysical limitation" upon the exercise of divine power.[8] This condition is not the same as the "moral limitation" the tradition at times places upon the exercise of divine power. For Hartshorne, God not only does not but in principle *cannot* completely control events in the world (OOTM, p. 6).[9] Traditional theologies have indeed said that persuasion is the divine *modus operandi,* but the limit is seen as self-imposed. That is, it is better (so that certain ends can be attained) for God to exercise persuasive rather than controlling power.

Hartshorne's position regarding the freedom of creatures is to be contrasted with that of the tradition in other important ways as well. This is seen most clearly in his critique of the compatibilist framework, which he directs from several angles. First he argues that their position lacks logical coherency.

> In spite of what Thomists say, it is impossible that our act should be both free and yet a logical consequence of a divine action which "infallibly" produces its effect. Power to cause someone to perform by his own choice an act precisely defined by the cause is meaningless (DR, p. 135).

Hartshorne raises the issue of religious viability: If we could affirm such "nonsense," all that we gain by saying that God is the cause of our free acts is divine responsibility for sin (DR, p. 135). In Hartshorne's view, such an assertion goes against our most basic religious intuitions and our most common hu-

---

[6]Hartshorne, "Whitehead and Berdyaev: Is There Tragedy in God?" p. 78.

[7]Perhaps Hartshorne means the "volitional" aspect to refer to the high degree of freedom that creatures manifest and that presumably God desires and lures them toward.

[8]Hartshorne would object to the term "limitation," since, in his view, the concept of power without this limitation is nonsensical.

[9]It is important to note in this regard that metaphysical categories, according to Hartshorne, are neither a function of divine volition nor a question of a higher law to which God is subject. They belong to the eternal essence of God. Metaphysical categories are necessary, cosmic laws are contingent. That there will be freedom is "necessary"; how much freedom there will be is "contingent."

man values. The frequently used analogy for deity is the parental role. But no parent—much less an ideal parent—seeks to control every detail of the child's life or make every decision for him or her (OOTM, p. 12). The idea of God fully determining without constraining our decisions[10] appeals more readily to the analogy of the hypnotist than that of the ideal parent. As in other arenas of discussion, Hartshorne measures this image against commonsense notions of what perfect power entails. "Is it the highest ideal of power to rule over puppets who are permitted to think they make decisions but who are really made by another to do exactly what they do?" (OOTM, p. 12).

Last, Hartshorne accuses the compatibilists of equivocating on the meaning of decision.

> The theistic version of strict determinism is the most glaringly inconsistent of all. For it splits decision into two forms which differ absolutely: the divine deciding back of which there is nothing whatever (neither any necessity of the agent's nature nor any influence of other agents), contrasted to our deciding, which is wholly determined by antecedent influences. So we have agents with no individuality of decision-making on the one hand, and an agent whose decisions are absolutely individual, totally uninfluenced or without social character, on the other.[11]

Neither decision *en vacuo* nor wholly determined decision makes sense to Hartshorne. In his system, all decisions are to some extent determined by antecedent conditions and to some extent a matter of choosing among alternatives. A supreme power, therefore, could conceivably set conditions more or less favorable to a particular choice, but the decision could not be in all respects inevitable. "Decision" by its very nature is not wholly inevitable and loses all meaning when inevitability is assigned, as it is in the compatibilist framework.

Hartshorne is defining creaturely freedom differently from Calvin and Barth. For them, freedom was defined as obedience to God, conformity to the all-determining divine will. It was claimed that this was "free" because it did not entail co-

---

[10]Classical theism does not intend to present this determination as coercive. The position is mitigated by the assumption that "when I act it is also God acting through me." Such identity of divine and human deciding/acting is not possible for Hartshorne. He sees self-decision and divine persuasion "as distinct but indispensable and complementary aspects of every act of freedom." Ford, *The Lure of God*, p. 19.

[11]Hartshorne, "A New Look at the Problem of Evil," p. 204.

ercion or compulsion. The inner working of the Holy Spirit is such that we will what God wills us to will and therefore act "freely." For Hartshorne, this minimalist definition of freedom is unacceptable. Freedom must involve more than simply the noncoercion or noncompulsion which Calvin and Barth claim. It must necessarily involve the exercise of a relatively independent will making real decisions, choosing from among real alternatives.

Hartshorne rejects not only the compatibilists' position but also the alternatives they had in view: the position of absolute determinism (that every event is determined by its causes) and the position of absolute indeterminism[12] (that at least some events have no cause). Hartshorne argues for a third option that sees freedom and determination not as contradictory but as complementary modes of ongoing experience— reality viewed from different standpoints. In such "relative determinism," or "relative indeterminism," each actuality is conditioned by its past and data of experience, but in its present "coming-to-be" it exercises freedom. "Causality is crystallized freedom, freedom is causality in the making."[13]

Hartshorne accepts universal causality but does not equate this with determinism. All events have causes but are not absolutely determined by them. The causes may limit[14] more or less sharply what can happen without fully determining happenings (LP, pp. 162ff.). The determinist assumes that if the causes can be fully known, then the effect can be infallibly predicted. Hartshorne admits an element of chance, a creative leap, the self- and other-creation of free creatures. All concrete individuals are momentary units of experience or processes of creative synthesis whereby a multiplicity of past experiences are prehended and integrated into a novel present actuality.[15] The synthesis is genuinely creative.

If Hartshorne's position of "relative determinism" (or "relative indeterminism") is accepted, the forced choice made by

---

[12]Hartshorne observes that absolute indeterminism is a doctrine no one defends, a fictitious position invented for the purpose of controversy. By ostentatiously burning this "straw man," deterministic writers frequently distract attention from the real opponent. Hartshorne, "Freedom Requires Indeterminism and Universal Causality," p. 793.

[13] Hartshorne, "A New Look at the Problem of Evil," p. 233.

[14]"That the freedom of one agent is limited by the freedom of others is the social structure of existence. That one's freedom now is limited by the freedom already exercised in the past is the temporal structure of existence." Hartshorne, "Introduction: The Development of Process Philosophy," p. 55.

[15]Davaney, p. 147.

the tradition between chance and providence[16] is shown to be a false alternative. We need not choose between unlimited chance which is sheer chaos and providential control of all things which amounts to divine determinism. Both "chance" and "providence" may be applied in different and more limited senses. The context of conditions may providentially set boundaries for chance, but decisions and details of events are not divinely decreed; they are left undetermined. God may be thought of as optimizing conditions under which local agents determine local happenings. "No longer do we face the cruel alternative: either no divine control or the deliberate divine contriving of all our woes" (DR, p. 137). In Hartshorne's opinion, this picture in no way diminishes the majesty of God.

> Only when viewed as a power inspiring yet not individually determining, countless acts of partial self-determination, wondrously coordinated to make a coherent world in which frustration and confusion, though real, are secondary, while fulfillment and harmony are primary can we adequately appreciate the "grandeur of reason incarnate" (LP, p. 189).

Hartshorne's account of the relation between creaturely freedom and divine determination is plausible. His principles are consistently and coherently applied to actuality at all levels, creaturely and divine. For this reason, he does not need to equivocate on such basic terms as "freedom" and "decision." The meanings for "freedom" and "decision" with which he is working are recognizably kin to commonsense notions of what these terms mean. They are not vulnerable to the same kinds of criticisms to which the traditional meanings were subjected. Creatures are granted real freedom that implies power, power that is not reducible to derivative, nonagential, instrumental power and power that cannot be revoked by divine volition.

What Is the Effect of Hartshorne's Understanding of Divine Power Upon His Approach to the Theodicy Problem?

Because Hartshorne understands divine power in this new way which provides a credible account of creaturely freedom, he is enabled to construct a credible theodicy based upon a

---

[16]A choice with which Calvin was preoccupied and which led him to an extreme position.

"free will" defense. In fact, because of Hartshorne's presuppositions about the nature of power (as relative/social and active/passive), the theodicy problem does not even arise for him in its usual form.

> In its appeal to the imagination [the theodicy problem] . . . will no doubt always be the most troublesome one in theology. But in pure logic it is not true that there is a sheer contradiction between the joint admission of divine perfection of goodness and divine perfection of power on the one hand and the fact of the reality of evil on the other, for the simple reason that the greatest possible power (which by definition is "perfect power") may not be the same as "all the power that exists united into one individual power," for such union of "all" power may be impossible. Had God "all the power there is," he must be responsible for all that happens. . . . The minimal solution of the problem of evil is to affirm the necessity of a division of powers, hence of responsibilities, as binding even upon a maximal power (MVG, p. 207).

In other words, Hartshorne's view of the problem is that it is a "pseudo problem" due to a "pseudo concept" of omnipotence. The blame for evil cannot be lodged in any one being; whatever happens is the outcome of multiple interacting freedoms. Evil springs from creaturely freedom, and without that freedom there could be no world at all.

Just as "good," for Hartshorne, is defined aesthetically as "harmony and intensity," evil is defined, correspondingly, as "discord and triviality." If discord—and the suffering it involves—were alone the essence of evil (as the tradition sometimes seems to assume), then the best way to have avoided evil would have been to avoid creating a world altogether. Once a "world"[17] has been created, discord is unavoidable.

Discord may be manifest in either metaphysical or moral evil.[18] Either form is a result of multiple freedoms pursuing incompatible values. All are "good" aims, but they are not all compossible. *Metaphysical evil* is often manifest in situations of "mutual obstruction," creatures making choices in ignorance of the choices of other creatures or in ignorance of the results of the combined choices. These, then, are choices "innocently" made. The relativity/sociality of existence makes

---

[17]For Hartshorne this must necessarily be a world of free creatures (with the accompanying risk of discord among them).

[18]Here I am using "moral evil" to mean evil *intentions* (sin) and "metaphysical evil" to mean evil *effects* (regardless of the intentions of the agency).

metaphysical evil inevitable. Yet it is *genuine evil,* because it would have been far better if the goods being sought could have been achieved without discord. The pain and suffering that result from the discord are regrettable. It is not presumed that the discord is instrumentally good, a "blessing in disguise."

Metaphysical evil (pain and suffering) may also be the result of *moral evil* when the discord has its source in deliberate self-centered action. Here the one acting *knowingly refuses* to take the interests of others (or the known negative outcome of combined actions) into account. The human being, for example, is self-transcending and able to consider the common good. To fail to do so, to ignore the needs of others in decision making, is moral evil.[19] This is even more obviously *genuine* evil.[20]

Hartshorne does not claim that his redefinition of omnipotence solves the problem of evil. But it does change the nature of the question. The question can no longer be, Why does God permit evil in the world? If the world is actual, its creatures will be free. If there are free creatures, they may be mutually obstructive (intentionally or unintentionally).[21] There will inevitably be the risk of evil. The question becomes quantitative. Does the opportunity for good made possible by the degree of freedom present in world process outweigh the risk of evil which accompanies that freedom? God might be indictable for the *high degree of freedom* that makes possible the *high degree of risk of evil.* Hartshorne's main defense here is three-pronged: (1) The opportunity for good is inextricably linked to the possibility for evil, (2) it is probable that the concrete outcome is in fact more good than evil, and (3) God suffers every evil that is suffered by any creature. Each of these will be discussed in turn.

---

[19]Problem: If God is luring all actual entities toward their greatest self-actualization, will there not be times when the greater values will be destroyed for the sake of lesser ones (i.e., the mosquito that spreads malaria)? John Cobb was the first to pose the problem in this way. Hartshorne is assuming that the good is social in character and does not lie in mindless pursuit of selfish interest. However, only creatures of a high level of development are able to take the interests of others into account.

[20]Hartshorne, "A New Look at the Problem of Evil," pp. 32ff.

[21]Hartshorne is clear that God does not will or do evil in any sense. "No concrete evil is divinely decided, whether as punishment, means of spiritual edification, or in view of any other end." Hartshorne, "A New Look at the Problem of Evil," p. 207. "Perhaps there is no *why* God sends us evils, since he does not send them at all. Rather he establishes an order in which creatures can send each other particular goods and evils" (NTOT, p. 120).

The possibility for evil is, for Hartshorne, inextricably linked to the possibility for good.[22]

> The risk of evil is inherent in multiple individuality since this means multiple freedom or self-determination. . . . The risk is worthwhile since multiple freedom is the condition of any opportunity for good.[23]

The matter can be put even more strongly. The "opportunity for good" and the "risk of evil" increase and decrease in proportion with each other.

> Great opportunity and great risk seem in fact to go together. And this is no mere accident. Great good means great sensitivity and intensity. But great evil arises from the same source. . . . Given beings of slight intensity, slight scope of alternative reactions, the harm they can do each other will be slight; for great suffering, high tragedy, is beyond their natures. But so is great joy, profound happiness. Great value consists in experiences characterized by wide ranges of freedom and capacity for intense sympathetic responses (DR, p. 136).[24]

By this particular line of argumentation Hartshorne may place in jeopardy his position's hopes of making reference (consistently) to genuine evil as opposed to *prima facie* evil. It is clear that he can claim, in the face of any concrete instance of evil (whether metaphysical or moral), that it would be better, all things considered, if this *particular* evil had not occurred. But can he make the claim more generally that, all things considered, it would be better if evil *in general* did not exist? He has so fully tied the risk of evil (as discord)—and even its inevitability, given the mutually obstructive nature of things—to any possibility for good (as intensity of experience)

---

[22]There is a tragic dimension here. The possibility for evil is a necessary precondition of the possibility of good—and even of there being any world at all. Nevertheless evil is *not* necessary in any of its concrete expressions, thus there is also the hope of its overcoming.

[23]Hartshorne, "Divine Absoluteness and Divine Relativity," p. 168.

[24]Here Hartshorne is following Whitehead very closely. "Decay, Transition, Loss, Displacement belong to the essence of the Creative Advance. . . . As soon as high consciousness is reached, the enjoyment of existence is entwined with pain, frustration, loss, tragedy. Amid the passing of so much beauty, so much heroism, so much daring, Peace is then the intuition of permanence. It keeps vivid the sensitiveness to the tragedy; and it sees the tragedy as a living agent persuading the world to aim at fineness beyond the faded level of surrounding fact. Each tragedy is the disclosure of an ideal—What might have been, and was not." Whitehead, *Adventures of Ideas*, pp. 368–369.

that this would be a difficult claim to maintain.[25] It might be argued that in Hartshorne's system genuine evil exists in particular but not in general.

In making the case that, in spite of evil, world process is more likely to be characterized by good, Hartshorne first observes that it is not evil that is inexplicable.

> That there is not perfect harmony and security is already explained by the notion of self-determining creatures, the only positively conceivable kind of creatures. What cannot be explained . . . is that in spite of all discord and peril a world of coexisting, and insofar mutually harmonious, things can exist and continue. This is the providential aspect, that it all adds up to a meaningful world (NTOT, p. 120).

The providential aspect is God's doing. God sets optimal conditions for maximum good and then supplies the ideal aim for each actual occasion.[26] This serves as a lure to harmony and intensity of experience. Because of God's constant, powerful, uniquely appealing persuasion, there is a meaningful world and one in which there is likely to be more good than evil. Nevertheless there is no guarantee in any particular instance that good will triumph—only a strong probability.[27]

Hartshorne has been much criticized for letting go of the tenet that God guarantees the triumph of the good. Hartshorne makes no apology for this "loss." It is the logical outcome of his alternative perspective on the nature of perfect power.

> Concerning the frequently alleged need for the worshiper to believe in "omnipotence" in order to feel wholly safe in the

---

[25]Intensity jeopardizes harmony. Hartshorne has associated "intensity," which is the overcoming of the evil of triviality, with the generation of the evil of discord (through the creation of a high degree of freedom that will be accompanied necessarily by the risk of this other form of evil).

[26]In Whitehead's phraseology, evil arises from the capacity of the actual entity not to conform to this "initial aim." Although the initial aim is given by God, the subjective aim is chosen by the subject. It is conditioned, though not determined, by the initial aim supplied by "the ground of all order and of all originality." Whitehead, *Process and Reality*, p. 108.

[27]Hartshorne is not able to offer this with the same certainty that Whitehead's system allowed. Whitehead provides for the "saving" of that which is "worth saving." Thus, presumably, only that which is good will remain everlastingly. Hartshorne, on the other hand, seems to call for a perfect preservation of both good and evil (in tact) forever in divine experience. Still, at any given moment we do have, added to that which has been preserved, God's good aims. The latter may tip the balance in the direction of the good.

hands of God, I can only submit that the longing for security is one thing, worship another.[28] Thus omnipotence in the form of a general providential tendency favoring the good and able to guarantee it a minimum of persistence through all future time answers to a general spiritual need. But for omnipotence which guarantees the exact degree and the last detail of future goods there is not only no need but also no possible place in an ethically significant world.[29]

In Hartshorne's system, God suffers every evil that creatures suffer. The God of classical theism may impose suffering as the punishment for sin but lacks passive power and therefore cannot be said to "suffer." In the neoclassical theism that Hartshorne advocates, God does not impose suffering; rather, we impose it upon ourselves and one another. God is to be viewed as "the fellow sufferer who understands" (Whitehead).[30] A God who is open to being affected—a victim and not an imposer of evil—is not so easily indictable as the God of classical theism.

In fact, Hartshorne's alternative definition of omniscience makes it certain that God will undergo whatever suffering there is to be undergone. "Omniscience, as conformative, inclusive, and preservative, leaves nothing out but brings everything into the divine life."[31] "God does not simply know that we suffer, but he knows our actual sufferings in their concreteness."[32] Thus "tragedy is not outside the divine life. The divine love takes all suffering upon itself."[33]

Hartshorne considers the ability to be affected a sign of excellence rather than a sign of imperfection (as classical theism regards it).

> Sympathetic dependence is a sign of excellence and waxes with every ascent in the scale of being. . . . The eminent form of sympathetic dependence can only apply to deity, for this form cannot be less than an omniscient sympathy, which depends upon and is exactly colored by every nuance of joy or sorrow anywhere in the world (DR, p. 48).

---

[28]Hartshorne, "Divine Absoluteness and Divine Relativity," p. 168.

[29]Hartshorne, "Redefining God," p. 11.

[30]"I hold that though God does not inflict suffering upon us (rather we inflict it upon ourselves and one another), the sufferings which occur are not simply outside the divine life." Hartshorne, "A New Look at the Problem of Evil," p. 207.

[31]Davaney, p. 220.

[32]Hartshorne, "A New Look at the Problem of Evil," p. 207.

[33]Hartshorne, "The Idea of God: Literal or Analogical?" p. 135.

The matter of God's being affected by our joy or sorrow is in part grounded in divine worshipfulness which entails divine all-inclusiveness. Hartshorne distinguishes his position on divine all-inclusiveness, which he characterizes as "panentheism," from "pantheism."[34] This is an important distinction for the present argument. Inclusion does not mean identity; our inclusion in the divine life is inclusion as objects of divine knowledge.[35] "It inheres in the very meaning of knowledge that it does not determine but accepts its objects."[36]

Intimations of divine suffering are present in the tradition but not treated with full seriousness, Hartshorne says. "The cross is a sublime and matchless symbol of this, partly nullified by theological efforts to restrict suffering and sympathy to God as incarnate" (MVG, p. 198). The cross is an instance of what is true of the divine life in every moment. It is not the sign of divine triumph over evil but rather the presence of God as "the fellow sufferer who understands."[37] God is "tortured, not by himself, but by the creatures who, in injuring each other, in some degree and manner crucify deity itself" (PSG, p. 210).

Some thinkers have proposed that this admission of divine suffering cannot further Hartshorne's theodicy argument. Everything seems to be resolved in the divine life because God "overcomes" evil in God's own experience, making the best of what has happened and then using it to further God's ideal aims. God seems even to gain from evil. This criticism stems from a misunderstanding of Hartshorne's position.[38] God does

---

[34] Hartshorne is careful to distinguish his position from pantheism in an argument that is lost on many of his critics. Pantheism is a special way of conceiving divine all-inclusiveness and not the way Hartshorne adopts. He agrees with classical theism concerning the importance of divine individuality and independence from any particular world. But he also agrees with pantheism that God is inclusive of all reality. He notes that while pantheism destroys the distinction between God and the world, deism destroys their interrelation (DR, p. 84), and he characterizes his position as being as far from the former as from the latter (DR, p. 88). " 'Panentheism' is an appropriate term for the view that deity is in some real aspect distinguishable from and independent of any and all relative items, and yet, taken as an actual whole, includes all relative items" (DR, p. 89).

[35] Self- and other-determination are powers of all actuality. In pantheism this would be collapsed into self-determination, since there would no longer be an "other."

[36] Hartshorne, "Divine Absoluteness and Divine Relativity," pp. 165–166.

[37] It has been observed that neoclassical theology because of this insight might well be understood as a systematized *theologia crucis* or radicalized patripassionism.

[38] The critics seem to be reading Whitehead's viewpoint into Hartshorne. For Whitehead, the evil is, in a sense, transfigured and resolved in the divine life. God

not desire, does not cause, and does not benefit from evil in world process. Nor does evil further God's aims—in any instance good could have done so much better. God literally participates in the suffering of creatures as it happens and suffers all the more by virtue of perfect knowledge (conformal, inclusive, preservative). To say that God has some gain from evil would be comparable to saying that human beings benefit from the ill-health of their own bodies.

In summary, Hartshorne has resolved the question of why God allows evil in world process. The question was shown to be a "pseudo question" based upon a "pseudo concept" of omnipotence. Once the nature of power is shown to be relative/social and active/passive, that question is resolved. Given the nature of actuality as entailing such power, the only way to avoid evil would have been not to create a world at all. Evil takes two forms: triviality and discord. Traditional theodicies have mistakenly concentrated exclusively on the latter. If preventing discord were the only consideration, then it would indeed have been best that a world *not* be created. However, in Whitehead's words, God's persuasive activity has led the finite realm out of a state of trivial chaos, and discord has appeared as a kind of "half-way house" between perfection and triviality.[39]

A different sort of theodicy question remains for Hartshorne to consider. Can God be justified in luring creation to such a state of complexity (freedom, intensity) that this high degree of evil is possible? Hartshorne responds with arguments from three directions: (1) Opportunity for good and risk of evil are inextricably bound and conversely proportional, (2) God is working for good and it is probable that there will be more good than evil in world process, and (3) God suffers with us in our suffering.

Hartshorne does not claim for his position that he has settled the quantitative theodicy question that remained after his redefinition of omnipotence settled the qualitative theodicy question. The quantitative question is one that, in a sense, cannot be answered.

> Of course I do not claim to have observed as an empirical fact that the ratio of risk and opportunity in the world, as deter-

---

only saves what is "worth saving." For Hartshorne, however, experience is perfectly preserved just as it was.

[39]Whitehead, *Adventures of Ideas*, pp. 255–260.

mined by deity, is as favorable as any possible, in view of antecedent decisions. Without being omniscient, how could anyone
make such an observation? What I have done is to formulate an
idea of adequate cosmic power that is apparently free from the
absurdities that haunt traditional notions of omnipotence (DR,
p. 138).

This is no small achievement.

Does Hartshorne's Critique Caricature the Tradition?

Hartshorne's interpretation of the traditional doctrine of omnipotence—as implying coercive, all-determining force, actual
or potential possession of all the power there is, and responsibility for everything that happens—has not gone unchallenged
by modern defenders of classical theism.[40] Nelson Pike, for example, has insisted that the "standard view" of omnipotence
does not reduce to Hartshorne's term "monopoly."[41] He
charges Hartshorne with treating power as if it were a fixed
quantity (like marbles), so that if God has all the power, we
have no power.[42] His claim is that creatures are *not* devoid of
power in the "standard view" of omnipotence. Pike does admit, however, that (in the standard view) God's power is understood to be greater power, so that God could "overpower"
any other power that exists. This being the case, the exercise of
any other power is importantly conditioned—contingent upon
God's self-limitation of power. It is arguable that, in effect, this
reduces to "monopoly" and that Pike is making a distinction
without a difference.

Nevertheless, orthodox theism cannot simply be identified
with the position Hartshorne is combating. The tradition is
filled with references to God that imply divine relatedness to
creation. Hartshorne's point is, rather, that these elements can
be added to a metaphysic of static perfection only by sheer
contradiction.[43] He does admit that certain tendencies within
the tradition—the development of mysticism and negative theology, for example—respond to the perceived inadequacy of
the all-too-Greek flavor of the dominant theologies. Hartshorne
characterizes the incorporation of Greek metaphysics as a

---

[40]Whitney, *Evil and the Process God*, p. 133.

[41]Pike, p. 154.

[42]In a later work, *Omnipotence and Other Theological Mistakes*, Hartshorne makes it
clear that it is not his intention to treat power quantitatively.

[43]Farley, p. 133.

theological mistake "half-realized" which drove the dominant theologies to indulge in "double-talk" (OOTM, p. 11).

The whole compatibilist position is a case in point. It was not the intention of the tradition to present divine power as coercive force or absolute determination. Creaturely freedom was assumed and a place was sought for it within the tradition. But, given the metaphysical presuppositions operating, a place could not be found without engaging in double-talk.[44] Hartshorne's invitation is to a more coherently conceivable theology. (Not everything verbalizable is coherently conceivable.) What is needed is a new metaphysical base.

> To mitigate these absurdities theologians introduce various more or less subtle equivocations. Would they not do better to take a fresh start . . . and admit that we have no good religious reason for positing the notion of providence as an absolute contriving of all events according to a completely detailed plan? . . . The religious value of such a notion is more negative than positive. . . . [It is an] arbitrary notion, which after all is invariably softened by qualifications surreptitiously introduced *ad hoc* when certain problems are stressed! (DR, pp. 23–24).

Hartshorne's position is not a caricature that disregards these corrective efforts. It is, rather, an invitation to bring the metaphysical base into closer alignment with these fundamental religious intuitions so that double-talk will no longer be necessary.

Does Hartshorne Place Limits Upon Divine Power?

It has become commonplace among critics of neoclassical theism to say that Hartshorne "places limits on divine power." The criticism seems to be based upon three presuppositions that Hartshorne has been disputing: (1) the cumulative/quantitative understanding of divine power, so that power granted to creatures necessarily reduces the amount of power God could potentially possess; (2) a view that actuality is not inherently powerful; that there could be a world in which creatures did not have freedom or power of their own; and (3) a meaning for power that is limited to active modes. These are in fact assumptions underlying the classical definition for power.

Hartshorne's defense has been to question whether these assumptions permit a meaning for power that is "the greatest

---

[44]Thus we find statements like the following: "The divine decision is that nevertheless the act shall be performed 'freely' " (OOTM, p. 12).

conceivable." In fact, he thinks it is neither "the greatest" nor
coherently "conceivable."[45] He has been urging a new meaning that is both. The meaning he supplies is a social notion for
power and one that admits both active and passive dimensions. Hartshorne has, in my opinion, successfully countered
the charge of having placed limits on divine power. He has so
shifted the *meaning* of power that the problems that the tradition encountered around omnipotence can be addressed without recourse to any limitation upon the *scope* of power.

Has Hartshorne Completed the Task He Began?

Hartshorne's redefinition of perfect power as active and
passive and as relative/social in nature could effectively de-
pose the understanding for power as domination and control.
We have seen that the redefinition makes possible a very different handling of both the relation between freedom and
determination and the theodicy problem. Upon surveying
Hartshorne's writings, however, we may have cause to wonder whether Hartshorne himself has realized the full implications of his redefinition. In several places, he himself seems to
slip back into the old way of thinking.

On occasion the "language of control" reasserts itself; the
word "control" appears even in his redefinition of omnipotence: "Omnipotence is influence (and the susceptibility to
influence) ideal in quality, degree, and scope, so that all beings are subject to its optimal (not absolute) control."[46] Also
note which parts of the traditional concept of God he retains.

> The strand which theologians on the whole still propose to re-
> tain, and which is alone self-consistent, as judged by its relation
> to the other strand, is the popularly familiar definition of God as
> everlasting, *all-controlling*, all-knowing, and ethically good or
> holy to the highest possible degree.[47]

---

[45]To quote again a passage that is especially well put: "It has become customary to say
that we must limit divine power to save human freedom and to avoid making deity
responsible for evil. But to speak of limiting a concept seems to imply that the concept,
without the limitation, makes sense. The notion of a cosmic power that determines all
decisions fails to make sense. For its decisions could refer to nothing except themselves.
They could result in no world; for a world must consist of local agents making their own
decisions. Instead of saying that God's power is limited, suggesting that it is less than
some conceivable power, we should rather say: his power is absolutely maximal, the
greatest possible, but even the greatest possible power is still one power among others, is
not the only power" (DR, p. 138).

[46]Hartshorne, "Omnipotence," p. 546.

[47]Hartshorne, "The Formally Possible Doctrines of God," p. 190.

To use the word "control" (rather than the word "influence" or some other) in these contexts significantly moderates the more radical position for which Hartshorne had appeared to be arguing elsewhere.[48] If these latter statements represent his central position, then it would seem that the alternative he offers is reduced to a modification of *scope* (how much power—with "power" still meaning "control") rather than *meaning* (what kind of power). Even though God does not possess a monopoly on power—other beings have power too—God still "controls," and the fundamental way of describing God's power is as "controlling."

In addition to isolated reappearances of the word itself, "control" is reasserted in one of Hartshorne's primary analogies for the relation between God and the universe, the mind-body relation.

> Our problem is now precise: *Over* what has man really direct control, and *of* what has he really immediate knowledge? For when we have found this area of quite immediately known and controlled objects we shall know that, as our relation to such objects, so, though in a more exalted way, is God's relation to the universe—in so far as the theological analogy has any validity. For if we have any knowledge and power that is immediate . . . , the immediate object of effective human volition is a change in the human body. . . . We thus arrive at the far-reaching conclusion: the power-relation in man which alone can be used as basis for the theological analogy is the mind-body relation. . . . God controls the world . . . by direct power of his will, feeling, and knowledge (MVG, pp. 178–179).

To use such an analogy for the power relation between God and the universe is problematic for several reasons. First, it seems inconsistent with Hartshorne's most basic principles. He has affirmed the sociality/relativity of all things. What we have in the mind-body relation is an *organic unity* that lets go of the social relation. It lends itself to a pantheistic interpretation, which Hartshorne has elsewhere rejected. This analogy also violates the principle of dual transcendence, which argues for passive as well as active power in God, both influence and susceptibility to influence held supremely. While the mind-body relation does not imply unidirectional influence, it does seem to weight the relation, giving God considerably more influence

---

[48]Admittedly he qualifies "all-controlling" with "to the highest possible degree." But this would still seem to imply that it is a perfection to "control" to the highest degree one can.

upon the world than the world has upon God, and conversely giving the world a greater power to be influenced. Theoretically, God should possess both active and passive power maximally. For all these reasons the mind-body relation seems a poor choice for an analogy expressing God's exercise of power in the universe. A genuinely social analogy such as that provided by the relation among human beings might be more fitting. It would model mutuality of influence and convey greater subtlety—even resistibility—in the operation of divine power.

The problem goes deeper than choice of words or analogies. Within the formal argument itself, certain elements are not unambiguously free of "control." Hartshorne names three ways in which divine power in its active form expresses itself: (1) in power to preserve and maintain worldly reality and divine existence in relation to it; (2) in power to order the world by general natural laws, setting limits to creaturely freedom; and (3) in power to provide for every actuality the stimulus to which it must respond. In points 2 and 3, controlling elements are insinuated. Each will be discussed in turn.

Hartshorne is clear that God does not possess absolute power, but God must possess power "absolute in adequacy" (DR, p. 134).

> Religious faith imputes to God at least the kind and degree of power that the world needs as its supreme ordering influence. Or, more briefly, it imputes power adequate to cosmic need (DR, p. 134).

Hartshorne has interpreted "absolute in adequacy" to include the power to impose cosmic laws as well as power to place limits upon creaturely freedom.[49] The world must be structured so as to prevent chaos and ensure "optimal conditions" for the attainment of aesthetic value.[50] A multitude of agents could not select a common world. Only God can do this for the universe.[51] In every moment the divine "synthesis" is received as a given by every actual occasion. In this way the laws of nature and the limitations upon creaturely freedom are imposed.[52]

---

[49]This is God's "wise and efficient limitation of the risks to the optimum point beyond which further limitation would diminish the promise of life more than its tragedy." Hartshorne, "A New Look at the Problem of Evil," p. 209.

[50]Davaney, p. 179.

[51]"God is the only individual with universal functions. Only God is related to everything that exists or could exist. God alone prehends all actuality and all possibility, and only God becomes the universal object for all subsequent prehensions." Davaney, p. 136.

[52]Ford, *Two Process Philosophers*, p. 76.

God's world-ordering operates by "irresistible persuasion," says Hartshorne, and here is where the difficulty arises.[53] How does this differ in its basic *meaning* from divine determination in the tradition? The tradition's "gracious determination" applies to everything, in general and in particular. Hartshorne's "irresistible persuasion" is here applied to cosmic law but also applies to the provision of the initial aim to each concrete actuality. Thus it too operates both generally and particularly.

As if to counter this difficulty, Hartshorne insists that the cosmic laws are not absolute. They are statistical[54] and modifiable from one cosmic epoch to another. But this can be relevant only for God. From our standpoint (within our own epoch), they are unchanging. We in no way contribute to them, nor can we escape from them.[55] Here Hartshorne diverges from Whitehead, who sees the laws of nature as immanent, not imposed; they are merely statistical generalizations of the actual regularity of behavior.[56] For Whitehead, limits upon creaturely freedom are set by the past actual world.[57]

I do not argue here that there is a problem with God's provision of cosmic laws in order to guard against chaos or to ensure optimal conditions for the achievement of value. I do question whether and how their irresistible imposition may be made consistent with a notion of power as persuasive and to what extent Hartshorne is committed to conceiving divine power in a persuasive rather than a controlling mode.

Hartshorne also differs from Whitehead with respect to the

---

[53]Throughout his discussion of divine imposition of cosmic laws, Hartshorne uses language that implies control. "God . . . sets limits by *constraint* to the destruction of mutuality" (MVG, p. 173). God uses "*coercion* to prevent the use of coercion to destroy freedom" (MVG, p. 173). "*God decides* upon the basic outlines of creaturely actions, the *guaranteed limits* within which freedom is to operate" (Hartshorne, "A New Look at the Problem of Evil," p. 209). We are able to "explain the outlines of the world order, the laws of nature, as *divine decrees*" (CSPM, p. 137). (All italics added.)

[54]How can such laws be statistical? How would that work with the law of gravity, for example?

[55]Barry L. Whitney has argued this point effectively and states his conclusion even more strongly. "The laws themselves were coercively imposed since their institution was, apparently, beyond our consent and control." Whitney, "Process Theism: Does a Persuasive God Coerce?" p. 136.

[56]Here Whitehead seems more consistent in his conviction that God's power is persuasive, not controlling. Hartshorne seems to see persuasion as a *means* of control: "God can rule the world and order it, setting optimal limits for our free action, by presenting himself as essential object, so characterized as to weight the possibilities of response in the desired respect. This divine method of world control is called 'persuasion' by Whitehead and is one of the greatest of all metaphysical discoveries" (DR, p. 142).

[57]Ford, *Two Process Philosophers*, p. 78.

third way in which divine power is actively expressed. Hartshorne attributes a greater determining power to the "initial
aim" that God provides; while the creature may or may not
choose to realize it, the initial aim does serve as the primary
and most influential element of the causal nexus the creature
receives.[58] Whitehead understands that the creature's "final
subjective aim" may be completely contrary to the lure God
provides, and he believes that the realization of the initial aim
depends upon how much the creature "values" it.[59]

Three factors[60] should be taken into consideration when one
is assessing whether Hartshorne's treatment of the initial aim
is an instance of power as "persuasion" or power as "control."
(1) The initial aim cannot simply be disregarded and is described by Hartshorne as an "irresistible datum." (2) The initial aim is peculiarly efficacious in that it presents what the
creature most wants in terms of intrinsic value and is therefore uniquely eloquent in its appeal.[61] (3) The initial aim is
unconsciously prehended; it is "felt" and "accepted" in the
depth of the creature. (Here Hartshorne makes no clear distinction between "felt" and "accepted.")

On a continuum between persuasion and control, these factors seem to push Hartshorne toward the "control" end. The
image of the "cosmic hypnotist" is evoked by his speaking of
the lure as irresistible, unconscious, and as felt and accepted
simultaneously.[62] Although Hartshorne rejected this image,[63]
it would seem that he has not altogether eradicated from his
system instances of divine power in the mode of domination
and control.

In any case, Hartshorne's position on omnipotence can still
be seen to be a significant departure from the traditional doc-

---

[58]Whitney, *Evil and the Process God*, p. 97.

[59]Ford describes Whitehead's position with respect to the "lures" in this way:
"Freedom is responsibly exercised in the light of future possibilities which become
lures insofar as they are valued." Ford, *Two Process Philosophers*, p. 36.

[60]These are summarized by Whitney in his article "Process Theism: Does a Persuasive God Coerce?" pp. 137ff.

[61]Hartshorne, "Religion in Process Philosophy," p. 258.

[62]Here again the "language of control" reasserts itself. "As this object changes, we
are compelled to change in response. . . . God molds us, by presenting at each moment a partly new ideal or order of preference which our unself-conscious awareness
takes . . . and . . . renders influential upon our entire activity" (DR, pp. 139, 142).

[63]"God is the unsurpassable genius of all freedom, not the all-determining coercive
tyrant, or (if possible) worse, the irresistible hypnotist who dictates specific actions
while hiding his operations from the hypnotized. The worship of power in any such
sense is idolatry in a rather brutal form." Hartshorne, "Divine Absoluteness and
Divine Relativity," p. 169.

trine and its modifications. They portray God either determining or able to determine everything, both in general and in particular. Hartshorne's position, even in its moderate interpretation, might be typified as one in which God "flexibly controls"[64] world process but *does not and cannot completely determine all things.*

If flexible control rather than persuasion turns out to be Hartshorne's central position, he is left with problems that would be avoidable if control were fully eradicated from his concept of divine power. In regard to the theodicy problem, for example, if God can exercise controlling power either by setting limits to creaturely freedom in general or by providing irresistible lures for each actual entity in particular, then the theodicy problem is not yet resolved. God is indictable for the amount of evil that is permitted in world process. While it is understood that evil cannot be altogether prevented, any failure to exercise controlling power to reduce and curtail evil is attributable to divine responsibility.

It seems clear that Hartshorne's fundamental intent is to redefine omnipotence so as to eliminate elements of coercion, compulsion, and control and to promote a new understanding of power as *persuasive* in character. He argues effectively for a multiplicity of powers and for power as entailing both active and passive expressions. For these reasons, I interpret this more radical reassessment to be Hartshorne's central position and I view the instances of the reemergence of "control" in word choices, analogies, and specific depictions of the exercise of divine power to be unfortunate and misleading lapses.

In this stronger sense, Hartshorne's position has far-reaching implications. The relativity/sociality of all things implies a world of free and self-creating creatures, a genuine "other" with which God relates. Creaturely decisions are then genuine decisions that have a real and lasting significance to the world and to God. A theodicy based on a "free-will defense" is thereby made credible. When perfections are drawn in accord with the principle of dual transcendence, relationship with a changing, temporal world is made coherently conceivable. God is then preeminently able to influence and to be influenced. Hartshorne has indeed fulfilled his intent (DR, p. 1) to construct a more "worshipful" concept of God[65] and

---

[64]Farley, p. 158.

[65]The question is whether we shall worship "mere power or independence, not the suffering love which I suppose is the deepest message of Christianity." Hartshorne, "Divine Relativity and Absoluteness: A Reply," p. 38.

has at the same time avoided the contradictions that have seemed inseparable from the idea of omnipotence as usually defined. Hartshorne's alternative looks promising and his argument is persuasive.

6

Feminist Perspectives

Certain difficulties present themselves in any attempt to provide a feminist perspective on divine power—much less *the* feminist perspective. To date, no one thinker has done a thoroughgoing critique and reconstruction of the meaning of divine power from a feminist perspective. Furthermore, there is no one position on the issue that may be identified as *the* feminist perspective. Feminists (from reformist to revolutionary) differ in their points of view. This chapter will consequently be limited to a preliminary exploration of feminist perspectives.[1]

Feminist thought has not drawn upon a particular metaphysical framework or consciously constructed a comprehensive system. There are, however, some indications of the direction of this emergent perspective. Certain images and themes and fundamental assumptions repeat themselves in varying forms, and they provide the resources that guide this exposition.

This consideration will comprise two steps: (1) a feminist critique of the traditional doctrine of omnipotence and (2) a brief

---

[1]It seems important to clarify my own position along this continuum of perspectives. I would describe myself as a *"Christian* feminist," and I am committed to staying in the church. I operate within the framework of Christian theology, and I value congruence with the biblical tradition. I believe that, at its essence and rightly interpreted, the fundamental message of the Christian faith is one that is liberating and life-enhancing. This does not mean that I am uncritical of the distortions that have been present in the dominant tradition or that I am unaware of its mixed history with respect to women. I would characterize my position as one of "critical appreciation" or perhaps "creative fidelity."

I understand and will give a sympathetic hearing to persons who explicitly reject the faith because of the distortions and mixed history. Some of the voices included here will be those of fairly radical, post-Christian feminists. My sympathetic hearing should not be mistaken for agreement on all points. Nevertheless I do consider the critique that post-Christian feminists are offering from the outside—as well as the critique that Christian feminists offer from the inside—important for the church as it strives toward greater faithfulness to its central vision.

exploration of the contributions that feminist perspectives may bring to the conversation concerning power in general and divine power in particular. The first step, which presents the critique, has two parts. First, it argues that the tradition's preoccupation with power is a typically male preoccupation and that the particular shape of the tradition's prevailing understanding of power (which I have called "power in the mode of domination and control") reflects a male bias. Second, it argues that the social consequences—here specified as oppression, exploitation, and violence—of elevating this kind of power by ascribing it to God have been disastrous. Here it will become clear that the feminist critique of the traditional doctrine is not concerned primarily with its coherence or with its religious viability as gauged by the adequacy of its account of human freedom or its resolution of the theodicy problem. Instead, the critique questions the religious viability of the doctrine from the standpoint of its *moral adequacy,* given the harmful social consequences that attend it. This approach will necessarily lead to consideration of a set of concerns somewhat different from those dealt with in the preceding chapters.

When the critique has been presented, the second step of this chapter will highlight some of the insights gained from feminist research. One particular image that is made available when God is conceived as female promises an alternative way of thinking about God's relation to the world and how God exercises power in the world. Certain themes emerging in feminist thought point to a genuinely different way of conceptualizing power.

Critique

A General Critique of the Male-Centeredness of Theology: Images and Concepts

That deity "is of male manufacture" (T. S. Eliot) is a recurrent observation in feminist literature. A male-centeredness is reflected in the theological language and images[2] as well as in the conceptual content of our doctrine of God. Feminists argue that this androcentrism has undesirable effects: it limits and

---

[2]The image of God as incarnate in Jesus of Nazareth, for example, "strongly suggests the idea of deity as highly spiritualized masculinity. It is a constant temptation to male chauvinism, and a temptation in historical fact not altogether resolutely resisted, to put it mildly." Hartshorne, OOTM, p. 60.

distorts our understanding of the divine, and it creates and legitimates attitudes and social structures destructive to human well-being.[3]

The first charge is that of idolatry. When God is conceptualized in analogy with male reality alone, a finite representation is being mistaken for and worshiped in the place of the infinite God.[4] Certainly male images that portray divine power, such as "father" and "king," are intended as symbols to point beyond human male power to an infinite power that judges all finite power. Nevertheless, as Mary Daly shows, these symbols more often function as idols, not pointing beyond themselves but allowing human beings to deify male power.[5] "If God is male, then the male is God."[6]

As Sallie McFague has pointed out, "It is not just that 'God the father' is a frequent appellation for the divine, but that the entire structure of divine-human and human-human relationships is understood in a patriarchal framework."[7] The male imagery for God has served to legitimate patriarchy and to suppress rebellion against it.[8] Thus there are both religious and social consequences attached to the exclusively male representation of God.[9] Many feminists are recognizing in the male im-

---

[3]Sharon Welch has observed that language and ideas are "embedded in networks of social and political control." The problem with such language is not only the negative effect of distorting (mystifying, falsifying) reality but—and in her view more seriously—the positive effect of *creating* particular realities (i.e., oppressive social structures). Welch, p. 10.

[4]Johnson, p. 443.

[5]Christ, p. 140.

[6]Daly, *Beyond God the Father*, p. 19.

[7]McFague, *Metaphorical Theology*, p. 9.

[8]"The image of the Father God, spawned in the human imagination and sustained as plausible by patriarchy, has in turn rendered service to this type of society by making its mechanisms for the oppression of women seem right and fitting. . . . What is happening, of course, is the familiar mechanism by which the images and values of a given society are projected into a realm of beliefs which in turn justify the social infrastructure. The belief system becomes hardened and objectified seeming to have an unchangeable independent existence and validity of its own." Mary Daly, "After the Death of God the Father," in Christ and Plaskow, p. 54.

[9]Anthropologist Clifford Geertz has noted that religious symbols shape a cultural ethos, defining the deepest values of a society. " 'Religion is a system of symbols which act to produce powerful, pervasive, and long-lasting moods and motivations' in the people of a given culture. A 'mood' for Geertz is a psychological attitude such as awe, trust, and respect, while a 'motivation' is the *social* and *political* trajectory created by a mood that transforms mythos into ethos, symbol system into social and political reality. Symbols have both psychological and political effects, because they create the inner conditions . . . that lead people to feel comfortable with or to accept social and political arrangements that correspond to the symbol system." As quoted by Carol Christ in "Why Women Need the Goddess," in Christ and Plaskow, p. 274.

agery for God an instrument of their betrayal and are leaving it behind.

To this end, changing language to be more inclusive is certainly important; however, the problem runs deeper than language. It is not just the gender references, but the particular *content of the concept* of God has been "masculinized," and this difficulty is less easily remedied. A sample of the problem will suffice for now.

It has been argued in previous chapters that the meaning for power that seems to underlie the traditional doctrine of divine omnipotence is "power in the mode of domination and control." Many feminists concur and insist that this understanding of power is a function of the male-formation[10] of the tradition. Rosemary Radford Ruether refers to this view as an "alienated paradigm of divine power, a paradigm of domination requiring subjection." This paradigm cannot be overthrown simply by changing language.

> It may be argued that the image of God as Holy Warrior, leading his people out of Egypt with a mighty arm and destroying the horses and chariots of the Egyptians cannot be salvaged with a simple change of genderized language. A female or neuter holy warrior would still be an alienated image of deity based upon male glorification of conquest and domination, not an image which appropriately describes the nature of divine power.[11]

If gender reference is changed and the content remains the same, the deeper difficulty will remain. Working on language is necessary but not sufficient.

Power: A Male Preoccupation and a Male-defined Term

On what grounds are feminists making the claim that the tradition's preoccupation with power is a typically male preoccupation and that the particular shape that the meaning for power has taken (domination and control) reflects a male bias? Many feminists join in this critique, but they differ substantially as to the level at which such a charge is directed. There seem to be at least four different stances from which feminists make these assertions.

Some feminists operate strictly at the level of *stereotypes.* They would insist there are no *real* differences in male and female attributes (other than the obvious physical differences).

---

[10]"Mal-formation" is the term Daly uses.
[11]Christ, p. 178.

Instead, there are stereotypes, which are strictly socially contrived, with no basis in reality. They are a limiting—and false—description of male and female. A stereotype prescribes that the male will be more concerned with power and that he will be dominant. The charge is being leveled at the stereotype, not at a distinctive male way of being in the world. Feminists in this camp do not endorse the traits in either the "feminine" or the "masculine" stereotype as in any way normative. Either is viewed as a limited and truncated description of human possibilities.

Other feminists take the stance that while gender differences are not biologically determined[12] and are not universal or even uniformly manifest in any one society, they do in fact exist. These differences are considered to be a function of the different *socialization* that males and females receive. Feminists who adopt this position admit that the nature-nurture debate over gender differences cannot be conclusively resolved as long as male and female children continue to be socialized differently. But they anticipate that if there were not differences in socialization, the gender differences would not appear. Feminists working from this perspective sometimes make value judgments, identifying normative human nature with certain feminine traits or—less often—certain masculine traits.[13] Many such feminists view male socialization with respect to power as damaging and, in this matter at least, grant normative status to feminine traits.

A third position taken by some feminists is that gender differences are real, grounded in *a combination of socialization and biological determination.* For example, some observe that the (potential or realized) reproductive role of women leads "naturally" to certain social roles (i.e., caring and nurturing roles), with a view to which they are then socialized. Here again value judgments may or may not be made with regard to the traits that women and men are respectively assigned. Those who, working from this perspective, criticize the male orientation toward power urge that men learn from women the "powers of caring and nurturing." They place a higher value upon "feminine" powers and think the society would be well served if these gained ascendancy.

---

[12]Anthropologist Peggy Sanday, for example, notes that sex roles and gender traits "are cultural not biological. . . . If sex-role plans were derived from the human biological structure we would not find the variety of plans that do exist." Sanday, p. 16.

[13]Ruether labels the latter "liberal feminists" and the former "romantic feminists." Ruether, *Sexism and God-Talk*, pp. 102–105.

A fourth option is to see the gender differences as real and as *biologically determined.* Here much is attributed to reproductive biology and to hormones. Testosterone, for example, is designated as the decisive factor that tends the male of the species toward aggressiveness and a desire to dominate. Jungian archetype psychology also falls in this category but sees gender traits as "flexibly determined." While "masculine" and "feminine" refer to gender-related characteristics, each individual possesses all the gender traits—to differing degrees according to gender. A woman can cultivate her "masculine" side (*animus*) and a man can cultivate his "feminine" side (*anima*). Even persons who accept this "biology is destiny" thinking seem to assume that what is biologically provided may be, to some extent, modified. Thus, value judgments can be made regarding whether traits such as aggressiveness should be "cultivated" or "overcome."

In the analysis that follows, feminists working from the second and third of these four perspectives—a kind of middle range position—will receive more careful attention. Their independently conducted research leads to remarkably similar analyses of gender differences with respect to power. Only four of the five presented here, however, assign normativity to the "feminine" orientation to power.

Gilligan

Carol Gilligan offers a theory to account for the reproduction within each generation of certain general differences that characterize masculine and feminine personality.[14] She attributes these differences to the fact that women as child-bearers[15] are almost universally assigned responsibility for child care, with the result that, "in any given society, feminine personality comes to define itself in relation and connection to other people more than masculine personality does."[16] Studies indicate that gender identity is firmly established by age three, and the dynamics of gender identity formation differ for male and female children. If the primary caretaker is female, individuation and differentiation from her is the developmental task that confronts boys, while connection and identification with the caretaker is the developmental task for girls. The result is

---

[14]This theory is based upon the work of Nancy Chodorow (1974). Gilligan, pp. 7–8.

[15]Gilligan attributes gender differences to a combination of socialization and biological determination.

[16]Gilligan, pp. 7–8.

that masculine gender identity is defined through "separation," while feminine gender identity is formed through "attachment." This difference has its effects in adult life and in the larger society.

Gilligan concerns herself primarily with ethical decision making. She notes that morality, for women, is focused upon "relationships and responsibilities," while, for men, morality is focused upon "rules and rights."[17] The morality of rights emphasizes separation and considers the individual rather than relationships as primary.[18] For men, the moral problem is how to exercise one's rights without interfering with the rights of others. For women, the problem is how to lead a life that takes into account competing needs for care. The "ethics of rights" has the obligation of noninterference, while the "ethics of care" has the obligation to respond to needs. Whereas male identity is seen as *qualified* by relation to others, female identity is seen as *realized* in relation to others. The former is an orientation toward independence, the latter an orientation toward interdependence.

Gilligan observes that these differences are often expressed imagistically, with males speaking in terms of hierarchical images and females in weblike[19] images. The power and persistence of these images and the feelings they evoke signify their embeddedness in male and female experience.

It is these differences—between separation and connection, "hierarchy" and "web"—which, according to Gilligan, constitute the differing orientations toward power. She reports in her study that while men represent powerful activity as assertion and aggression, women portray acts of nurturance as acts of strength.[20] Furthermore, the reality of connection is experienced by women as a given rather than as something freely entered into from a prior stance of autonomy. Consequently, they arrive at an understanding of life that reflects "greater limits upon both autonomy and control."[21] According to the

---

[17]Here we see the beginning of "law and order" thinking and what Soelle has called "that masculine set of mind intent on domination and regulation." Soelle, p. 46.

[18]Gilligan, p. 19.

[19]"The ideal of care is thus an activity of relationship, of seeing and responding to need, taking care of the world by sustaining the web of connection so that no one is left alone." Gilligan, p. 62.

[20]Gilligan, pp. 167–168.

[21]Gilligan, p. 168. That women differ in their orientation to power is also confirmed in Jean Baker Miller's analysis. She distinguishes between relationships of temporary and permanent inequality, the former representing the context of human

study, women also generally manifest a stronger repulsion to violence. Gilligan sees male aggression and more ready acceptance of violence as originating in the "failure of connection."[22] Because women *do* feel more connected to others, there is a common thread running through their ethical decision making, that is, "the desire not to hurt" others and the hope that there may be a way to resolve conflicts so that no one will be hurt.[23]

Keller

Gilligan's proposal that males are generally more oriented toward separation and females are more oriented toward connection is corroborated by Catherine Keller's research. Keller goes on to observe that it is the male perspective on selfhood (separate self) and not the female perspective (soluble self) that predominates in our culture.[24] She questions the adequacy of this dominant model for understanding selfhood, suggesting that it does not speak to the experience of women. Women find themselves enmeshed in relational complexities[25] that blur the boundaries of self and other.[26] She sees in

---

development, the latter the condition of oppression. In relationships of temporary inequality, such as parent and child or teacher and student, power ideally is used to foster the development that removes the initial disparity. In relationships of permanent inequality, power cements domination and subordination, and oppression is rationalized by theories that "explain" the need for its continuation. While both men and women find themselves on both sides of the temporary inequality relationship, by virtue of their *gender* they are fixed in dominant and subordinate roles in a relationship of permanent inequality. Miller, pp. 3–12.

[22]Gilligan, p. 173.

[23]On the Thematic Apperception Test, there is a statistically significant sex difference in the number of places where violence is seen and in the kinds of circumstances construed as violent. Far greater incidence of violence is found in responses written by men. Where violence is projected, men are more likely to project violence into situations of personal affiliation and women are more likely to project violence into impersonal situations of achievement. It is hypothesized that males associate images of intimacy with danger, while females associate images of competition with danger. Regardless of the situation, it is concluded that danger is more often responded to with violence by men than by women. Gilligan, p. 39.

[24]"Common sense identifies separateness with the freedom we cherish in the name of 'independence' and 'autonomy.' " Keller, p. 1.

[25]With respect to social power, Keller notes that "women's traditional specialization in relationships seems to have taken the place of both strength of individual identity and real social power." Keller, p. 2.

[26]Keller does not interpret this way of being as unqualifiedly good even though she is more critical of the separative orientation. The dangers implicit in the soluble self are dependency and the tendency to "absorb" others or to dissolve emotionally and devotionally into another. Keller, pp. 7–8.

women's experience and even in the nature of reality itself a "pull toward connection"—not a separative universe of isolated atoms. "Fluidity and interpermeability show themselves to be the character of every being; every entity in the universe can be described as a process of interconnecting with every other being."[27]

Going beyond the level of Gilligan's work, Keller pursues theological questions suggested by her analysis. She finds that the traditional understanding of the divine perfections is based upon the model of the male separative ego;[28] it reads like a catalog of the male heroic ego's ideals for himself.[29] She asks why it is "embarrassing" to imagine a creator interdependent with the creation. Her conclusion is that our male-formed notions of perfection require that God be "the Absolute" which is complete in itself, independent of and separate from everything else, creating and reigning in utter omnipotence, before whom all humanity (male and female) trembles, emasculated and dissolved into the role of feminine dependent. In the tradition the soul is feminine, "melting into the unity of ecstatic subservience to a masculine image."[30] Keller observes that unless this way of defining divine perfection is reexamined, it does no good simply to alter language and genderized images; the God concept itself promotes a pattern of domination and subordination.

Keller sees this image of the divine as contrary to true religion, which she describes in terms more reminiscent of the rejected alternative vision of ultimate reality—a vision of connection rather than separation.

> Religion true to its name activates connection. It "ties together," binding up the wounds of breaking worlds. It is the bridging, bonding process at the heart of things. There is no reason not to call this process Love: the Eros that seeks to get things together, no matter what.[31]

Schaef

Anne Wilson Schaef's analysis illustrates the way in which such male-female differences affect the dynamics of power.

---

[27]Keller, p. 5.

[28]"It is less precise to call this ego separate than *separative*, implying an activity or an intention rather than any fundamental state of being." Keller, p. 9.

[29]Keller, p. 38.

[30]Keller, p. 35.

[31]Keller, p. 218.

She notes a dualistic and hierarchical mode of thinking about power in what she refers to as the White Male System.

> Things have to be either this way or that. One must be either superior or inferior. One must be either one–up or one–down. . . . One is either controlled or controlling, depending on where one is in the hierarchy.[32]

In the White Male System, power is conceived of in a "zero sum" fashion or on a "scarcity" model. There is only so much power available and "one had better scramble for it and hoard it." In the Female System, on the other hand, power is viewed as limitless, and when it is shared, it regenerates and expands (more like love). There is no need to hoard it, because it increases when it is given away.[33] In the White Male System, power is conceived of as power to exert domination and control over others. In the Female System, power is seen as *personal* power, which has nothing to do with power or control *over* another.[34]

Maguire

The fourth feminist thinker to be consulted here is Daniel Maguire. Maguire is not so much seeking the origins of gender differences (as Gilligan and Keller did) as seeking to describe the negative social consequences of the priority our culture attaches to the masculine traits. He lists five traits that he considers to be "the principal liabilities of the macho-masculine blight":[35] (1) a proneness to violent modes of power; (2) an anticommunitarian, hierarchical proclivity; (3) a disabling abstractionism; (4) a consequentialist bias; and (5) a culturally devastating hatred of women.[36]

The focus of attention here will be upon "abstractionism,"[37]

---

[32]Schaef, p. 12.

[33]Schaef, pp. 124–125.

[34]Schaef underlines the association of male power with domination and control and connects preoccupation with this kind of power with "a desire to be God." It is interesting that she seems to take for granted the popular view that by "God" we mean "the One with controlling power." She speaks of the White Male System in parallel terms as "a father figure" who wants to be in control and requires all others to be dependent on him. Keller, p. 125.

[35]Maguire, pp. 59–67.

[36]Maguire, p. 63. He does not imply that all men possess these liabilities or that any one man possesses all of them in their full vigor. These are said to be *tendencies* in "macho-masculine" culture.

[37]Gilligan confirms Maguire's findings on the male tendency to abstract from reality.

since others of these liabilities are explored elsewhere. Many have observed that patterns of the present male-formed system necessitate a way of thinking that is objective, Aristotelian, data-centered, descriptive, measuring, hierarchical, systematic, fragmentizing, logical, and sequential. It is also antiemotional, impersonal, unfeeling, and sterile.[38]

Maguire sees several of the other liabilities as growing out of this "pernicious abstractionism." The tendency to abstract and objectify is what makes misogyny possible. Presumably it is more difficult to hate real, concrete, individual women than an abstract image that represents women. The "consequentialist bias" is also a form of abstractionism. "Bottom line" thinking is intoxicated with an abstract *end* and tends to be less than careful in evaluating the *means*[39] used to attain it.[40] Maguire sees violence as another outcome of abstractionism. An "image of the enemy," an abstract mythic creation,[41] is needed to engender sufficient hatred to sustain a violent, nonrelational approach to another human being.

Ruether

Rosemary Radford Ruether traces to dualistic thinking the phenomenon being described in various terms by Gilligan, Keller, Schaef, and Maguire.[42] Dualism's most basic expression seems to her to be the self-other duality. It has been said

---

She sites a three-year study of adolescents and their parents which indicates that the moral judgments of males and females differ in the extent to which females were concerned with resolution of real as opposed to hypothetical dilemmas. There was a decided tendency in males toward abstraction and in females toward concretion. Gilligan, p. 69.

[38]Barbara Starrett, "The Metaphors of Power," in Spretnak, p. 186.

[39]"To be specific, only a man could have stood in the ashes of the totally destroyed village of Ben Tre during the war in Viet Nam and announced, as one colonel did: 'We had to destroy this village to save it.' . . . The colonel at Ben Tre is brother to the tearless politicians who have prepared for us the end of the world and stored it in their silos, all in the name of security. The question is not whether women could function in intrinsically moral enterprises such as politics. The burden of proof has been classically misplaced." Starrett, in Spretnak, p. 61.

[40]Many feminist thinkers have of late insisted that the means *are* the end.

[41]"Countless Viet Nam veterans have spoken of the fact that they were able to kill the Vietnamese because they thought of them as 'gooks,' as a mindless, subhuman species, rather than as people like themselves." Sheila Collins, "The Personal Is Political," in Spretnak, p. 365.

[42]Ruether, *Sexism and God-Talk*, pp. 72ff. A basic dualism has been set up between mind and body, culture and nature, man and woman.

that woman is for man the primordial "other." Male thinking has objectified "woman" and made the relationship with "woman" the paradigm for relating to all other "others." This division is not a simple duality of difference but is a "graded dualism" of dominant and subordinate, and therefore the model for relating to all other "others"[43] is a dominant-subordinate relation. There is a fear[44] and hatred and desire to dominate the "other" whether it be the female, or the male foreigner, or the tribal enemy.[45]

An important consideration, which Ruether underscores, is that assignment of gender traits is not strictly arbitrary. The traits conducive to domination are assigned to males and those conducive to subordination are assigned to females.[46] This artificial polarization of human qualities constitutes the traditional sex stereotypes and is designed to serve and perpetuate patriarchal society.[47] The gender differences assigned have more to do with domination and subordination than with gender as such. It is by virtue of the fact that males are the dominant group that this particular set of traits comes to be identified as masculine. Thus it is not a male way of being in the world as such that leads to preoccupation with power as domination and control but male being in the context of patriarchal society that provides a certain socialization in power.

The point being made here is that this "gender complemen-

---

[43]De Beauvoir, p. 14.

[44]Cynthia Adcock, "Fear of the 'Other': The Common Root of Sexism and Militarism," in McAllister, p. 210.

[45]Judith Plaskow has made an interesting observation concerning the effect of the doctrine of chosenness on how differentiations are treated and perceived in the Jewish tradition. The concept of chosenness claims a *special* difference. It is not simply that the Jews are different in their own community of uniqueness as all others are different in theirs. Jews are "different, differently" because only they are chosen. They are set apart for an unparalleled role in history. Even if this role is seen in terms of servanthood, it still provides a heightened status. Chosenness becomes emblematic for other differences, and graded differentiation becomes the way of doing differentiation. This sets up a hierarchical mode of thought about differences, with superiority attached to one side and inferiority to the other (i.e., kosher vs. non-kosher, clean vs. unclean, Sabbath vs. weekday, male vs. female). The result is a "system of separations." Internal others (women) mirror external others (Gentiles). Evil is projected upon the internal other (women) as a way of explaining the why of suffering which seems to contradict the enlarged self-concept. Judith Plaskow, "Israel from a Feminist Perspective: Redefining Community," unpublished paper delivered at the American Academy of Religion, December 1987.

[46]Feminists have observed that "femininity" is always defined as oriented to the needs of men, while "masculinity" is never defined primarily as serving the needs of women.

[47]Ruether agrees with this description of the origin of gender differences.

tarity,"[48] as it is sometimes called, is based upon an *artificial polarization of gender traits created by patriarchy for its own purposes*—it is not grounded in any kind of necessity. "Socialization in power and powerlessness distorts integration further and creates what appears to be dichotomized personality cultures of men and women, that is, masculinity and femininity."[49] What is being rejected here is the view that certain attitudes or qualities are inherently "feminine" or "masculine" either biologically or because of biology-related socialization.

Ruether differs markedly from the other four feminists presented above in that she refuses to assign a normativity to the "feminine" side of the artificial polarization created by patriarchy.

> Neither masculinity traditionally defined nor femininity traditionally defined discloses an innately good human nature, and neither is simply an expression of evil. Both represent different types of alienation of humanity from its original potential.[50]

Neither male nor female being can be "whole" in the context of patriarchy. For Ruether the answer lies not in rejecting male notions of power (formed from their socialization in power) and adopting female notions of power (formed from their socialization in powerlessness)[51] but in rejecting the larger systemic context of patriarchy and the dualism which is at its root. Only then can wholesome understandings of power be formulated.

Social Consequences of Elevating Power in the Mode of Domination and Control

The word "power" has drawn its connotations—domination and control—from the dominant male culture. The formation of the concept has rested almost solely in the hands of people who have lived with a constant need to maintain an irrational dominance, and in their hands it has acquired overtones of tyranny.[52]

---

[48]Feminists almost universally see the "complementarity" theme as fallacious and oppressive. Daly, *Beyond God the Father*, p. 99.

[49]Ruether, *Sexism and God-Talk*, p. 90.

[50]Ruether, *Sexism and God-Talk*, p. 110.

[51]While these might have much to recommend them in the face of the particular distortions of "male" notions of power, they too are "deformed" by the context of patriarchy. Ruether, *Sexism and God-Talk*, p. 110.

[52]Miller, p. 115.

Feminists argue that this particular conceptual/behavioral content is not only not necessary to the meaning of power but is positively damaging. There has been considerable damage done to the concept of God. Dorothee Soelle comments:

> As a woman I have to ask why it is that human beings honor a God whose most important attribute is power, whose prime need is to subjugate, whose greatest fear is equality. (When God drives Adam and Eve from the garden it is because they will become "like one of us.") What kind of a God is that, whose major interests have to be described in these terms? A being who is addressed as "Lord," a being whom his theologians describe as all-powerful because he cannot be satisfied with being merely powerful . . . ? (A "phallocratic fantasy"). Why should we honor and love a being that does not transcend but only reaffirms the moral level of our present male dominated culture? Why should we honor and love this being . . . if this being is in fact no more than an outsized man . . . ?[53]

Thus the religious viability of this concept of God is called into question.

When the social consequences that feminists attribute to this theological construct are brought to light, its religious viability comes under fire once again—this time from the standpoint of *moral adequacy.* When power in the mode of domination and control is attributed to God, human exercise of power in this mode gains a certain legitimacy. The negative social consequences that feminists observe will be discussed briefly under the categories of oppression, exploitation, and violence.

Oppression

Mary Daly argued in her book *Beyond God the Father* that a distorted image of divine power has in fact given rise to a mentality of conquest and domination. She claims that this concept of God is ideologically "a dangerous mask for relationships of domination."[54] Oppression has been given a kind of "holy space," with the divine as the apex of a system of privilege and control.[55]

---

[53]Soelle, p. 97.

[54]"Compared to Mary Daly's critique of Christian faith and theology, the challenge of Feuerbach seems genteel and innocuous. Her challenge is not just to the conceptual inadequacy of Christian theology. She questions the moral adequacy. . . . Mary Daly claims that Christian faith itself is an expression of patriarchy and necrophilia." Welch, p. 3.

[55]Ruether, *Sexism and God-Talk*, p. 61.

Ruether has offered the disclaimer that there is within the Judeo-Christian tradition a prophetic voice *against* oppression. A strong view of the sovereignty of God was sometimes used as a way of negating the claims of oppressors (i.e., Pharaoh in the Old Testament and "authorities" in the New Testament—"we will obey God rather than men").[56] Nevertheless she admits that oppressors also appealed to this divine power, claiming it as the basis for their authority (divine right of kings). She notes that we need God language that is not so easily coopted by systems of domination.

This discussion will focus on the oppression of women as the paradigm for all oppression.[57] Feminists believe the tradition's vision of God functions to legitimate the oppression of women: (1) through scriptural references that convey that women's subordinate status is "God's will"; (2) through male language and images of God, which elevate and "deify" the male; (3) through the concept of God as dominating and controlling power, a concept that gives domination a divine sanction;[58] and (4) through women's internalization of patriarchal religion in their religious socialization.

The focus will be upon the fourth of these influences, since the first three have been discussed. Dorothee Soelle has said that many women have so internalized patriarchal religion that they live their lives "on someone else's terms. They do not know what self-determination is."[59]

Feminists insist that there is a strength-destroying quality inherent in acceptance of some traditional theological constructs. Salvation by faith, for example, has meant that "there is nothing we can do"; our destiny is "in God's hands." Although this construct is meant purely theologically, it nevertheless has social consequences that cannot simply be ignored. Theological constructs that emphasize divine controlling power have the effect of exaggerating human helplessness. It seems that the weaker we are, the stronger that makes God; that there is an inversely proportional relationship between our power and God's power.[60] We are disempowered by God's omnipotence.[61]

---

[56]Ruether, *Sexism and God-Talk*, p. 64.

[57]The situation between the sexes is a case of what Max Weber has defined as *herrschaft*, a relation of dominance and subordinance. This is the institutionalized birthright priority whereby males rule females. Millett, p. 24.

[58]This latter is considered especially deadly in combination with item no. 2

[59]Soelle, p. 93.

[60]This is power on the "zero sum" or "scarcity" model.

[61]Soelle, pp. 95–96.

Alongside the affirmation of divine power has been the affirmation of divine benevolence.[62] This makes the image all the more powerful and irresistible. Since God is the embodiment of kindness, how can we want to rebel against God and what God has willed for us? Willing obedience[63] and quietism are promoted by this attribute.

> The concept of an omnipotent providential deity serves to subvert rebellion and remove the imperative of responsibility for social change: This function is not only ideological, masking the nonnecessity of conditions that are oppressive; it also insures or enhances the survival of a social system by eliciting accommodation to it.[64]

The way in which emphasis upon divine controlling power (benevolent as it is) becomes an accomplice in oppression can be summed up in these outcomes: our ready acceptance of a superior power that controls our destiny, willing submission to this power which needs no moral legitimation outside itself, and denial of human power to act responsibly or affect one's destiny.[65] These tendencies—religiously inspired—are reenacted in the realm of human affairs with disastrous results. For this reason the task of reassessing the nature of divine power takes a high priority for feminists who would oppose oppression (their own or anyone else's).

Exploitation

Exploitation is another social consequence of the elevation of power in the mode of domination and control, as several

---

[62]The benevolence of God is not being challenged in the feminist critique, but it should be noted in passing that benevolence really does not change the nature of the meaning for power which is at work. Power as domination and control can be exercised benevolently or not; it still remains power of this sort. A kindly slaveholder may be more beloved but is still a slaveholder. The benevolence of the slaveholder may in fact make resistance even more difficult (the "happy slave" syndrome).

[63]There are extreme dangers in the "ethic of obedience" promoted by this God concept. This is true not only for women but also more generally. In the Milgram experiment, for example, the vast majority of ordinary people obeyed authority (the experimenter) when instructed to subject others to painful electric shock for the sake of scientific research. Soelle proposes and gives evidence that Christian preoccupation with dependence and obedience prepared the way for Nazism in Hitler's Germany. The atrocities committed were, by and large, not resisted by Christians. This in itself should be enough to "rob this concept of all its theological innocence." Soelle, p. 109.

[64]Welch, p. 70.

[65]Soelle, p. 110.

feminists have argued. This discussion will be limited to consideration of the exploitation of nature as a case in point.

Ruether has observed that a kind of hierarchical dualism underlies traditional patterns of thought about reality: God/world, culture/nature, man/woman, spirit/body, good/evil. Not only is each of these contrasted with its opposite but one in each pair is assigned superior status. Furthermore, the superior realities are associated with one another and the inferior realities are associated with one another (i.e., world, nature, woman, body, and evil are associated). In every case, it is assumed that the superior should by right rule over the inferior. The inferior is in the service of the superior. God, as the apex of the model, is clearly the exemplary instance of how the "superior" is to relate to the "inferior." If God exercises power in the mode of domination and control over the world, then this is the mode of power that culture should exercise over nature, man over woman, and so forth.

With regard to culture and nature, feminists point out, this pattern has been followed with a vengeance. High priority has been attached to controlling nature. It is understood that nature is there to be exploited for human enjoyment and gain. An adversarial relation is established, "man *against* nature." Every advance in the ability to control is greeted as a triumph. Yet technical controlling knowledge and intervention now border upon destruction of the natural environment.

> Within a brief century and a half the optimistic vision of expanding control, leading to Paradise, takes on the frightening visage of global disaster, the universal outbreak of uncontrollable pollution, famine, poverty, and warfare, which threatens the very survival of the planet.[66]

The good of the whole human and natural community is laid aside in favor of the immediate advantage of the dominant class, race, and sex.[67]

This situation, in which "control" is the primary model for how human beings relate to nature, is in stark contrast to that of cultures in which cooperation with nature is the pattern and nature is seen as having its own inherent value apart from its usefulness to humanity. It has also been observed that in cultures that conceive divine power as in some sense cooperative rather than controlling (i.e., in Native American religion),

[66]Ruether, *Sexism and God-Talk*, p. 84.
[67]Ruether, *Sexism and God-Talk*, p. 91.

an alternative model for cooperative relationship with the environment is the norm.[68]

Violence

Barbara Zannotti writes of her conviction that increasing militarism and the danger of nuclear war are deeply linked to institutionalized male dominance.[69] Donna Warnock, a peace activist, insists that the peace movement, to be effective, must commit itself to overthrowing patriarchy. "We must dismantle the mental weaponry as well as the military."[70]

Here again the nature of power is a fundamental question. Jo Vellacott has observed that in our culture, "power is exercised through violence, that indeed the potential for physical, economic, and psychological violence is almost the definition of power."[71]

It is possible that violence as a social consequence may in large part be understood through use of the same interpretive tool by which Ruether got at the root of what makes power in the mode of domination and control an attractive option in the first place. That interpretive tool is dualism. The self-other duality is the most useful for this discussion. In this case it is further delineated as the "self over against other" duality.

Starrett has referred to the operation of dualism in this form as the "adversary system."[72] Competition, "one-upmanship" is the attitude. Person is set against person, group against group, nation against nation, idea against idea, with an expected win/lose outcome. Opposition is the spirit of the "adversary habit." What is sought is *domination and control* of the opponent, or the playing field, or the market, or land, or resources.

---

[68]It might be argued that (instead of taking the approach proposed here) a simple rejection of the whole system of dualisms listed above and "great chain of being" thinking in general would more likely attack the problem at its roots. However, as long as our concept of divine power functions as the model upon which the exercise of human power is fashioned, reassessing this model in particular will be a useful strategy for working to salvage the natural environment.

[69]Barbara Zannotti, "Patriarchy: A State of War," in McAllister, pp. 16–20.

[70]Donna Warnock, "Patriarchy Is a Killer," in McAllister, p. 20.

[71]Jo Vellacott, "Women, Peace, and Power," in McAllister, p. 32.

[72]Legal structures of our society are based upon the adversary system. One attorney opposes another attorney not directly in order to achieve truth but to win. Truth and justice are sincerely presumed to be corollaries of victory. It may be argued that most male-dominated realms of human endeavor are organized in this mode; scholarship, politics, and sports are prime examples. Starrett, in Spretnak, p. 186.

Gordon Kaufman, in his treatment of the nuclear threat, has argued from a somewhat different angle that the traditional way of understanding divine power as controlling exacerbates the problem of violence in yet another way. He proposes that the situation in which humanity now finds itself—"in which we are able by the mere press of a button to destroy our entire world as well as humankind itself" (the ultimate instance of violence)—tends to be discounted by the central tradition's claim about God's utter sovereignty over the world. Persons who believe that God is in control give two kinds of answers to the nuclear problem. Some say that if nuclear destruction comes, it will be because God wills it. Others say God will simply not allow it to happen. Either answer, based upon belief in God's controlling power, "cuts the nerve of human responsibility."[73]

In Kaufman's view, the traditional understanding of divine sovereignty proves unable to contain or interpret our new situation; in fact, it proves positively dangerous.[74] Those who seek an antidote for the the pell-mell rush to nuclear annihilation will need to look elsewhere.

Images and Themes Suggestive for Reconceiving Divine Power

Feminists believe that an exploration of feminine images for the divine holds promise for numerous reasons. A range of the possibilities is enumerated here.

1. The pluriform richness of feminine images quickly exposes the nonnecessity of both the exclusively masculine language/symbolism and the peculiar understanding of God (as possessing primarily stereotypically male attributes) that has grown out of these limited representations. The hold of the male God who has become idol may be broken.

2. Making available female representations of the divine may have an effect for women similar (in one sense) to that which male representations of the divine have had for men. That is, they might provide an affirmation and elevation of "femaleness" just as male representations provide an affirmation and elevation of "maleness." The refusal to represent

---

[73]Kaufman, p. 8.

[74]If, as Kaufman proposes, the supreme test of the viability and truth of Christian symbols is their capacity to provide insight and guidance in our present situation, then the traditional doctrine of omnipotence clearly fails in this regard. Kaufman, p. 28.

God with female images has consigned woman to secondary status in self-concept as well as in other ways.

3. A positive symbolizing of female sexuality and bodily experience may serve to offset the denigration of these at the hands of patriarchy. Celebration of the powers of the female body would include but would not be limited to female reproductive powers as symbolic of divine creativity.

4. Recovery of the religion of the Goddess may make available symbols—lacking in the patriarchal tradition—of the legitimacy and beneficence of the female will and independent female power. "Religious symbol systems focused around exclusively male images of the divine create the impression that female power can never be fully legitimate or wholly beneficent."[75] The Goddess, in her obvious strength, capability, and transcendence, provides a needed model and a validation of female power.

5. The history and practice of Goddess religion may point to alternative ways of conceiving divine power. A long-range possibility is the overturning of some of the social consequences (oppression, exploitation, and violence) of elevating power in the mode of domination and control.

6. A shorter-range goal is the revitalization of the doctrine of God. The images from Goddess religion have a metaphoric power today, while traditional masculine images have become commonplace.[76]

Within the scope of this exposition, it is not possible to enumerate, much less fully present, all the insights and contributions from feminist perspectives that might aid in the reshaping of the doctrine of omnipotence. Nevertheless a brief exploration of feminist research into—and in some cases recovery of—the religion of the Goddess may reveal some of the potential that is there.

The Promise of the Ancient Goddesses

Historical research into the ancient religion of the Goddess uncovers many promising features. The roles and characteris-

---

[75]Christ, p. 140. Male power is legitimated by these symbols, while female power is denigrated. Elizabeth Janeway has argued that female power, while not altogether denied in patriarchy, is not recognized as legitimate. Power that is not recognized as legitimate cannot be expressed directly but only deviously, secretly, or through manipulation—and thus is always suspect of being dangerous or evil. The illegitimacy of female power within the Western tradition is epitomized in the story of Eve.

[76]"God the father," for example, is an image that has become literalized and commonplace; it has lost its disclosive power. In a sense, it has become both idolatrous and irrelevant. McFague, *Metaphorical Theology*, p. 2.

tics of the gods and goddesses of antiquity were not defined according to later stereotypes of "masculine" and "feminine." In them the gender division is not yet the primary metaphor for imaging the dialectics of human existence, nor is the idea of gender complementarity present.[77] Either gender could represent the full range of divine attributes and actions. Male and female are equivalent—not complementary—images of the divine.[78] Gender as a category is not seen as a necessary or natural correlative of power or powerlessness.[79] Neither the level of activity nor the scope of power is contingent upon gender. Nor is there any dualism of body and spirit; both gods and goddesses manifested sexual potency as well as social power. As Ruether notes, "It is precisely this aspect [of equivalency] that provides the most striking alternative to the symbolic world generated by male monotheism."[80]

This discovery reveals the nonnecessity of what has heretofore operated as a guiding (and limiting) principle in divine attribution. Gender complementarity has not always been— and need not always be—determinative of the attributes that may properly be assigned to the deity (whether represented in male or female images). The nonnecessity of masculine language, symbolism, and (stereotypical) attributes is established.

It was also hoped that the imaging of the divine in female form would affirm femaleness and female being, thereby making possible a heightened self-concept for women. Merlin Stone's observation seems to make this conclusion self-evident: "A religion in which the deity was female and revered as wise, valiant, powerful, and just, provided very different images of womanhood than those offered by the male-oriented religions of today."[81] Stone has also documented that the characteristics attributed to the Goddess were often lived out in the lives of women who worshiped her. Where the Goddess was worshiped as a powerful, courageous hunter or warrior and a leader in battle, we find accounts of women as hunters and warriors. Where Ishtar (Directress, Prophetess, Lady of Vision)

---

[77]"Ishtar is addressed as the expression of divine power and sovereignty in female form, a deity who performs the divine works of dividing heaven from earth, setting captives free, waging war, establishing peace, administering justice, exercising judgment, and enlightening human beings with the truth—as well as presiding over birth, healing the sick, and nurturing the little ones." Johnson, p. 461.

[78]Johnson, p. 461.

[79]Ochshorn, p. 89.

[80]Ruether, *Sexism and God-Talk,* p. 52.

[81]Stone, p. 5.

was worshiped, women served as judges and magistrates in the courts of law.[82]

Two other desired outcomes of the exploration of the religion of the Goddess also appear to be realistic. Although the connection between religion and social practices is extremely complex, and there *were* cultures in which the Goddess was worshiped and women were not given full social equality with men, generally, where the Goddess was worshiped, the social status and political power of women increased accordingly.[83]

Where worship was directed toward a male deity or deities exclusively, the male tended to dominate socially and politically.[84] The situation among the worshipers of Yahweh is a case in point. The economic, legal, and social position of Israelite women contrasted sharply with that of women all about them. Israelite wives had no right of divorce, were counted among their husband's possessions, and were treated as slaves. Vows made by women had to be validated by their fathers or husbands, and a man could sell his daughter.[85]

In the light of such findings, a reclaiming of the Goddess may be expected to have a positive effect upon the social status and political power of women. This is part of the promise that the resacralizing of the Goddess holds for women.

The Goddess as Manifesting Power in the Mode of Life-Giving and World-Generation

The fundamental intention of this exploration of the image of the Goddess is to gain fresh resources for the effort to reconceptualize divine power. And, in fact, the Goddess does prove a rich source of alternative meanings for power. We find in the religion of the Goddess that power is valued and expressed primarily in the mode of "life-giving" and "world-generation."

According to Merlin Stone,[86] primitive peoples who did not

---

[82]Stone, p. 3.

[83]Diodorus wrote at length of the worship of the goddess Isis. Describing the social consequences of this religious practice, he wrote, "It is for these reasons, in fact, that it was ordained that the queen should have greater power and honor than the king and that among private persons the wife should enjoy authority over the husband, husbands agreeing in the marriage contract that they will be obedient in all things to their wives." Stone, p. 36.

[84]"Almost always in male-dominated societies, the godhead is defined in exclusively masculine terms." Sanday, p. 6.

[85]Stone, p. 55.

[86]Merlin Stone, "The Great Goddess: Who Was She?" in Spretnak, pp. 8–10.

understand biological paternity or the necessary connection between sexual intercourse and conception revered the female as the "Giver of Life." These cultures were matrilineal in descent, matrilocal in marriage, and frequently matriarchal in governance.[87] Names, titles, possessions, and territorial rights were passed along through the female line. In these societies, women not only were venerated but actually had social and political power. Archaeological evidence indicates that these matriarchal cultures tended to be egalitarian, democratic, and peaceful.[88]

The earliest concepts of religion probably took the form of ancestor worship. Idols used were generally female and represented the human origins of the whole tribe. This is a result of the fact that accounts of ancestry were reckoned only through the matriline. The concept of the "creator of all human life" may have been formulated by the clan's image of the woman who had been their most ancient ancestress, which became deified as "Divine Ancestress."

It was thought that woman, like the Goddess, brought forth life alone and unaided. Awe of the universe was transformed into reverence for woman herself, whose body became the symbol for birth and rebirth. Woman's creative power was embodied in a multitude of female figurines[89] that emphasized her breasts, belly, and hips. These "Mother Goddesses" were worshiped everywhere and have been discovered in the remains of civilizations all over the world.

The pregnant human female was the central metaphor for the powers of life for peoples who domesticated neither

---

[87]Care must be taken here not to assume that matriarchal cultures are the reverse image of patriarchal cultures. This is to assume that the only way of ruling and exercising power is in the oppressive-controlling pattern of patriarchal societies. While some matriarchal cultures may have adopted this pattern, there seems to be little evidence to suggest that this was the usual pattern of matriarchal governance. Nor is a simple reversal of male and female roles in modern culture what is desired by feminists who work for the substantial increase of social and political power for women.

[88]Judy Chicago, "Our Heritage Is Our Power," in Spretnak, p. 152. Proto-Indo Europeans who were patriarchal, nomadic, and warlike infiltrated the matrifocal, agricultural, peaceful societies where the Goddess was worshiped between 4500 and 2500 B.C.E. As a result, the Goddess was deposed, either slain or made wife, daughter, or mother to the male deities of the warriors. By the time of decipherable written records, we begin to see evidence that societies are ruled by warrior-kings worshiping warrior-king divinities. Societies are hierarchical and slave-based. Christ, pp. 161–162.

[89]These date back as far as 25,000 B.C.E. and continue well into Roman times. Stone, in Spretnak, p. 11.

animals nor plants but were totally dependent on the spontaneous forces of the earth for gathering food.[90] The symbolism continued even after nomadic peoples herded livestock
and after the invention of agriculture. The images of fertility
and earthiness predominate in the images of Goddess as
life-giver.

> The Goddess is first of all earth, the dark, nurturing mother
> who brings forth all life. She is the power of fertility and gener-
> ation; the womb, and also the receptive tomb, the power of
> death. All proceeds from Her, all returns to Her. As earth, She
> is also plant life; trees, the herbs and grains that sustain life. She
> is the body and the body is sacred.[91]

A theme of cooperation with nature characterized Goddess
religion. Spirit and matter were not dichotomized.[92]

It is important to note[93] that the major fertility goddesses
were hardly viewed as mere breeders. Beyond the bearing
and nurturing of life, their association with the earth and fertility signified an important measure of participation, not only
in the creation of the universe but also in its organization and
maintenance.[94] Thus the Goddess is not only life-giver but also
world-generator. As such, she generates and encompasses all
reality; she is transcendent even in her immanence.[95] She is
the One[96]

---

[90]Ruether, *Sexism and God-Talk*, p. 48.

[91]Starhawk, p. 78.

[92]Ruether, *Sexism and God-Talk*, p. 85.

[93]Ochshorn, p. 3.

[94]According to Stone, descriptions of the female deity as creator of the universe
and inventor or provider of culture often were given only a line or two. If the female
deity was mentioned at all, scholars quickly disposed of these aspects of the female
deity as hardly worth discussing. Despite the fact that the title of the Goddess in most
historical documents of the Near East was Queen of Heaven, some writers were
willing to know her only as the eternal "Earth Mother." Stone, pp. xx–xxi.

[95]One of the earliest and most enduring images is the "Goddess Creatress," the
"Lady of the Animals." Classic representations include appearances of the Goddess
with animals or as having herself animal characteristics. The Lady of the Animals
"was not a power transcendent of earth but rather the power which creates, sustains,
and manifests in the infinite variety of life forms on earth." Christ, p. 165.

[96]There is a richness and diversity of titles, roles, and images of the Goddess that go
well beyond simple "Earth Mother" designations. She is also Sea Goddess, Queen of
Heaven, Creator of the Universe, force of existence, the one who takes in death,
provider of law and cosmic pattern, provider of herbs and healing, and the essence of
wisdom. Anthropomorphic images include hunter, judge, warrior, tribal ancestress,
protector of animals, prophetess, inventor of fire, guardian of the celestial chamber of
grain, teacher of carpentry and masonry, and scribe of the tree of life. These images
in themselves refute generalized archetypes, stereotypes, and simplistic dualities.

within which all things, gods and humans, sky and earth, human and non-human beings are generated. Here the divine is not abstracted into some other world beyond this earth but is the encompassing source of new life that surrounds the present world and assures its continuance.[97]

She has meaning as a symbol of the holistic nature of life on earth in which all forms of being are intrinsically connected and are one.

The Womb of the Goddess:
A Promising Image for the God-World Relation
and for Divine Power

Among the many images that are being proposed by theologians reconstructing the doctrine of God from a feminist perspective, the metaphor of the divine womb[98] is selected for special focus here.[99] This image stands out as particularly useful in providing an alternative to traditional images for the God-world relation and for divine power exercised in that relation. Instead of an image of the God-world relation as being like that existing between a king and his kingdom, it is thought of as being like the relation between a mother and the child she carries in her womb. The nature of the exercise of power shifts accordingly from images of ruling to images of life-giving and world-generation.

The selection of this metaphor as expressive of the relation of God and the world is well grounded in the Judeo-Christian tradition. Phyllis Trible has noted that the word for "womb" (*rehem*) comes from the same root as the adjective "merciful" (*rahum*) which is used exclusively for the Creator, never for creatures. When Yahweh is spoken of as "merciful and gracious" (Ps. 86:15; 111:4; 145:8; Neh. 9:17), this is the term that is used. "In many and various ways, then, the maternal metaphor *rahûm* witnesses to God as compassionate, merciful, and loving."[100] Given the frequency with which mention of

---

[97]Ruether, *Sexism and God-Talk*, p. 48.

[98]It is interesting that the caves where Paleolithic worship of the Goddess was performed were understood to be the "womb of the Creatrix." Christ, p. 192.

[99]The choice of this image is inspired by and dependent upon the work of Sallie McFague in her book *Models of God: A Theology for an Ecological, Nuclear Age.* She has said of the model of God as "mother" that "there is simply no other imagery available to us that has this power for expressing the interdependence and interrelatedness of all life with its ground" (p. 106).

[100]Trible, *God and the Rhetoric of Sexuality*, p. 39.

God's merciful compassion appears in scripture, it can hardly be said that such female imagery is peripheral to the tradition even though, until recently, it has gone unnoticed.[101]

The entire process of birthing has in fact been attributed to deity. In various passages, God conceives, is pregnant, writhes in labor pains, brings forth a child, and nurses it.[102] Given the patriarchal stamp of scripture and the systematic repression of female voices and images within it, the wealth of these images is remarkable.[103]

In terms of its potential for illumining the meaning of divine power, this metaphor effectively conveys the theme of power as life-giving and world-generating in contrast to power as dominating and controlling. It fleshes out this basic meaning by highlighting in the God-world relation the features of connectedness, relatedness, and interdependence. These features prove decisive for an effective addressing of the problems of separation, self-other duality, and independence, which, as the feminists who were considered earlier have argued, lead us to an "alienated paradigm of divine power."

The Theme of "Power in Relation": Mutual Empowerment and Synergy

The theme of "relation"[104] keeps surfacing in the writing of feminists and seems to offer a genuinely different approach to thinking about power. Carter Heyward takes the bold step of equating divine power with the power found in the bonds of our relationships.[105] "The experience of relation is fundamental and constitutive of human being; . . . it is good and powerful; . . . it is only within this experience . . . that we may realize that *the power in relation is God.*"[106]

---

[101]Johnson, p. 447.

[102]Trible, *God and the Rhetoric of Sexuality*, p. 69.

[103]Some of the references include God as conceiving and being in labor (Isa. 42:14), giving birth (Deut. 32:18), nursing (Isa. 49:15), engaged in traditional mothering activities (Hos. 11:3–4; Isa. 46:3–4; Isa. 66:13–14), God as midwife (Ps. 22:9–11), God as mother bear (Hos. 13:8), God as mother hen (Matt. 23:37), and God as mother eagle (Deut. 32:11–12).

[104]Jill Raitt, for example, proposes "a theology built upon the category of relation" in her article "Structures and Strictures: Relational Theology and a Woman's Contribution to Theological Conversation," pp. 3–17.

[105]"The power of God . . . is the power of our relational bonding, a persistent power which makes 'justice roll down like waters.' " Heyward, *Our Passion for Justice*, p. 118.

[106]Heyward, *The Redemption of God*, p. 1.

Rita Nakashima Brock[107] speaks of this power as "erotic power" and sees it operating in the community. "Erotic power is the power of connectedness." Christ, not as the person of Jesus, but as the relational power of Christa/Community is life-giving, life-saving power. It is power that heals and makes whole, *empowers* and liberates. It comes from the heart, the center of one's being (Latin: *cor*). It is not about control, dominance, or authority but about our primal interrelatedness. Connection is the basic power of all existence, the root of life.

The character of the operation of divine power in relation is best characterized as "empowerment." It is loving and persuasive power that empowers—and does not coerce—action and response.[108] This understanding of power does not assume that one gives up power in order to empower others. It is not a "zero sum" or "scarcity" model of power. Rather, power is an expansive phenomenon—like love—that is not reduced by being shared or by being given away. In feminist literature, "mutuality" and "reciprocity" are often emphasized as essential ingredients of relationality. "Mutual empowerment" is one of the expressions that is often used in discussions of power.

Another important way of characterizing the operation of this "generating" power is as "synergy." That is, it *cooperates* with other powers. There is a decided emphasis on the "collective functioning" of this energy. When energies are joined with one another, power is built through synergy, and they may together generate energy greater than the sum of their separate generations.

Many thinkers—including both scientists and feminists—have begun to speak of the fundamental nature of reality as "energy" rather than substance or matter.

> The universe is a fluid, ever-changing energy pattern, not a collection of fixed and separate things. What affects one thing affects, in some way, all things: All is interwoven into the continuous fabric of being.[109]

In this sense, God may be thought of as the world's "life

---

[107]These insights are taken from Rita Nakashima Brock, "Beyond Jesus the Christ: A Christology of Erotic Power," paper delivered at the American Academy of Religion, December 1987.

[108]"The power of God at work in Christ is experienced by most Christians as a gentle, persuasive power. It does not coerce rectification and the acceptance of the love God offers, for a loving response can never be coerced." Raitt, p. 12.

[109]Starhawk, p. 129, in a section with the intriguing title "Energy: The Cone of Power."

force" (*dynamis zōtikē*), "energizing" all reality. Divine energy (power) flows within, between, and among us. It is the "source" of our power.[110]

The Implied Ethic of a "Power in Relation": Solidarity

If divine power consists in domination and control, then the implied ethic is one of obedience. One humbly submits to the divine will. Sin consists in prideful self-assertion and rebellion against the divine will.[111]

If, however, divine power is power in relation, power in the mode of life-giving and world-generating, which operates as empowering and synergy, then the ethical imperative is completely reshaped. The theory of virtue which seems most suited to the new model is an *ethics of solidarity*, centering on strengthened and enriched relationships with God and with one another.

Solidarity with God (more often spoken of as union with God) has roots in the mystical tradition, which developed alongside the dominant tradition, and from which many feminists draw. The mystical tradition has no place for deferring to a higher power, submitting to alien rule, or denying one's own strength. It does not urge that God be honored and obeyed because of God's power over us. Rather, it calls one to immerse oneself in God as in the depths of a sea of love.[112] We become one with God and one with God's movement in the world. Our solidarity with God is made possible by God's

---

[110]Some feminists use "power" and "energy" interchangeably. Both Barbara Starrett and Sally Gearhart do so in their articles entitled, respectively, "The Metaphors of Power" and "Womanpower: Energy Re-sourcement," in Spretnak, *Politics of Women's Spirituality*. The emphasis in the feminist literature seems to be placed first upon the energy within us (our intrinsic power) and then upon the energy among us. Sally Gearhart proposes that "womanpower" is built up by energy "re-sourcement." "To re-source is to find another source, an entirely different and prior one, a source deeper than the patriarchy and one that allows us to stand in the path of continuous and cosmic energy." Spretnak, p. 195.

[111]"The conception of sin as primarily a kind of personal disobedience or violation of the divine will, and salvation as being rescued from that condition of alienation and guilt, is rooted almost completely in the mythic picture which presents God as a divine king and father, and our relationship to God as the interpersonal and political one of subjects and children." Kaufman, p. 55.

[112]"Symbols from nature are preferred where our relationship with God is not one of obedience but of unity, where we are not subject to the commands of some remote being that demands sacrifice and the relinquishing of the self, but rather where we are asked to become one with all life." Soelle, p. 102.

prior solidarity with us as symbolized in the traditional account of the incarnation and as imaged in the metaphor of the womb.

Solidarity with one another (as opposed to separation, self-other duality, and independence) is also entailed in this ethic. Our shared power is mutually empowering and synergetic. Our power is not power *over* community (as in paternalism) or power *without* community (as in autonomy) but power *within* the community (as in solidarity).[113]

Social consequences of such an ethic would be very different from those associated with power in the mode of domination and control and the ethic of obedience[114] that accompanies it. These consequences can be alluded to only briefly here. Power exercised in solidarity with others discourages independent, arbitrary assertion of the individual will[115] over against the needs and desires of others.[116] It seems that solidarity would by its very nature seek to avoid oppression, exploitation, and violence. This is the case because harm done to another with whom one stands in solidarity is perceived as harm done to oneself.

Conclusion

In this chapter we have considered the feminist critique: that the tradition's preoccupation with power is a typically male preoccupation and that the prevailing model for power found there reflects a male bias. The several different levels at which feminists are directing this charge have been illustrated as have their grounds for doing so. Social consequences that feminists attribute to the exercise of "male power" have been summarized. Images emerging from feminist research into the religion of the Goddess have been explored in hopes of discovering there fresh insights that will assist us in reconceiving divine power. The image of God as a pregnant human female and the world as a child in the womb was found to present a

---

[113]Letty Russell makes similar distinctions in her book *Household of Freedom*.

[114]The dangers of the ethic of obedience were presented in the section that dealt with social consequences of power in the mode of domination and control, specifically under the topic of oppression.

[115]"One possible reason the will is denigrated in a patriarchal religious framework is that both the human will and the divine will are often pictured as arbitrary, self-initiated, and exercised without regard to the will of others." Christ, p. 128.

[116]Power that is shared power can be good, creative, and redemptive, but it is "nothing less than evil when we possess it as ours and ours alone." Heyward, *Our Passion for Justice*, p. 122.

promising alternative metaphor for the God-world relation and for God's exercise of power in that relation. Power having the character of life-giving and world-generation is displayed in this image. The theme of "power in relation" which recurs in feminist writing was noted along with frequent references to "empowerment" and "synergy." An ethic of solidarity is a logical implication of this image and these themes.

7

Constructive Proposal:
A Process-Feminist Synthesis

A Brief Review of the Classical Model
and One of Its Modifications

That the traditional doctrine of omnipotence stands in need of reassessment in the face of the problem of evil has been a fairly commonplace observation in contemporary theology. In recent studies that undertake this task, the end in view—redefining omnipotence in such a way that God is not seen as indictable for evil—has been largely determinative of the form the redefinition has taken. Redefinitions have tended to alter the scope of the concept by restricting in some way *how much* power is implied in the term "omnipotence." This study has argued that the question of the meaning of the concept and *what kind* of power is to be attributed to God is more fundamental and a more pressing question. This latter question has rarely been addressed. The reason seems to be that there is within the tradition an implied consensus as to the meaning of the term "power."

As we have seen, for Calvin omnipotence meant "the effectual exercise of the divine personal will in accomplishing divine purposes." Calvin rejected two moves made by theologians of the Middle Ages to deal with the cluster of problems surrounding omnipotence. He refused to distinguish between God's "absolute" power and "ordained" power, and he refused to restrict the range of divine power to the set of things that are logically possible.

Calvin's understanding of divine power cannot be reduced to the notion of absolute power (the view preferred by his contemporary Duns Scotus), because God's power is *defined by the divine personal will*, which is never arbitrary but is always in conformity with the divine nature. Here Calvin is admitting a kind of internal (moral) limitation upon divine power. Nor can Calvin's doctrine of omnipotence be reduced to the sheer determinism of the Stoics because of the *freedom* of the divine will, which is not caught up in necessity. It might be said that everything downward from God is completely determined by God, but Calvin sees this as a very different position from that of the Stoics, which leaves the world in the hands of blind fate. Necessity is excluded. Calvin portrayed God's power as "personal and particular care," displayed in the creation, governance, and final disposition of the world. This power operates universally and continuously. Chance is excluded.

An important emphasis in Calvin's doctrine of omnipotence is his decided focus upon God's "ruling and governing." What comes to be in world process directly corresponds with the divine will. This is not merely a potentiality of divine power but power that God actively exercises everywhere and always,[1] determining not just generalities but all the particulars of world process—even the will and actions of free creatures. When Calvin discusses divine "ruling and governing," the term "control" appears frequently. Because of this choice of words and the content with which Calvin fills out his doctrine of omnipotence, the power Calvin ascribes to God has been described as "power in the mode of domination and control."

This meaning for "power" raises problems of coherence and religious viability. A challenge has been brought concerning whether Calvin can affirm divine determination of all things and still make other affirmations that seem important to him (e.g., creaturely freedom sufficient to make "relationship with God" and "moral responsibility" conceivable). The theodicy problem is exacerbated by this way of meaning omnipotence.

Calvin responds by, to a large extent, admitting divine responsibility for evil but then insisting that what appears evil to us is serving God's good purposes. As a second line of argument, Calvin relies upon a "free-will defense." Here he argues that in evil human actions—which God completely determines—God has good intentions and is therefore blameless, while human beings have evil intentions and are therefore guilty. This argument runs aground, however, when Calvin elsewhere insists that even the will is determined by God.

When power is taken to mean the ability to dominate and

---

[1]Calvin accepts the understanding of God as *actus purus*. He does not admit unrealized potentiality in divine power. This is evident in the reasoning behind his rejection of the distinction between absolute power and ordained power.

control and the qualifier "omni" is attached to this meaning, insurmountable problems are created. Many thinkers who work within the same general understanding of omnipotence have seen the problems and have sought to ameliorate them by in some way restricting the scope of the power attributed to God. This is done in hopes of allowing for greater creaturely freedom and ensuring that God is not indictable for evil.

Barth, for example, maintains the traditional meaning for omnipotence with its emphasis upon divine control. He locates his explicit discussion of omnipotence under the description of divine perfections. For Barth, perfections are divided into two categories, "perfections of love" and "perfections of freedom." He insists that the division is only for purposes of discussion and divine love and freedom imply one another. However, he does locate the doctrine of omnipotence under the category of freedom rather than love—a placement that turns out not to be arbitrary. The terms "freedom" and "power" become almost interchangeable for him. In his elaboration of the doctrine of omnipotence, Barth seems more concerned to illustrate divine freedom than love. Like Calvin, he develops an all-determining notion of power that demonstrates divine freedom well enough but makes the possibility of genuine relationship between God and a real "other" difficult to imagine.

Basically, divine power takes two forms for Barth: (1) Divine *self-determination* as the capacity for God to be Godself. This specification excludes all abstract notions of power and any idea of unlimited power or of power as *potentia* apart from *potestas*. (2) Divine *world-determination* is the capacity to determine completely all other realities. These realities are conceived as distinct but not independent from Godself.

God's power is *conscious* and *purposive* for Barth. With Calvin, he maintains that divine power operates personally, universally, and particularly. Unlike Calvin, Barth accepts the medieval distinction between God's absolute power and God's ordained power. God exists omnipotently apart from any activity in the world. Therefore God's power is not to be seen as "dissolved and disappearing" in God's actual willing and acting. Barth seems at first to accept also the medieval limitation of the scope of divine power to include only those things which are logically possible. However, he then lodges "possibility" in God. Consequently, his position turns out not to differ greatly from Calvin's on this latter point.

Barth takes two steps in the direction of modifying the scope of divine power. The first is his acceptance of the possibility of *voluntary self-limitation* of divine power. The divine nature is understood by Barth not simply as a given but as something self-determined. God can therefore place limitations upon Godself. In the decision to create, for example, God decided to be "God in relation" and in creating accepted a voluntary self-limitation.

Two difficulties with this step have been noted. First, this way of speaking introduces a "before and after" in God which Barth elsewhere shows that he does not want to admit. Second, because of the *voluntary* nature of this self-limitation, it cannot advance the theodicy problem toward resolution. A voluntary self-limitation is as good as no limitation at all, for it can be removed at will.

The second step Barth takes toward modification of the scope of divine power lies in his christological orientation. In principle, Barth understands Jesus Christ to be the embodiment of divine power and our only guide to what power means in relation to God. There is no question that such a starting point could significantly alter the doctrine of omnipotence derived. In Jesus Christ, what we see most obviously is divine suffering love, vulnerability, humility, and weakness.

If Barth consistently followed through with his christological orientation, the meaning of power—and not just the scope of power—that is attributed to God would be transformed. However, Barth does not consistently follow through. Power in the mode of domination and control is allowed to serve as the grid through which he interprets what is seen in the incarnation and the crucifixion. Barth denies that power, in the sense of control, is in any way relinquished. Even the cross event is interpreted as a display of God's active power of self-determination and world-determination, despite the apparent vulnerability we see in the incarnation and the crucifixion. It is interpreted by and swallowed up in Barth's preconceived notion of power as completely active and all-determining.

Neither of these attempted limitations in the scope of divine power advances Barth very far in the direction of ameliorating the difficulties that are inherent in the traditional doctrine of omnipotence. It may be that no attempts at modifying the scope of divine power can be adequate to this task as long as the underlying meaning for power remains intact. It would seem that a reconsideration of the meaning for power is indicated.

The extent to which the classical model out of which both Calvin and Barth are operating is formed and limited by the classicist worldview has been noted. The "supernaturalism" which sets God and the world in opposition, as well as the particular way of understanding "perfections" which leads to convictions of divine immutability, independence, and pure activity, profoundly affects their construction of the meaning of divine power.

Calvin has difficulty consistently affirming divine relation to the world because the classicist framework out of which he operates imposes a concept of God that is fundamentally non-social. Calvin does press the limits of the classical concept in his use of personal metaphors that imply relation (and consequently imply a kind of mutability, dependence, and passive power for the receptivity and responsiveness that are ingredient to relation). His concept and his metaphors, then, remain in tension with one another.

Calvin's presentation of omnipotence parallels his doctrine of God. His concept of God's power is essentially a nonsocial concept of unidirectional, all-determining power. Here again his concept is in tension with his metaphors, for in the human arena we nowhere experience fathers, kings, or lords with all-determining power. Calvin's doctrine of God and his doctrine of omnipotence are at least consistent with each other, though each of these has its own internal tensions.

With Barth the situation is somewhat different. His doctrine of God is intended to be fully social/relational. The intertrinitarian life itself is social/relational. However, Barth grafts onto his social notion of God a nonsocial notion of power. He maintains the same unidirectional, all-determining meaning for power that Calvin proposed and that I have referred to as "power in the mode of domination and control."

In the discussion that follows, it will be demonstrated that the very problems the classical worldview created for the doctrine of God and the doctrine of omnipotence are significantly addressed by the construction of an alternative metaphysical framework.[2] The new framework makes possible consistent articulation of central convictions that Calvin and Barth both hold but cannot articulate consistently because of the constraints of classical metaphysics. The proposal will adopt the metaphysical framework of process thought fleshed out by images and themes emerging from feminist thought. The al-

---

[2]Hartshorne's critique of classical theism is more immediately addressed to the Aristotle/Aquinas tradition. However, the "classicist worldview" with its supernaturalism and its assumptions about the nature of perfection is pervasive—not strictly localized in Aquinas. It takes in Calvin and Barth as well. Thus I find the critique and alternative proposed by process thought to be fairly readily transferable.

ternative approach provided by this synthesis is intended as a reconstruction of the doctrine of omnipotence that can express the central convictions of the tradition while avoiding the pitfalls of the classical model.

The Possibility of a Process-Feminist Synthesis

Feminism and process thought have commonalities both in their respective critiques of the classical tradition and in their basic presuppositions.[3] Perhaps the central point of unity that issues in the many accompanying commonalities is their firm rejection of the dualism in the classical tradition. Proponents of feminism and process thought see the dualistic vision of reality as existentially and intellectually inadequate. They differ, however, as to the angle from which they are addressing their criticisms.

Process thinkers trace this vision of reality to its intellectual roots—to a worldview and a metaphysical system that they insist is no longer defensible in the light of modern science and its discoveries and theories (i.e., relativity theory). They seem most concerned with the *intellectual inadequacy* of this perspective.

Feminists, on the other hand, seem more concerned with the *existential inadequacy* of this worldview. They trace this vision of reality to its existential roots in the "oldest and most fundamental dualism," the hierarchical differentiation between women and men. They criticize this perspective for its social consequences—for justifying and perpetuating oppression.

The classical tradition's ways of conceiving self, world, and God are clearly dualistically defined and hierarchically patterned. This worldview draws dichotomies: mind/body, spirit/nature, good/evil, being/becoming, subject/object, activity/passivity. In each of these sets, one is given priority over the other and considered to be more valuable. Hartshorne attacked this approach at its intellectual roots. He noted that all basic metaphysical ideas come in pairs of contraries that are inseparable and that mutually imply each other, but in themselves these are empty abstractions; every actual entity is in fact co-constituted by these contraries. The separation of

---

[3]My summary has been helped by the work of Sheila Greeve Davaney, Valerie Saiving, John Cobb, and Marjorie Suchocki whose articles on the interface between feminism and process thought appear in Sheila Greeve Davaney, ed., *Feminism and Process Thought.*

these can only be an abstracting from reality. Furthermore, Hartshorne argued, it is not self-evident that perfection (or even superiority) is to be associated with one side of these contrasts any more than with the other. For this reason, he argues (in his "dipolar theism," or doctrine of "dual transcendence") that God is to be thought of as possessing both poles "in uniquely excellent ways" (OOTM, p. 44).

Feminists add to this criticism. Not only has the classical tradition imposed an artificial and hierarchical dualism on reality but it has consistently correlated the dichotomies with a male-female dualism, associating male with the "superior" pole. It is assumed that inherently or ideally the superior pole should prevail over and control its inferior opposite.[4] In terms of gender traits, those which will ensure domination are assigned to the male and those which will ensure subordination are assigned to the female. A pattern of male domination and female subordination is upheld and promoted in this way of construing reality. The moral inadequacy of this thought system becomes clear as we see the extent to which it provides the ideological underpinnings for the social structures that oppress women.[5]

Feminists and process thinkers, approaching from different angles, are unified by their rejection of the graded dualism found in the classical tradition, and this rejection calls forth from them a fairly unified set of corollary criticisms of the classicist worldview. They refuse the elevation of being over becoming and stasis over dynamic activity.[6] They deny that self-completeness and independence are superior to relatedness and interdependence. They reject the primary and absolute differentiations between God and the world, men and women, and humanity and nature. Each of these dualities is one more "graded differentiation" in which one side has been understood as "subject" with intrinsic value and power, while the other has been understood as "object" and valued only in its relation to the subject.

In addition to their similar criticisms of the classicist worldview, feminists and process thinkers share many basic

---

[4]Valerie Saiving, "Androgynous Life: A Feminist Appropriation of Process Thought," in Davaney, p. 18.

[5]Ruether has drawn out the damage of this graded dualism more broadly, adding to it the self-other duality. Domination and subordination become the pattern for relating to all "others." The social consequences as I have described them are oppression, violence, and exploitation.

[6]Here the importance of affirming immutability and refusing mutability in God is denied.

presuppositions. Methodologically they share a commitment to experience as a starting point. Both perspectives are working toward a holistic rather than a dualistic understanding of reality. There is a shared emphasis upon becoming rather than being, process rather than product or consequence.[7] They tend to work from dynamic and organic models that emphasize potential and growth.

Both affirm the essential "subjectivity" of all that exists and suggest that this subjectivity is social, creative, and processive in nature. Whitehead's panpsychism, which Hartshorne also adopts, implies that nothing can be viewed strictly as "object." This connects well with the feminist refusal of "object status." Both thought systems are, in their own way, contending against mind-body dualism.

For our purposes, perhaps the most interesting of the similarities between process thought and feminist thought lies in their parallel campaigns against traditional monarchical,[8] unidirectional, all-determining concepts of divine power. They opt for power that is "power in relation," empowering and working-with-other-powers (in synergy), allowing for both "influence" and "being influenced," and persuasive rather than coercive in its exercise.

One of the more central shared emphases concerns *relationality*. Feminists have stressed personal and social dimensions of relationships, including connectedness, openness to the other, and mutuality. Process thought, as it has been illustrated in Hartshorne, is equally strong in its affirmation of the sociality/relativity of all things.

A companion conviction has been the *interdependence* of all

---

[7]The consequentialist bias of the dominant tradition which Maguire criticized from a feminist perspective is rejected by both process and feminist thinkers. Maguire, pp. 59–67.

[8]There is a sense in which the tradition is unfairly criticized for its monarchical understanding of power. In a predemocratic political system, this is the only live option available in the thought world. This is not an altogether negative model. A good monarch has the positive value of minimizing conflictual and chaotic elements in the society and may even serve to protect the weak from the strong. This kind of power, or something like it, is a necessary condition of the possibility of the existence of any "society" at all.

The critique from the standpoint of a democratic political system cannot be avoided, however. For it opens up a whole range of heretofore unavailable options for thinking about the exercise of power. This political innovation presents the possibilities of "social" power, shared power, self-rule, government by the consent of the governed, order created by mutually agreed upon laws, etc. These political developments make thinkable many of the changes that process and feminist thinkers propose in the way divine power is conceived.

things. No subject is considered to be absolutely dependent or independent. Every subject has dimensions of both independence and dependence—each is uniquely and intrinsically valuable in itself, but each exists in relation to others. Each subject is affected by and affects other subjects.

In contrast to the tradition which assigns all *freedom and power* to God, feminist thought and process thought see freedom and power as essential to every subject. All subjects possess freedom and power within limits—none possess them absolutely. In the process framework, each subject emerges from its past which is simply "given." This places a limit upon freedom. However, the way the past will be integrated in the moment of becoming is a function of the free self-creativity of the subject.

Both feminists and process thinkers assign limited *active and passive power* to all subjects. In the language of process thought, there are two forms of power: the power of self-creativity in response to the influence of others (passive power) and the power of other-creativity in one's influence upon others (active power). Power of influence is always power within limits. It is qualified by the fact that no one is the sole influence upon another and by the fact that no free subject can be totally externally determined by the influences of others.

Both their critique of the classicist worldview and their fundamental presuppositions provide substantial grounds for collaboration between feminists and process thinkers. Even Mary Daly,[9] who has cautioned against adopting the ideas of any particular thinker or thought system "ready made" into which feminist thought can be fitted, recognizes the attractiveness of process thought and its compatibility with feminist insights. To date, feminists have not concentrated on developing a distinctive metaphysical vision. It may be that process thought can provide a conceptual framework to articulate more effectively feminist insights and themes and put them in helpful relation with the insights of others.

Hartshorne's Understanding of Divine Power

Hartshorne defines power as "the capacity to influence and to be influenced." He employs this meaning for power consistently for both divine and creaturely power. His alternative

---

[9]Daly, *Beyond God the Father*, pp. 37, 188.

meaning for divine power is made possible by his beginning at a new starting point. Along with the tradition, Hartshorne affirms that God must be "that than which nothing greater can be conceived." He does not begin, however, with the same assumptions regarding what constitutes "greatest conceivable"—immutability, independence, pure activity, and so forth. Instead, Hartshorne seeks to work out a "religious" definition of perfection, as "worshipfulness."

Two concepts in particular shape the content of the term "worshipfulness" for Hartshorne: unsurpassability and all-inclusiveness. *Unsurpassability* is a term chosen in acknowledgment of the sociality/relativity of all things. With respect to power, this principle requires that God be viewed as one power among others. Thus it is inconceivable that God should literally possess all the power that is—a monopoly. Actual entities by virtue of being *actual* possess power of their own.[10] The existence of these other powers places a metaphysical limitation upon God's power.[11] The perfection of divine power is not in its monopoly but in its unsurpassability. God possesses power—as with all other qualities—preeminently, in unsurpassable form.

All-inclusiveness is another term that fills in the content of "worshipfulness" for Hartshorne. It affirms that divine being includes within itself all positive values. This is a working out of Hartshorne's principle of dual transcendence. Hartshorne notes that all metaphysical ideas come in pairs that are inseparable and mutually imply each other. He criticizes the tradition for its one-sidedness in associating perfection with one side of the metaphysical contrasts and denying the other. Hartshorne insists that God incorporates *both* poles of the metaphysical contrasts (i.e., immutability *and* mutability, independence *and* dependence, active power *and* passive power), and each in the sense in which it is most excellent. This is why Hartshorne's definition of power includes both active power (influence) and passive power (being influenced). In the tradition, active power (intrinsic, agential, determinative, causal power) is assigned to God and passive

---

[10]Classical theism has, in Hartshorne's view, confused omnipotence with "omnificence," universal agency. It has acted as if God were the *only* agent (or actual entity) and therefore had a monopoly on power. As long as there are other actualities, there will be other agents, other powers.

[11]This is a very different kind of limitation from the moral limitation which Calvin admits, based upon divine nature, or the voluntary self-limitation which Barth admits, based upon the divine willing.

power (derivative, nonagential, determined, causal only in an instrumental sense) to the creature.

A Preliminary Definition

This constructive proposal will begin with Hartshorne's stated definition of power as "the capacity to be influenced and to influence." Attaching the qualifier "omni" to this meaning results in a definition of omnipotence as "the capacity to be influenced by *all* and to influence *all*." Furthermore:

1. This power *entails intentionality*. Here we are adopting a meaning consistent with the tradition as exemplified by Calvin and Barth, for we are assuming the exercise of divine will in a certain direction, with a certain teleology. This exercise of divine power is, using Barth's terms, "conscious and purposive."

2. This power *is present both in actuality and in potentiality*. This position agrees with Barth who allows for a distinction between God's absolute power and God's ordained power, and disagrees with Calvin, whose refusal of the distinction was intended as a rejection of "absolute power" abstracted from divine personal willing.

3. This power *is power in relation* and the relation is *of a personal sort*. This is something Barth and Calvin both seek to affirm, although each has difficulty doing so consistently because of the meaning for "power" they presuppose. Their meaning implies divine determination of creatures to a degree that makes any notion of real relation (which in any ordinary meaning entails some degree of reciprocity) difficult to conceive.

4. This power *does not entail a conflict of interests engendering resistance which is overcome*. It need not be thought of in terms of "overpowering," as the traditional meaning often is. Neither Barth nor Calvin thinks of the exercise of the divine will in these terms, yet in their systems the *will* of the creature is brought into conformity with the divine willing and there is not even an opportunity for resistance, since the creature is not genuinely independent.[12] In this new definition, it

---

[12]There is no conscious resistance for either Barth or Calvin. The divine power is not seen as an extrinsic force that controls the activities of creatures against their will but rather as a force that operates internally, determining the will of the creature from within. The conflict is not joined, in part, because real independence of existence for creatures is never granted in the first place. In Barth this is illustrated in the divine control of both the event of revelation and the human response to it.

is assumed that creatures have real independence and may or
may not respond to the divine influence.

How This Power Operates

This constructive proposal is adopting the model of "knowing," which Hartshorne uses to describe the nature of the
operation of power as the capacity to influence and to be influenced. This model, like the definition, is usable to describe
both creaturely power and divine power without equivocation. The model of knowing serves well in this regard. The
mind is *influenced* by what it knows. As God receives the
world—in its entirety and in all its particularity—as an object
of awareness, God is influenced by the world. The divine response of integrating that experience with the divine willing
in an act of divine self-creativity becomes influential in the
world as God in turn becomes an object of awareness for the
world. God's successive consequent states have influence on
the world (as do the world's upon God). The operation of this
power is *persuasive, not coercive,* just as the mind is persuaded—not coerced—by what it knows.

The Sense in Which Divine Power as Newly Defined
Is Omnipotent

The capacity to influence and to be influenced is the meaning for power that will underlie the reconstructed doctrine of
omnipotence. When this meaning is applied to God, the qualifier "omni" is to be added. The resulting definition of omnipotence is "the capacity to influence *all* and to be influenced
by *all.*" What we have is a new meaning for "omnipotence"
constructed upon the foundation of a new meaning for power.

It is important at this point to show whether and in what
sense this new meaning ascribes to God a power that is
uniquely excellent and qualitatively superior. Here it will be
argued that the difference between the limited "influencing
and being influenced" ascribed to creatures and the unlimited
"influencing and being influenced" ascribed to God is a
quantitative difference that makes a qualitative difference.
This qualitative difference will be described in terms of "all-
inclusiveness" and "unsurpassability."

To elaborate the difference made by the "all-inclusiveness"
of divine power, it may be useful to recall terminology used in
the social sciences to quantify power. The notion of power
base, for example, acknowledges the fact that power is always

in reference to a structure of relationships with respect to which one has power. Creatures may be said to have a narrow power base, while God's power base is not only broad but unlimited (all-inclusive). "Range of influence"—that is, how many others one may be said to influence—is similarly limited for creatures and unlimited (all-inclusive) for God.[13]

Two other quantifying phrases are *zone of acceptance,* which refers to the region in which power may be exercised, and *intensity of power,* which refers to the degree of influence within a given zone. The zone of acceptance for divine power has no boundaries—it is all-inclusive—and in any prescribed zone, divine power has the highest intensity (unsurpassable intensity) of any powers present.

This definition makes no "zero sum" presumption, that there is a finite sum of power to be distributed and the more power one has, the less another possesses. Divine influence over all, for example, in no way inhibits or restricts the influence of creatures upon one another or upon God.

Omnipotence in its new meaning is as "unlimited" in its scope as even the most absolute interpretations of the traditional definition. The "metaphysical limitation" introduced by the nature of reality does not really imply a limitation upon the scope of power but rather shapes the meaning that can be given to power. Omnipotence, in the new definition, is *the ideal and maximal case of power assuming a division of power.* A division of power must be assumed if actuality entails power and there exist other actualities besides God. Once the new meaning is accepted, the scope of divine power "as the capacity to influence all and to be influenced by all" can be seen to be unlimited.

Hartshorne's requirement of "unsurpassability" is also met by this new definition. God surpasses all others in power in several ways. (1) *God alone is the universal object of awareness.* This grants to God unsurpassable influence which cannot be attributed to any creature. (2) *Divine power is maximal in both aspects of the meaning of the term:* its maximal capacity to influence and its maximal capacity to be influenced. This is in part because the divine knowing, unlike that of creatures, is

---

[13]Hartshorne might view this differently. There is a sense in which the actual entity in its transition might be said to influence everything that comes after it by virtue of the relationality of all things. But that influence is only direct influence in a limited range. In the larger range, the farther away the other actual entities, the more indirect—and negligible—the influence becomes. God's influence is direct in an unlimited range.

perfectly conformal and all-inclusive. This enables both receptivity and responsiveness to be unsurpassable. (3) *Divine influence is unsurpassable in its persuasiveness.* This is so because God is able to provide ideal aims that are truly fitting and attractive for each actual occasion. No creature has the ability to do this; the result is that the influence of creatures upon one another and upon God is of a different quality.

The all-inclusiveness and unsurpassability of divine power make it possible for God to exercise influence in ways not open to creatures. There are things which only a "universal object of awareness" can accomplish for the world. God exercises power uniquely in (1) preserving and maintaining the world, (2) ordering the world by general natural laws that ensure against chaos and guarantee optimal conditions for the attainment of value, and (3) providing for every actuality an ideal aim to be integrated into its experience. These distinctly divine abilities further the argument for the unique excellence and qualitative superiority of divine power.

It might seem that, because the same kind of power is being attributed to God and to creatures, the difference between the two is merely quantitative. But on closer examination, it has been shown that this quantitative difference makes a qualitative difference, worthy of the term "omnipotence."

The Way in Which This Definition of Divine Power Avoids Connotations of Domination and Control

The new definition for power is designed to avoid the connotations of domination and control present in the traditional meaning for power. To review the prior description, *to control* means "to exercise restraint upon the free action of, to hold sway over, to exercise power or authority over; to dominate, command; to hold in check, curb, restrain from action, hinder, prevent; to overpower, overmaster, overrule."[14] To this term we add the word "domination"[15] primarily because it conveys more effectively the *personal* nature of this control which was an important ingredient in the tradition surrounding divine power. "Domination" is rooted in the Latin term *dominus*, which means lord or master. These two terms taken together are used to describe the meaning for power underlying the traditional doctrine of omnipotence. That meaning for omnip-

---

[14]OED.

[15]"The action of dominating, the exercise of ruling power, lordly rule, sway or control, ascendancy, lordship or sovereignty, predominance, prevalence." OED.

otence is further elaborated as "the effectual exercise of the divine personal will in accomplishing divine purposes." This meaning implies a monopoly on power, which is unidirectionally exercised, and involves complete self-determination and world-determination. It operates continuously and universally and attends to particulars.

The new way of meaning *power* is also universally operative and attends to particulars, but it is very different in its nature than power in the mode of domination and control. It is a power that "influences" but does not "control." The world may or may not be brought into conformity with the divine purposes. All-inclusive and unsurpassable influence—which is uniquely "powerful" influence—is exercised in the direction of the divine purposes. But the response of the world is a function not only of divine influence but also of other influences and of the freedom of self-creativity that belongs to each actuality. The "effectuality" of the divine willing is thus made dependent upon creaturely response. It cannot be said that God is "world-determining," since the freedom/power of all actualities is assumed. There is no divine monopoly on power in this new understanding, since God is one power among other powers. Nor is the power unidirectional; it flows both ways. God influences and is influenced. It cannot be said that God is completely self-determining, because God is influenced by the world. Passive power as well as active power is admitted in this new definition. The purely one-way causal action attributed to God by the tradition, which allowed for no reaction to or interaction with other actualities, is denied.

Many of the values that have made affirmation of "control" seem important in the tradition can be met in other ways by an affirmation of "influence." One such value, protection against chaos, will be explored here by way of example. Religious faith attributes to God at least the kind and degree of power necessary for the ordering of the world—a necessary condition of the possibility of there being any world at all. In my view, this requirement can be met by a concept of God as a *supremely powerful ordering influence* and does not necessitate divine control of all particulars.

Hartshorne incorporates this ordering influence into the set of powers that God possesses uniquely.[16] A "uniquely excel-

---

[16]In discussing these powers, Hartshorne himself slips back into the language of "control." But I do not think this is a necessary step in order to convey his meaning. It seems ill-advised in the light of the baggage that this term carries. It also appears inconsistent in the light of Hartshorne's complete repudiation of divine control else-

lent" and "qualitatively superior" divine influence would be sufficiently pervasive and sufficiently "powerful" to order the world by natural laws,[17] ensuring against chaos and guaranteeing optimal conditions for the attainment of value. World-determining control of all things in their particularity is *more than is needed to ensure against chaos.* The "control" that was emphasized in the tradition has positive content in providing this ordering influence. Unfortunately, as we have seen, the term carries with it much more than this ordering influence, and when "control" with its fuller implications becomes the primary notion of power in general and of divine power in particular it lends itself to excesses.

Hartshorne's basic definition of power has been incorporated into this constructive proposal, as has his description of how power operates. This provides a coherent metaphysical grounding for a reconstructed doctrine of omnipotence. The theoretical framework being in place, what is needed now is some fleshing out through the use of appropriate images and a thematic elaboration of the character of the divine power.

Images and Insights from Feminist Thought

The step of fleshing out through the use of appropriate images will draw upon insights emerging from feminist thought. There has been a decided preference for masculine images for God and a tendency to delineate divine attributes in ways congruent with a "masculine" stereotype. Varied approaches to the reconstruction of the doctrine of God are being employed with a view to overcoming the "male bias" of traditional theology. Before this minor contribution to that major effort is launched, it may be helpful to review the approaches and defend the particular approach which this book adopts.

Feminists working on this problem seek to reconstruct the doctrine of God in one (or more) of four ways: (1) by ascribing stereotypically "feminine" qualities (nurturing, compassion) to God who is still understood primarily as a male being, (2) by uncovering a "feminine dimension" in the male God,[18] which is then emphasized, (3) by assigning the "feminine

---

where. It would be more consistent if he maintained the "language of influence" throughout.

[17]There is a significant difference between the exercise of power immanently through natural laws and the exercise of power extrinsically with such regularity that there is the mere *appearance* of natural law (Calvin's model).

[18]This is the approach that seeks a Jungian androgyny in which the male God now comes to express and integrate his "feminine" side (*anima*).

principle" to one person of the Trinity—usually the Holy Spirit—while the other two persons are presumed to be male, or (4) by using a female personal image—just as the tradition used male personal images—to portray God in God's fullness.

This constructive proposal will take the fourth approach because of what I perceive to be real inadequacies of the other three. The other three all make needed steps forward in their incorporation of stereotypically "feminine" attributes, whether through the addition of traits or a "feminine dimension" or a "feminine principle." These stereotypically "feminine" traits have been underemphasized in the traditional concept of God to the impoverishment of that concept. Balance is being sought, and to some extent achieved, by these approaches as they broaden and enrich the traditional concept of God. However, all three of these approaches seem at some level to buy into and work within the limits of gender stereotypes. In doing so, they presuppose and reinforce at the level of the divine being the artificial polarization of traits into categories of "masculine" and "feminine." This seems to play into and perpetuate a way of thinking that most feminists are seeking to overcome.

Another limitation of these three approaches is that they do not advance very far in the direction of offering a thoroughgoing reconstruction of the doctrine of God. The first approach simply "adds on" traits that are stereotypically "feminine." The stereotypically "masculine" traits are not reexamined or altered in any way. It is questionable whether a coherent concept of God can be constructed in this way. Divine "androgyny" seems to be the goal of the second approach. In seeking a "feminine dimension"—a kind of divine *anima* to complement the divine *animus*—this approach accepts and ratifies in the divine life the categorization of attributes as "masculine" or "feminine." It has the advantage, however, of insisting that divine being (like the human being) is complex enough to incorporate and integrate these "opposite" dimensions. The third approach does not seek even to integrate these attributes. It simply assigns "feminine" traits to one person of the Trinity. Furthermore, it seems to endorse the stereotypically "feminine" auxiliary[19] role in its assignment of the "feminine

---

[19]In traditional theology, the Holy Spirit often seems an edifying appendage, lacking the strength and vividness of the other persons of the Trinity. It is a vague, amorphous background figure, despite all the claims of unity and equality of persons. Furthermore, this approach leaves the male principle dominating (two-to-one). The Holy Spirit proceeds from the Father and the Son. In the same way, woman receives

principle" to the Holy Spirit.[20] The approaches of adding "feminine" traits, dimension, or principle—accepting the stereotype as they do—all augment the traditional doctrine of God, but they do so in ways that maintain and do not overcome the androcentric pattern that they seek to unseat. God remains "masculine" but now possesses in addition a "feminine" set of traits, dimension, or principle which makes God more attractive. This continues the stereotypical role of the "feminine" as supporting and enhancing the more important role of the "masculine."[21]

The fourth approach selects a female image to represent the fullness of the divine. The theological presupposition is that, while God is neither male nor female, both male and female are created in the image of God and are equally appropriate for imaging God in God's fullness. This is not to say that whatever female image is chosen will be a complete and adequate expression of the divine but to affirm that it is capable of at least as complete and adequate an expression of the divine as the masculine images in the tradition.[22]

Another important presupposition behind this choice is that theological constructs have social and political consequences. It seems to be the case that imaging God in strictly masculine images to the exclusion of feminine images has had the effect of reinforcing the secondary status of women. While the evidence is not unambiguous and notable exceptions can be found, it appears to be the case historically that where God

---

her identity and existential stamp from her husband and children. While the intention of this approach is to rehabilitate the feminine principle in the divine, the effect is subordination to a male principle. Johnson, p. 457.

[20]Ruether summarizes well the difficulties with these approaches. "We should guard against concepts of divine androgyny that simply ratify on the divine level the patriarchal split of the masculine and the feminine. In such a concept, the feminine side of God, as a secondary or mediating principle, would act in the same subordinate and limited roles in which females are allowed to act in the patriarchal social order. The feminine can be mediator or recipient of divine power in relation to creaturely reality. She can be God's daughter, the bride of the (male) soul. But she can never represent divine transcendence in all fullness. For feminists to appropriate the 'feminine' side of God within this patriarchal gender hierarchy is simply to reinforce the problem of gender stereotyping on the level of God–language." Ruether, *Sexism and God-Talk*, p. 61.

[21]Johnson, p. 455.

[22]It should be noted that the project advocated here is not a revival of the ancient religion of the Goddess. It is, rather, a bringing to expression of images already present in the Judeo-Christian tradition, but underemphasized there, and it is an invitation to act upon the theological insight that God is neither male nor female but we are created in God's image—male and female.

has been imaged with female personal images, women have experienced heightened social and political status.[23] This is another reason why I advocate the approach of imaging God in female personal images.

A distinct advantage of this approach over the other three approaches is that it can *refuse* the artificial polarization of human qualities into categories of "masculine" and "feminine." It does not work from the traditionally given base of a "masculine" deity, historically circumscribed by the "masculine" stereotype—beginning there almost *requires* an approach of "adding on" missing attributes. This approach begins fresh with what is largely—to our tradition, at least—a *new* image. It does not carry with it the limiting factor of a history of interpretation within the tradition which has assigned it a limited set of attributes. Admittedly, the popular mind may quickly jump to think of the image in stereotypically feminine terms, but this step need not be taken. Selecting a female image does not necessarily presuppose the content of the God concept in any particular direction.[24] All worthy features can be attributed to a female personal image. Furthermore, if gender stereotypes are *refused* in a given female representation—whereas they have been allowed to function as limiting principles in the traditional male representations—it is quite possible that the image may be allowed to offer a more complete and adequate expression of the fullness of divine power and care.

Another advantage of this step is that masculine images for God have become so commonplace that they have lost much of their disclosive power as metaphors. The tension between the "is" and the "is not" has been lost. And these images (i.e., God as "father") have become so literalized that they almost function as idols—the fact that these *are* only images (meta-

---

[23]Riane Eisler, *The Chalice and the Blade: Our History, Our Future* (San Francisco: Harper & Row, 1987). Eisler has concluded from her research that before the advent of male monotheism, in cultures where the Goddess was worshiped, the status of women was indeed heightened. More than this, there was an entirely different pattern of social organization. What existed was not "matriarchy"—the mirror image of patriarchy. Rather, there was what Eisler refers to as the "partnership" model which is to be contrasted with the "dominator" model of patriarchy (or matriarchy) that assumes there must always be a dominant-subordinate pattern to all social relations.

[24]"To image God in female personal terms is not to identify God with any particular set of characteristics, unless one is slipping in feminine stereotypes under the cover of simple gender appellation. . . . We are not attributing passive and nurturing qualities to God any more than we are attributing active and powerful qualities." McFague, *Models of God*, p. 99.

phors) has been forgotten. It seems unlikely that female personal images for God will quickly become commonplace or readily be literalized in the near future. This being the case, it may be that, for the time being, these images have greater possibility for disclosive power and less risk of idolatry.[25]

The constructive proposal offered in this chapter will be fleshed out by an imaginative exploration of a particular image made available when God is thought of in female personal terms. Framing and guiding this exploration is an assumption that the problem with the symbol of God goes deeper than the problem of genderized language or attributes. It will not be sufficient to work with the same old concept of God and simply change gender references to feminine or neuter. Nor will it be sufficient to add on stereotypically feminine qualities. The end in view is not just a more inclusive set of attributes to be ascribed to God. More is needed than an "adding up" of stereotypically "masculine" and stereotypically "feminine" qualities into a kind of collection of attributes. A sifting, rejecting, and reintegrating process is needed as the entire doctrine of God is reassessed. That is a project well beyond the scope of this book. Nevertheless the approach being advocated here is, I think, helpful in reassessing the meaning of divine power.

A Female Personal Image for God

In this imaginative exploration the female personal image for God will be the image of God as mother. One particular aspect of this image, namely, the nature of the relationship between the mother and the child in her womb, will receive special attention. This rich image proves extremely illuminating as a metaphor for the relation of God and the world and for the way in which God exercises power in the world. The traditional image of God as king presents the relation of God to the world as being like that of a king to his kingdom. The nature of the exercise of divine power implied in this image is "ruling." In contrast to this image and its implications, I offer the image of God as mother and the relation of God to the world as being like that of a mother to the child in her womb. The nature of the exercise of divine power implied in this image is "life-giving" and "world-generating." The power

---

[25]These insights are presented and fully explored by Sallie McFague in her book *Metaphorical Theology*.

that we see at work in this image is much more the power of "influencing and being influenced" than the power of "domination and control." The implications of the image will briefly be explored here.

Several disclaimers are in order before that exploration to make clear what is *not* being claimed for this image. The image of God as mother is not being assumed to be the only available or appropriate female personal image. Nor is it being claimed as the central female personal image—as if the reproductive capacity of woman is her most important capacity. This image is one among many. This particular choice of God as mother carrying the world as a child in her womb is selected because of its richness and its suggestiveness for the specific issue at hand.

It is important to note that God is being identified in this image with the *person* of the mother and not with her womb. It is being assumed that God is more than the vessel or container for the world. The image goes beyond God as "the great womb" which was the root image of the divine in the ancient Mediterranean world and in India. God is more than the Primal Matrix. A pregnant woman is more than her womb and its contents—she has life and activity of her own beyond her life-giving activity. So also, God is more than a vessel for the world and more than the world. God has life and activity beyond the divine life-giving, world-generating activity. It is not assumed that a woman's reason for being is her reproductive activity, nor is it assumed that God exists for the sole purpose of enlivening and generating the world. In other words, a *panentheism* (the world in God) is being proposed with this image rather than a *pantheism* (which completely identifies the world and God).[26] This image maintains the transcendence of God.

I acknowledge that this image is not a new one. In fact, it is an image more ancient than the image of God as king, which it is designed, in this proposal, to challenge. The reproductive powers of women were recognized and celebrated from antiquity; they were readily identified with divine power. The present constructive proposal seeks to reclaim this ancient im-

---

[26]Notions of God as the world's "soul" (Plato) and the world as God's "body" (Grace Jantzen, *God's World, God's Body;* Philadelphia: Westminster Press, 1984) are also being intentionally excluded by this choice of image. Each of these in its own way communicates the connectedness that is being sought in my own choice of images, but both lend themselves to too close an identity between God and the world. God's transcendence and otherness are compromised.

age by drawing out its potential as a metaphor that can illumine the dynamics of the God-world relation and the nature
of divine power exercised in that relation.

At the outset, however, it should be admitted that there are
problems with this image. It lends itself to a certain romanti-
cism and sentimentality. When used as fixed image for the
relation between human beings and God, it might be criticized further as promoting a human stance of unhealthy dependency that is characterized as infantile clinging to
consolation, comfort, and protection which the womb provides. A healthy child in the womb comes to birth, grows, and
matures to adulthood achieving a status similar to that of the
mother. This is the proper trajectory for persons—not perpetual dependency. This cluster of problems can be offset
somewhat if the image is used in the more restricted sense
intended here—as a model for the God-*world* relation and not
for the relationship of individuals to God. The state of the
world in relation to God is not one of gradually maturing and
eventually rivaling God; the state of the world is properly
imaged as one of continuing dependency.

The limitations that apply to the metaphor of God as father
may also apply to the metaphor of God as mother. One such
limitation is the experiential context in which people hear and
interpret these metaphors. If one's relationship to one's father
or mother is ambivalent, or even negative, then the image
may not serve well as an image for God. The associated com-
monplaces that attend the metaphor in a given context may
adversely affect its interpretation. If negative experiential
images of a stern disciplinarian father have translated into
theological concepts of God as "wrathful judge," then negative experiential images of a "nagging mother" probably will
fare no better.[27] As with any images we might choose to use
for God, this image, when pushed to its limits, will show its
inadequacies.

Another obvious inadequacy is the semiautomatic way in

---

[27]There is also the problem of "matriphobia," which for many people will make
the image unattractive. "Dorothy Dinnerstein provides an intriguing explanation of
why both males and females find it comfortable to defer to the power of men in
religion and society. According to Dinnerstein, all mother-reared children develop a
deep ambivalence toward the power of women because of their early intimate dependence upon women (for meeting all basic needs). As they begin to assert their independence of the mother, mother-reared children wish to forget their dependence on
her, and thus they willingly transfer their allegiance to the father, whose power,
because it is more distant and less connected to intimate bodily dependence, seems
more manageable." Christ, p. 142.

which the mother's body provides for the child in her womb. While she can enhance or inhibit the process, the process itself is a natural and spontaneous giving and generating which elicits her conscious attention but does not really require it. That divine activity in relation to the world is conscious and purposive may not be fully conveyed in this image.

The most important problem with this model, from a feminist perspective, is its limited focus upon the reproductive powers of women. Motherhood in no way exhausts female experience, nor does it provide in itself all the symbolism needed for a fully adequate female representation of the divine. A plurality of images (male and female) will be needed when the larger task of reconstructing the concept of God is undertaken. The metaphor used here is selected in full awareness of these limitations. It is chosen for its particular usefulness and suggestiveness, not as an image in any way exhaustive of the range of possibilities. It does have the advantage—over some other images that could have been chosen—of displaying the only distinctly female power that remains after the stereotypes have been seen through and set aside. It is an irreducible biological remainder just as the distinctly male power of "begetting" is an irreducible biological remainder.

With a clear view of the limitations of this image and what is *not* being claimed for it, it is now possible to move on to consider its positive content—what the image does have to offer. Its contributions will first be evaluated in terms of its ability to flesh out the proposed new meaning for power.

Power as "the capacity to influence and to be influenced" has been proposed to displace the meaning for power as "domination and control." This image can be shown to convey the new meaning very well. A mother does not control the child in the womb—as any mother can testify. Mutual influence characterizes the relation. As in the process scheme, the "self-creativity" of each becomes "other-creativity" by virtue of their intimate relation. The two are, in a sense, interdependent and the well-being of the one depends upon the well-being of the other. Nevertheless the relation is an asymmetrical relation. In this relation, the mother's power is "uniquely excellent" and "qualitatively superior." The mother has much greater influence upon the child than the child has upon the mother. There is a greater degree of dependency on the part of the child and a greater degree of independence on the part of the mother. The influence of the mother upon the child is "all-inclusive" and "unsurpassable," while the child in the womb is only one aspect of the life of the mother.

The "ordering influence" which Hartshorne proposed as a uniquely divine power—and which is a necessary prerequisite for there being a world at all—may be compared to the way in which the mother provides an environment that in one sense contains and limits the possibilities but in another sense provides all that is necessary for growth, setting "maximal conditions for the attainment of value."

In these ways and many others the image is a good metaphor for communicating the proposed new meaning for power and for exemplifying the mode of operation of that kind of power. The image can also prove useful in terms of its corrective potential in relation to particular problems that the traditional doctrine of omnipotence carried with it.

The connectedness, relationality, interdependence, and organic unity communicated by this image prove decisive for directly addressing the problems of separation, self-other duality, and independence which, in the feminist critique and elsewhere, have been argued to be major shortcomings of the traditional meaning for power.

Ultimate reality, to which we are all intimately connected, is the source of all life and the source of all that sustains and enhances life.[28] In the divine womb we are organically united with one another. Following the imagery of the womb, the interconnection is symbolized by the umbilical cord.[29]

Connection rather than control is the relevant feature. God's power is here manifest in "internal relations" rather than "external manipulation."[30] If we, in turn, are internally related with one another by virtue of our organic unity in the womb, then there cannot be a self-other duality that permits

---

[28]Kaufman seems to support this way of thinking about God. "God should today be conceived in terms of the complex of physical, biological, and historico-cultural conditions which have made human existence possible, which continue to sustain it, and which may draw it out to a fuller humanity and humaneness. Devotion to a God conceived in terms other than these will not be devotion to *God*, that is, to that reality which has (to our best understanding) in fact created us, and a living connection with which is in fact needed if our lives are to be sustained and nourished. It will be, in short, devotion to an idol, a pretender to divinity, and as such will be debilitating and destructive, and may in the end be disastrous." Kaufman, p. 42.

[29]Judy Grahn speaks of our interconnection in this way: All beings come tied to the matrix of interconnection by "the one true cord/the umbilical line/unwinding into meaning/transformation/the web of thought and caring and connection." Keller, p. 248.

[30]Keller has argued that "control is the age-old alternative to connection" (p. 200).

an objectification of and distancing from the other and invites the development of strategies of domination and control. Habits of division and domination will have no benefit and will be decidedly out of place if we are radically connected as this image suggests. An ethic of solidarity is the logical implication of the image; it is grounded in our reality.

Relationality is presupposed in this image, and it is a relation of greater intimacy than that communicated by most traditional images. Even the personal familial image of "father" seems distant by comparison. There is transcendence here— God is more than the world—but it is transcendence that is not distant or over and above but rather embracing and surrounding in an immanent fashion.[31]

The assumption is that relationality as such does not diminish but enhances existence (divine and human). This is illustrated in the process scheme as self-creativity actually becomes other-creativity as each actual entity contributes to the "becoming" of all others. Openness to the other in relationship is preeminently displayed in God's relation with the world. God's consequent nature is perfectly receptive to the world in all its consequent states, and God's primordial (antecedent) nature is "open" as the source and provider of novel possibilities for the world's future.[32]

While there is a clear implication of dependence of the world upon the divine, it is not to be assumed that the divine is independent, in the traditional sense of separate from and unaffected by the world. Genuine *interdependence* can be communicated through this image. There is a mutuality of influence—though an asymmetrical one—between the mother and the child in the womb. In a very real sense God's well-being depends upon the well-being of the world. Process thought assumes that God's "perfect" knowledge is conformal, corresponding perfectly to whatever is. God "feels our feelings." When we suffer, God does not stand in independent

---

[31]Hartshorne finds fault with the traditional parent-child analogy for the divine-human relation because it implies too great a separation. It fails to communicate that God "is 'nearer to us than breathing and closer than hand or foot.' . . . It is the mother, not the father, who furnishes by far the best symbol of deity. The fetus-mother relationship is decidedly more intimate than the fetus-father relationship." Furthermore, the "radical inferiority of human beings in comparison with deity is only weakly or misleadingly modeled by that of a child in comparison with its parent." As the child matures, it comes to rival and surpass the parent in some values and powers. OOTM, pp. 54, 60.

[32]Marjorie Hewitt Suchocki, "Openness and Mutuality in Process Thought and Feminist Action," in Davaney, p. 64.

isolation from our pain but in fact is among us as a "fellow sufferer who understands." Like relationality, interdependence is seen as enhancing the divine life. Without this kind of interdependence, how would genuine relationship—which entails a certain reciprocity of influence—be possible? If relationality is a value for the tradition, it would seem that interdependence must also necessarily be admitted.

From this working out of the metaphor, it is shown to be a rich resource for a fresh interpretation of the nature of the God-world relation and of how divine power is exercised in that relation. Connectedness, relationality, and interdependence are carried as implications of the image and effectively counter the separation, self-other duality, and independence carried as implications of the traditional image.

It may be argued that precisely because of its focus upon connectedness, relationality, and interdependence as opposed to separation, self-other duality, and independence, this new way of understanding divine power has let go of the transcendent dimensions of divine power. I would counter that the transcendent dimension is retained but not in the ordinary way.

In what sense is transcendence transcendent? It may be that the particular spatial metaphors often used to talk about transcendence—"over" and "above" as opposed to "under" and "below"—place limitations upon our ways of thinking about transcendence. These spatial designations may even lend themselves to reinforcing power as domination and control. "Power over" and "power above" carry this connotation. Other spatial metaphors are available. Is power *over* necessarily more transcendent than power *within?* Images of embracing, grounding, and surrounding express power in ways compatible with the proposed image for divine power without allowing the world to be completely identified with God so that God's transcendence is utterly absorbed into immanence.

In response to the criticism that feminist theology has no place for a transcendent God, Carter Heyward argues that by "transcendent" these critics mean "a God at the top who is in control." This is a power congruent with hierarchical dualism but not with mutual relation. This transcendence is a projection of the patriarchal value system. The meaning of the term "transcend" is to "cross over" and therefore "to bridge, to make connections, to burst free of particular locations." Transcendent power is "a wonderful mysterious power truly crossing over into . . . the lives of all created beings. . . . This power is indeed God, transcendent precisely in the fullness of her immanence among us."[33] This perspective on transcendence allows for divine power to be seen as operating intrinsically, not from the outside to dominate and control, but from *within*, in synergy, to enliven and energize. It does not overpower but *empowers*. God's power acting quietly from within may be likened to the power of the leaven or the mustard seed, or the womb of the Virgin.[34]

The Character of Divine Power

The image of God as mother with the world as a child in her womb carries important implications for the character of divine power and consequently the nature of reality. To say that divine power is life-giving is to affirm that a biophilic and altruistic orientation lies at the very heart of reality. Affirming divine power as "world-generation" implies that God is involved in creating, ordering, and sustaining the world.

The power conveyed by this image is properly characterized as "power in relation." It is *empowering* in its character, as the mother empowers the child for living. It works with other powers (in *synergy*); it does not replace them or overpower them. The mother's body must work with the dependent/independent unfolding of the life within her. "Solidarity," which feminists have been urging as an ethical imperative, is an appropriate outworking of this image and its elaboration.

As the image is mined for its conceptual implications, it becomes increasingly evident that the character of the power being modeled here is generalizable beyond the literal interpretation of the image. It is a way of exercising power that is clearly available and appropriate for both male and female.

How the New Model Addresses the Problems of Coherency and Religious Viability

Coherency

The process-feminist proposal for a new understanding of divine power makes possible a more consistent articulation of certain central affirmations of the tradition. The affirmation of genuine relationship between God and creatures and the

---

[33]Heyward, *The Redemption of God*, p. 7.
[34]Heyward, *The Redemption of God*, p. 7.

affirmation of creaturely freedom and responsibility is in serious tension with the traditional understanding of divine power. The unsuccessful struggle for coherency can be seen vividly in the tradition's equivocation on the central terms "power" and "freedom."

In the tradition, the term "power" when applied to God means intrinsic, all-determining, agential, causal power. But when the same term is applied to creatures, it means derivative, nondeterminative, nonagential power which is only causal in an instrumental sense. In the feminist-process synthesis, on the other hand, the same meaning for "power," "the capacity to influence and to be influenced," is applied to *both* divine and creaturely realities.

A similar equivocation can be seen in the way the term "freedom" is used in the tradition. In Barth's usage, for example, "freedom" applied to God entails self-determination, but applied to human beings, it consists in "obedience to God" and does not imply self-determination. The feminist-process understanding of freedom, by contrast, entails self-creativity and other-creativity for *both* God and creatures.

Where the classical model seems to require equivocation on such key terms as power and freedom, the process-feminist synthesis does not. The genuine relation between God and creatures and the genuine creaturely freedom and responsibility, which were important to both Calvin and Barth, can be more coherently expressed in connection with the new meaning for power offered in this constructive proposal.

Religious Viability

The prevailing model for understanding divine power aggravates the theodicy problem and has negative ramifications in the realm of human affairs. The greater religious viability of the new meaning for power can be demonstrated in relation to both of these problems.

The new meaning for power being proposed attributes genuine freedom to creatures and gives a credible account of what is meant by freedom. Creatures are neither absolutely free nor absolutely determined. There is a freedom within limits. The past is "given" for creatures, but they are free with regard to their self-creativity in relation to it. Because this is the case, a credible "free-will defense" can be mounted in response to the theodicy problem.

Furthermore, a "metaphysical limitation" is admitted in this new model which is denied by the classical model. That is, given the existence of other actualities and the fact that actuality entails power, a limitation is placed upon what "omnipotence" can mean. It cannot mean "possessing all the power there is," as the tradition at times seems to imply. It means, rather, the "ideal maximum of power given a division of powers." The power of creatures provides a metaphysical limitation—not so much upon the scope of divine power as upon the meaning for power that can be admitted. This metaphysical limitation is far more helpful in resolving the theodicy problem than the "voluntary self-limitation" of God's power introduced by Barth. Because this limitation is a matter of the will, it can presumably be removed at will, and God is indictable for *not* removing it in order to prevent evil.

The process-feminist synthesis offers a credible account of creaturely freedom and creaturely power and presents a metaphysical limitation on the meaning of omnipotence. For these reasons, it can offer a credible theodicy based upon a free will defense.

The questions surrounding the moral adequacy of the traditional definition of omnipotence are also effectively answered. When power in the mode of domination and control is ascribed to God, that kind of power is elevated and "divinized." The result is that power in this mode is legitimatized and promoted in the realm of human affairs. Some of the negative ramifications observed by the feminist critique were oppression, exploitation, and violence. The effect of attributing to God power "to influence and to be influenced" is clearly very different. This kind of power can be safely elevated and legitimatized and can be reenacted in the realm of human affairs without the damaging social consequences feminists have connected with the traditional notion of divine power. "Divinizing" power that has the character of "life-giving" and "world-generation" promotes a way of living that values and enhances life, that is "generating" and "creative" with respect to the world rather than draining and destructive. It promotes an ethic of solidarity, the notion of "power in relation," and the exercising of power in cooperation with other powers (synergy) with a view to empowering rather than overpowering.

Some Other Points of Continuity with the Tradition

There is very little in this new definition of power that will not assist the most basic insights into divine power to be found in Calvin and Barth. Both affirmed the "universal, personal, and particular caring" nature of the divine power. This can be comfortably—and more consistently—affirmed in the process-synthesis model. Calvin's concern that God have sufficient power "to create" and "to save" can also be addressed by this model. It is simply not assumed that these require power in the mode of domination and control. Pervasive and "powerful" influence of the "uniquely excellent" and "qualitatively superior" kind is what is necessary. Furthermore, the process-feminist proposal successfully addresses Calvin's concern that the world not be left to chance on the one hand or to necessity on the other. A "divine ordering influence" ensures against chaos and also mere chance. There is sufficient freedom at both divine and human levels to assure that the world is not left in the hands of blind fate.

Barth's most fundamental concerns are not foreign to the new understanding of power either. It is assumed here that divine power is "conscious and purposive," just as Barth assumed it is. God is granted something like self-determination and world-determination, though in a significantly modified form. The difference is that the process-feminist model draws on "creativity" rather than "determination," and God's self-creativity *is* God's world-creativity. God's consequent states influence the world. Creatures too have self-creativity and other-creativity, which Barth's scheme did not permit them. Had Barth worked with this alternative meaning for power, he might have more convincingly articulated how God is "the one who *loves* in freedom." Without genuine relation, which his meaning for power makes difficult to conceive, the term "love" is without relevant content. The process contributions make relation conceivable, and the feminist contributions flesh out the character of divine power in such a way that the term "love" has meaning.

Barth's preoccupation with God's active, all-determining power kept him from seeing passivity, vulnerability, weakness, or divine suffering love even in the cross event. Had he not been misled by his preconceived notion of what power means, he might indeed have developed a doctrine of divine omnipotence—according to his own intention—based upon what is revealed in Jesus Christ. Such a doctrine of omnipotence would have entailed a new *meaning* for divine power, not just a modification of the *scope* of that power.

Conclusion

I have argued that a reconstructed doctrine of omnipotence based upon a new meaning for power is both possible and desirable. The alternative model presented here rests upon the metaphysical foundations of process thought, which are taken to be more tenable for our time than those of classical metaphysics. In this constructive proposal, omnipotence means "the power to influence all and to be influenced by all." The insights and images appropriated from feminist thought ascribe to this power a character that is "life-giving" and "world-generating." Its operation is synergistic (cooperating with other powers) and empowering rather than overpowering. The implied ethic which accompanies this model is one of solidarity rather than obedience.

The questions by which I would most want this new proposal to be judged—and which I think are the most urgent ones by which all our theological endeavors are to be assessed—are: Does it bring honor to God? Does it promote the well-being of God's creatures?

God is unfathomable mystery. The vastness of God's glory and holiness and power is too great for the human mind to grasp. This realization undergirds and relativizes all our speaking about God. Our religious language never possesses its subject but leads ever more profoundly into an attitude of awe and adoration.[35] The very incomprehensibility of God invites a proliferation of images, metaphors, and symbols, with each one acting as a corrective to the others and offsetting the tendency toward literalization, reification, and idolatry. Realizing that all our concepts of God are human creations, we seek constructions that are coherent and religiously viable (bringing honor to God and promoting the welfare of creatures).

This reconstruction of the doctrine of omnipotence is an imaginative adventure aimed at achieving an understanding of divine power that is both more coherent and more religiously viable. The ideas being entertained here are not unprecedented; the primary themes are fundamental to the Judeo-Christian tradition—when the "ideological mystifications"[36] are stripped off. In fact, the new understanding proposed here makes possible a more consistent articulation of some central affirmations of the tradition. And it has the advantage of avoiding the usual difficulties created by ascribing to God power in the mode of domination and control. While I believe the reconstruction is persuasive, I do not cherish any hope of having

[35]Johnson, p. 441.
[36]Ruether, *Sexism and God-Talk*, p. 31.

conclusively settled the issues surrounding divine power. It has been said that it is easier to affirm the power of God than to develop a satisfactory understanding of it. This is "the endeavor of many and the achievement of none."

Bibliography

Power

Benn, Stanley I. "Power." In *The Encyclopedia of Philosophy*, edited by Paul Edwards, vol. 6. New York: Macmillan Co., 1967.

Böckle, Franz, and Jacques-Marie Pohier, eds. *Power and the Word of God*. New York: Herder & Herder, 1973.

Burkle, Howard R. "God's Relation to the World: The Issues Between St. Thomas Aquinas and Charles Hartshorne." Ph.D. thesis, Yale University, 1954.

————. *God, Suffering. and Belief.* Nashville: Abingdon Press, 1977.

Clarke, W. N. "Potency." In *New Catholic Encyclopedia*, vol. 11. New York: McGraw-Hill Book Co., 1967.

Clifford, Paul. "Omnipotence and the Problem of Evil." *Journal of Religion* 41 (April 1961): 118–128.

Dahl, Robert A. "The Concept of Power." In *Introductory Readings in Political Behavior*, edited by S. Sidney Ulmer. Chicago: Rand McNally & Co., 1961.

de Jouvenel, Bertrand. *On Power: Its Nature and the History of Its Growth.* Translated by J. F. Huntington. New York: Viking Press, 1949.

de Muralt, André. *Souveraineté et Pouvoir.* Lausanne: Revue de Théologie et de Philosophie, 1978.

Eising, H. "Chayil." In *Theological Dictionary of the Old Testament*, edited by G. Johannes Botterweck and Helmer Ringgren. Grand Rapids: Wm. B. Eerdmans Publishing Co., 1977.

Flew, Antony. "Compatibilism, Free Will and God." *Philosophy* 48 (1973): 231–244.

Foerster, Werner. *"Exousia."* In *Theological Dictionary of the New Testament*, edited by Gerhard Kittel, vol. 2, pp. 562–575. Grand Rapids: Wm. B. Eerdmans Publishing Co., 1964.

Gendin, Sidney. "Omnidoing." *Sophia* 6 (1967): 17–22.

Glare, P. G. W., ed. *Oxford Latin Dictionary.* London: Oxford University Press, 1976.

Grave, S. A. "On Evil and Omnipotence." *Mind* 65 (1956): 259–262.

Grundmann, Walter. *"Dynamai/dynamis."* In *Theological Dictionary of the New Testament,* edited by Gerhard Kittel, vol. 2, pp. 284–317. Grand Rapids: Wm. B. Eerdmans Publishing Co., 1964.

Guthrie, W. K. *A History of Greek Philosophy.* Cambridge: Cambridge University Press, 1969.

Haroutunian, Joseph. *Lust for Power.* New York: Charles Scribner's Sons, 1949.

Hemmerle, Klaus. "Power." In *Sacramentum Mundi: An Encyclopedia of Theology,* vol. 5. New York: Herder & Herder, 1970.

Keene, G. B. "A Simpler Solution to the Paradox of Omnipotence." *Mind* 69 (1960): 249–275.

Lasswell, H. D.; C. E. Merriam; and T. V. Smith. *A Study of Power.* Glencoe, Ill: Free Press, 1950.

Loomer, Bernard. "Two Kinds of Power." *Criterion* 15 (Winter 1976): 13–29.

Lukes, Steven. *Power: A Radical View.* London: Macmillan & Co., 1974.

Mackie, J. L. "Theism and Utopia." *Philosophy* 37 (1962): 153–158.

Migliore, Daniel L. *The Power of God.* Philadelphia: Westminster Press, 1983.

Murray, J. A. H., et al., eds. *Oxford English Dictionary.* 13 vols. in 2 vols. Oxford University Press, 1971.

Nietzsche, Friedrich W. *The Will to Power.* Translated by Walter Kaufmann and R. J. Hollingdale. New York: Random House, 1967.

Otto, Rudolf. *The Idea of the Holy.* Translated by John W. Harvey. 2d ed. London: Oxford University Press, 1950.

Peters, Francis E. *Greek Philosophical Terms: A Historical Lexicon.* New York: New York University Press, 1967.

Pike, Nelson. "Of God and Freedom: A Rejoiner." *Philosophical Review* 75 (1966): 367–379.

Plantinga, Alvin. "The Free Will Defense." In *Philosophy in America,* edited by Max Black. Ithaca, N.Y.: Cornell University Press, 1965.

Ramsey, I. T. "The Paradox of Omnipotence." *Mind* 65 (1956): 263–266.

Ross, Floyd Hiatt. *Personalism and the Problem of Evil.* New Haven: Yale University Press, 1940.

Roxburgh, G. "Omnipotence." In *New Catholic Encyclopedia,* vol. 10. New York: McGraw-Hill Book Co., 1967.

Rubinoff, Lionel. *The Pornography of Power.* Chicago: Quadrangle Books, 1968.

Russell, Bertrand. *Power: A New Social Analysis.* New York: W. W. Norton & Co., 1938.

Sampson, Ronald Victor. *The Psychology of Power.* New York: Pantheon Books, 1966.

Schleiermacher, Friedrich. *The Christian Faith.* New York: Harper & Row, 1963.

Sennett, Richard. *Authority.* New York: Vintage Books, 1980.

Simon, H. A. "Notes on the Observation and Measurement of Political Power." In *Models of Man: Explorations in the Western Educational Tradition,* by Paul Nash. New York: John Wiley & Sons, 1968.

Stallmach, J. *Dynamis und Energia.* Monographien zur philosophischen Forschung, 21. Meisenheim, 1959.

Taylor, J. C. "Potency and Act." In *New Catholic Encyclopedia,* vol. 11. New York: McGraw-Hill Book Co., 1967.

Tracy, Thomas F. *God, Action, and Embodiment.* Grand Rapids: Wm. B. Eerdmans Publishing Co., 1984.

Wainwright, William J. "Freedom and Omnipotence." *Nous* 3 (1968): 293–301.

Young, Robert. "Omnipotence and Compatibilism." *Philosophia* 6/1 (1976): 49–67.

Calvin

Augustine. *De Diversis Quaestionibus,* Book I. In *Augustine: Earlier Writings,* edited by John H. S. Burleigh. Library of Christian Classics, vol. 6. Philadelphia: Westminster Press, 1953.

Bratt, John H., ed. *The Heritage of John Calvin.* Heritage Hall Lectures, 1960–1970. Grand Rapids: Wm. B. Eerdmans Publishing Co., 1976.

Calvin, John. *Calvin: Commentaries.* Edited by Joseph Haroutunian. Library of Christian Classics, vol. 23. Philadelphia: Westminster Press, 1958.

―――. *Calvin: Institutes of the Christian Religion* (1559). Edited by John T. McNeill and translated by Ford Lewis Battles. Library of Christian Classics, vols. 20 and 21. Philadelphia: Westminster Press, 1960.

―――. *Calvin: Theological Treatises.* Translated, with introductory notes by J. K. S. Reid. Library of Christian Classics, vol. 22. Philadelphia: Westminster Press, 1954.

―――. *Calvini Opera,* 59 vols. in *Corpus Reformatorum.* Edited by W. Baum, E. Cunitz, and E. Reuss. Braunschweig: C. A. Schwetschke, 1863–1900.

―――. *Calvini Opera Selecta.* Edited by P. Barth and W. Niesel. 5 vols. Munich: Kaiser, 1926–1952.

———. *Calvin's Commentary on Seneca's De Clementia.* Translated by Ford Lewis Battles and Andre Malan Hugo. Leiden: E. J. Brill, 1969.

———. "Calvin's Treatise 'Against the Libertines.' " Introduction by Allen Verhey and translated by Robert Wilkie and Allen Verhey. *Calvin Theological Journal* 15/2 (November 1980): 190–219.

———. *Concerning the Eternal Predestination of God.* Translated by J. K. S. Reid. London: J. Clarke, 1961.

———. *Institutes of the Christian Religion, 1536 Edition.* Translated and annotated by Ford Lewis Battles. Atlanta: John Knox Press, 1975; Grand Rapids: Wm. B. Eerdmans Publishing Co., 1986.

———. *Sermons from Job.* Grand Rapids: Wm. B. Eerdmans Publishing Co., 1952.

———. *Tracts and Treatises.* Translated by Henry Beveridge. Grand Rapids: Wm. B. Eerdmans Publishing Co., 1958.

———. *Treatises Against the Anabaptists and Against the Libertines.* Translated and edited by Benjamin Wirt Farley. Grand Rapids: Baker Book House, 1982.

Dakin, Arthur. *Calvinism.* Port Washington, N.Y.: Kennikat Press, 1972.

Danielson, Dennis Richard. "Reformation Theology and the Battle of Theodicy," in his *Milton's Good God: A Study in Literary Theodicy,* pp. 66–75. Cambridge: Cambridge University Press, 1982.

DeKlerk, Peter. "Calvin Bibliography." *Calvin Theological Journal* 18/2 (December 1983): 206–224.

Dowey, Edward A. *The Knowledge of God in Calvin's Theology.* New York: Columbia University Press, 1952.

Farley, Edward. *Ecclesial Reflection: An Anatomy of Theological Method.* Philadelphia: Fortress Press, 1982.

Forstman, H. Jackson. *Word and Spirit: Calvin's Doctrine of Biblical Authority.* Stanford, Calif.: Stanford University Press, 1962.

Gerrish, Brian Albert. *The Old Protestantism and the New: Essays on the Reformation Heritage.* Chicago: University of Chicago Press, 1982.

Gilson, Etienne. *The Spirit of Medieval Philosophy.* Translated by A. H. C. Downes. New York: Charles Scribner's Sons, 1936.

Gustafson, James M. *Ethics from a Theocentric Perspective.* Chicago: University of Chicago Press, 1981.

Harkness, Georgia. *John Calvin: The Man and His Ethics.* New York: Henry Holt & Co., 1931.

Heppe, H. L. J. *Reformed Dogmatics: Set Out and Illustrated from the Sources.* Translated by G. T. Thomson. London: George Allen & Unwin, 1950.

Hunter, A. Mitchell. *The Teaching of Calvin: A Modern Interpretation.* 2d ed., rev. Westwood, N.J.: Fleming H. Revell Co., 1950.

Klooster, Fred H. "The Uniqueness of Reformed Theology." *Calvin Theological Journal* 14/1 (April 1979): 32–54.

Knudsen, R. D. "Calvinism as a Cultural Force." In *John Calvin: His Influence in the Western World,* edited by W. S. Reid. Grand Rapids: Zondervan Publishing House, 1982.

LeCerf, A. "La souveraineté de Dieu d'après le Calvinisme." In *Études Calvinistes.* Neuchâtel, Switzerland: Delachaux & Niestlé, 1949.

Leith, John H. *Introduction to the Reformed Tradition: A Way of Being the Christian Community.* Atlanta: John Knox Press, 1977.

Loeschen, John R. *The Divine Community: Trinity, Church, and Ethics in Reformation Theologies.* Kirksville, Mo.: Sixteenth Century Journal Publishers, 1981.

McNeill, John T. *The History and Character of Calvinism.* New York: New York University Press, 1954.

Murray, John. *Calvin on Scripture and Divine Sovereignty.* Grand Rapids: Baker Book House, 1960.

Nichols, David. "Images of God and the State: Political Analogy and Religious Discourse." *Theological Studies* 42 (June 1981): 195–215.

Niesel, Wilhelm. *The Theology of Calvin.* Translated by Harold Knight. Philadelphia: Westminster Press, 1956.

Ntoane, L. R. Lekula. *A Cry for Life.* Kampen: Uitgeversmaatschappij J. H. Kok, 1983.

Oakley, Francis. "The 'Hidden' and 'Revealed' Wills of James I: More Political Theology." *Studia Gratiana* 15 (1972): 365–375.

———. "Jacobean Political Theory: The Absolute and Ordinary Powers of the King." *Journal of the History of Ideas* 29 (1968): 323–346.

———. *Omnipotence, Covenant, and Order: An Excursion in the History of Ideas from Abelard to Leibniz.* Ithaca, N.Y.: Cornell University Press, 1984.

Parker, T. H. L. *The Doctrine of the Knowledge of God: A Study in the Theology of John Calvin.* Edinburgh: Oliver & Boyd, 1952.

Partee, Charles. "Calvin and Determinism." *Christian Scholar's Review* 5/2 (1975): 123–128.

———, ed. *Calvin and Classical Philosophy.* Leiden: E. J. Brill, 1977.

Rashdall, Hastings. "Personality: Human and Divine." In *Personal Idealism: Philosophical Essays by Eight Members of the University of Oxford,* edited by Henry C. Sturt. London: Macmillan & Co., 1902.

Reardon, P. H. "Calvin on Providence: The Development of an Insight." *Scottish Journal of Theology* 28/6 (1975): 517–533.

Reid, W. S., ed. *John Calvin: His Influence in the Western World.* Grand Rapids: Zondervan Publishing House, 1982.

Rudavsky, Tamar, ed. *Divine Omniscience and Omnipotence in Medieval Philosophy.* Boston: D. Reidel Publishing Co., 1985.

Seeberg, Reinhold. *Textbook of the History of Doctrines.* Grand Rapids: Baker Book House, 1952.

Spykman, Gordon J. "Sphere Sovereignty in Calvin and the Calvinist Tradition." In *Exploring the Heritage of John Calvin,* edited by David E. Holwerda. Grand Rapids: Baker Book House, 1982.

Stauffer, Richard. *Dieu, la création et la providence dans la prédication de Calvin.* Bern: Peter Lang, 1978.

Taylor, Henry Osborn. *The Medieval Mind.* 4th ed. 1925. Reprint. London: Macmillan & Co., 1938.

Teall, John L. "Witchcraft and Calvinism in Elizabethan England: Divine Power and Human Agency." *Journal of the History of Ideas* 23 (1962): 21–36.

Venema, Cornelius P. "History, Human Freedom, and Idea of God in the Theology of Wolfhart Pannenberg." *Calvin Theological Journal* 17/1 (April 1982): 53–77.

Verhey, Allen, and Robert Wilkie, trans. See under Calvin: "Calvin's Treatise 'Against the Libertines.' "

Warfield, B. B. "Calvin's Doctrine of God." *Princeton Theological Review* (1909): 381–436.

Weber, Max. *The Protestant Ethic and the Spirit of Capitalism.* Translated by Talcott Parsons. London: George Allen & Unwin, 1930.

Wendel, François. *Calvin: The Origins and Development of His Religious Thought.* Translated by Philip Mairet. New York: Harper & Row, 1963.

Barth

Allen, Edgar Leonard. *The Sovereignty of God and the Word of God: A Guide to the Thought of Karl Barth.* London: Hodder & Stoughton, 1950.

Balthasar, Hans Urs von. *The Theology of Karl Barth.* Edited and translated by J. Drury. New York: Holt Rinehart & Winston, 1971.

Barth, Karl. *Church Dogmatics.* Edited by G. W. Bromiley and T. F. Torrance. Edinburgh: T. & T. Clark, 1936–1962.

———. *Dogmatics in Outline.* Translated by G. T. Thomson. New York: Harper & Brothers, 1959.

———. *The Faith of the Church: A Commentary on the Apostle's Creed According to Calvin's Catechism.* Edited by Jean-Louis Leuba; translated by Gabriel Vahanian. New York: Meridian Books, 1958.

———. *The Humanity of God.* Translated by John Newton Thomas. Richmond: John Knox Press, 1960.

———. *Prayer According to the Catechisms of the Reformation.* Philadelphia: Westminster Press, 1953.

Berkouwer, G. C. *The Triumph of Grace in the Theology of Karl Barth.* Translated by H. R. Boer. Grand Rapids: Wm. B. Eerdmans Publishing Co., 1956.

Bromiley, Geoffrey W. *Introduction to the Theology of Karl Barth.* Grand Rapids: Wm. B. Eerdmans Publishing Co., 1979.

Davaney, Sheila Greeve. *Divine Power: A Study of Karl Barth and Charles Hartshorne.* Philadelphia: Fortress Press, 1986.

Duthie, Charles. "Providence in the Theology of Karl Barth." In *Providence,* edited by Maurice Wiles. London: SPCK, 1969.

Griffin, David Ray. *God, Power, and Evil: A Process Theodicy.* Philadelphia: Westminster Press, 1976.

Gunton, Colin E. *Becoming and Being: The Doctrine of God in Charles Hartshorne and Karl Barth.* London: Oxford University Press, 1978.

Hartwell, Herbert. *Theology of Karl Barth.* London: Gerald Duckworth & Co., 1964.

Hick, John. *Evil and the God of Love.* New York: Harper & Row, 1966.

Jensen, Robert W. *God After God: The God of the Past and the God of the Future, Seen in the Works of Karl Barth.* Indianapolis: Bobbs-Merrill Co., 1969.

Jüngel, Eberhard. *The Doctrine of the Trinity: God's Being Is in Becoming.* Translated by Horton Harris. Grand Rapids: Wm. B. Eerdmans Publishing Co., 1977.

Kant, Immanuel. "On the Failure of All Philosophical Theodicies." In *Kant on History and Religion,* edited by M. Despland. London: Edward & Arnold, 1930.

Ruether, Rosemary Radford. "The Left Hand of God in the Theology of Karl Barth." *Journal of Religious Thought* 25 (1958–1959).

Hartshorne

Brown, Delwin; Ralph E. James, Jr.; and Gene Reeves, eds. *Process Philosophy and Christian Thought.* Indianapolis: Bobbs-Merrill Co., 1971.

Cobb, John B. *God and the World.* Philadelphia: Westminster Press, 1969.

Cobb, John B., and David Ray Griffin. *Process Theology: An Introductory Exposition.* Philadelphia: Westminster Press, 1976.

Davaney, Sheila Greeve. *Divine Power: A Study of Karl Barth and Charles Hartshorne.* Philadelphia: Fortress Press, 1986.

Farley, Edward. *The Transcendence of God: A Study in Contemporary Philosophical Theology.* Philadelphia: Westminster Press, 1960.

Ford, Lewis S. *The Lure of God.* Philadelphia: Fortress Press, 1978.

————. *Two Process Philosophers.* Tallahassee, Fla.: American Academy of Religion, 1973.

Gragg, Alan. *Charles Hartshorne.* Edited by Bob Patterson. Waco, Tex.: Word Books, 1973.

Griffin, David Ray. *God, Power, and Evil: A Process Theodicy.* Philadelphia: Westminster Press, 1976.

Gunton, Colin E. *Becoming and Being: The Doctrine of God in Charles Hartshorne and Karl Barth.* London: Oxford University Press, 1978.

Hartshorne, Charles. *Anselm's Discovery: A Re-examination of the Ontological Proof for God's Existence.* LaSalle, Ill.: Open Court Publishing Co., 1965.

————. *Aquinas to Whitehead: Seven Centuries of Metaphysics of Religion.* Milwaukee: Marquette University Publications, 1976.

————. *Creative Synthesis and Philosophic Method.* LaSalle, Ill.: Open Court Publishing Co., 1970.

————. "Divine Absoluteness and Divine Relativity." In *Transcendence,* edited by Herbert W. Richardson and Donald R. Cutler, pp. 164–171. Boston: Beacon Press, 1969.

————. *The Divine Relativity: A Social Conception of God.* New Haven, Conn.: Yale University Press, 1948.

————. "Divine Relativity and Absoluteness: A Reply." *Review of Metaphysics* 4 (1950): 31–61.

————. "The Formally Possible Doctrines of God." In *Process Philosophy and Christian Thought,* edited by Delwin Brown, Ralph E. James, Jr., and Gene Reeves, pp. 188–210. Indianapolis: Bobbs-Merrill Co., 1971.

————. "Freedom Requires Indeterminism and Universal Causality." *Journal of Philosophy,* September 1958, pp. 793–811.

————. "God as Absolute, Yet Related to All." *Review of Metaphysics* 1 (1947):24–51.

————. "God and Man Not Rivals." *Journal of Liberal Religion,* Autumn 1944, pp. 9–13.

————. "The Idea of God: Literal or Analogical?" *Christian Scholar,* June 1956, p. 135.

————. "Introduction: The Development of Process Philosophy." In *Talk of God,* edited by G. N. Veesey, pp. 152–167. New York: St. Martin's Press, 1969.

————. "Is Whitehead's God the God of Religion?" *Ethics,* April 1943, pp. 219–227.

————. *The Logic of Perfection.* LaSalle, Ill.: Open Court Publishing Co., 1962.

———. *Man's Vision of God, and the Logic of Theism.* Chicago: Willett, Clark & Co., 1941.

———. *A Natural Theology for Our Time.* LaSalle, Ill.: Open Court Publishing Co., 1967.

———. "A New Look at the Problem of Evil." In *Current Philosophical Essays: Essays in Honor of Curt John Ducasse,* edited by Frederick C. Dommeyer. Springfield, Ill.: Charles C Thomas, Publisher, 1966.

———. "Omnipotence." In *Encyclopedia of Religion,* edited by Vergilius Ferm, p. 545. New York: Philosophical Library, 1945.

———. *Omnipotence and Other Theological Mistakes.* Albany: State University of New York Press, 1984.

———. "Philosophical and Religious Uses of 'God.' " In *Process Theology: Basic Writings,* edited by Ewert H. Cousins. New York: Newman Press, 1971.

———. "Redefining God." *New Humanist,* July–August 1934, pp. 8–15.

———. "Religion in Process Philosophy." In *Religion in Philosophical and Cultural Perspective: A New Approach to the Philosophy of Religion Through Cross-Disciplinary Studies,* edited by J. Clayton Feaver and William Horosz, pp. 152–167. Princeton: D. Van Nostrand Co., 1967.

———. "Whitehead and Berdyaev: Is There Tragedy in God?" *Journal of Religion,* April 1957, pp. 71–83.

Hartshorne, Charles, and William L. Reese. *Philosophers Speak of God.* Chicago: University of Chicago Press, 1953.

James, Ralph. *The Concrete God: A New Beginning for Theology— The Thought of Charles Hartshorne.* Indianapolis: Bobbs-Merrill Co., 1967.

Madden, Edward H., and Peter H. Hare. "Evil and Persuasive Power." *Process Studies* 2 (1972): 44–48.

———. "Evil and Unlimited Power." *Review of Metaphysics* 20 (1966).

Peters, Eugene H. *Hartshorne and Neoclassical Metaphysics: The Creative Advance.* Lincoln, Neb.: University of Nebraska Press, 1970.

Pike, Nelson. "Process Theodicy and the Concept of Power." *Process Studies,* Fall 1982, pp. 150–167.

Reese, William, and Eugene Freeman. *Process and Divinity: The Hartshorne Festschrift.* LaSalle, Ill.: Open Court Publishing Co., 1964.

Richardson, Herbert W., and Donald R. Cutler, eds. *Transcendence.* Boston: Beacon Press, 1969.

Whitehead, Alfred North. *Adventures of Ideas.* New York: Macmillan Co., 1933.

———. *Process and Reality*. New York: Macmillan Co., 1929.

———. *Religion in the Making*. New York: Macmillan Co., 1926.

———. *Science and the Modern World*. New York: Macmillan Co., 1926.

Whitney, Barry L. *Evil and the Process God: The Problem of Evil in Charles Hartshorne's Thought*. New York and Toronto: Edwin Mellen Press, 1985.

———. "Process Theism: Does a Persuasive God Coerce?" *Southern Journal of Philosophy*, 1979, pp. 133–143.

Feminist Perspectives

Andolsen, Barbara Hilkert; Christine E. Gudorf; and Mary D. Pellauer. *Women's Consciousness, Women's Conscience: A Reader in Feminist Ethics*. Minneapolis: Winston Press, 1985.

Belenky, Mary Field; Blythe McVicker Clinchy; Nancy Rule Goldberger; and Jill Mattuck Tarule. *Women's Ways of Knowing: The Development of Self, Voice, and Mind*. New York: Basic Books, 1986.

Brock, Rita Nakashima. "Beyond Jesus the Christ: A Christology of Erotic Power." Unpublished paper presented at the American Academy of Religion, December 1987.

Burkhart, John E. *Worship*. Philadelphia: Westminster Press, 1982.

Carson, Anne. *Feminist Spirituality and the Feminine Divine: An Annotated Bibliography*. Trumansburg, N.Y.: Crossing Press, 1986.

Christ, Carol. *Laughter of Aphrodite: Reflections on a Journey to the Goddess*. San Francisco: Harper & Row, 1987.

Christ, Carol, and Judith Plaskow, eds. *Womanspirit Rising*. New York: Harper & Row, 1979.

Cornwall Collective. *Your Daughters Shall Prophesy: Feminist Alternatives in Theological Education*. New York: Pilgrim Press, 1980.

Daly, Mary. *Beyond God the Father: Toward a Philosophy of Women's Liberation*. Boston: Beacon Press, 1973.

———. *The Church and the Second Sex*. London: Geoffrey Chapman, 1968.

———. *Gyn/ecology: The Metaethics of Radical Feminism*. Boston: Beacon Press, 1978.

———. *Pure Lust: Elemental Feminist Philosophy*. Boston: Beacon Press, 1984.

Davaney, Sheila Greeve, ed. *Feminism and Process Thought*. New York: Edwin Mellen Press, 1981.

de Beauvoir, Simone. *The Second Sex*. New York: Vintage Books, 1974.

Englesman, Joan Chamberlain. *The Feminine Dimension of the Divine.* Philadelphia: Westminster Press, 1979.

Gilligan, Carol. *In a Different Voice: Psychological Theory and Women's Development.* Cambridge, Mass.: Harvard University Press, 1982.

Gilman, Charlotte Perkins. *His Religion and Hers.* New York: Century, 1923.

Goldenberg, Naomi R. *Changing of the Gods: Feminism and the End of Traditional Religions.* Boston: Beacon Press, 1979.

Heyward, Isabel Carter. *Our Passion for Justice: Images of Power, Sexuality, and Liberation.* New York: Pilgrim Press, 1984.

———. *The Redemption of God: A Theology of Mutual Relation.* Lanham, Md.: University Press of America, 1982.

Hooks, Bell. *Feminist Theory: From Margin to Center.* Boston: South End Press, 1984.

Johnson, Elizabeth A. "The Incomprehensibility of God and the Image of God as Male and Female." *Theological Studies* 45 (1984): 441–465.

Kaufman, Gordon D. *Theology for a Nuclear Age.* Philadelphia: Westminster Press, 1985.

Keller, Catherine. *From a Broken Web.* Boston: Beacon Press, 1986.

McAllister, Pam, ed. *Reweaving the Web of Life: Feminism and Nonviolence.* Philadelphia: New Society Publishers, 1982.

McFague, Sallie. *Metaphorical Theology: Models of God in Religious Language.* Philadelphia: Fortress Press, 1982.

———. *Models of God: A Theology for an Ecological, Nuclear Age.* Philadelphia: Fortress Press, 1987.

Maguire, Daniel. "The Feminization of God and Ethics." *Christianity and Crisis* 42/4 (March 15, 1982): 59–67.

Miller, Jean Baker. *Toward a New Psychology of Women.* Boston: Beacon Press, 1976.

Millett, Kate. *Sexual Politics.* Garden City, N.Y.: Doubleday & Co., 1970.

Mollenkott, Virginia Ramey. *The Divine Feminine: The Biblical Imagery of God as Female.* New York: Crossroad Publishing Co. 1983.

Moltmann-Wendel, Elisabeth, and Jürgen Moltmann. *Humanity in God.* New York: Pilgrim Press, 1983.

Mud Flower Collective. *God's Fierce Whimsy: Christian Feminism and Theological Education.* Edited by Carter Heyward. New York: Pilgrim Press, 1985.

Ochshorn, Judith. *The Female Experience and the Nature of the Divine.* Bloomington, Ind.: Indiana University Press, 1981.

Olson, Carl, ed. *The Book of the Goddess, Past and Present: An Introduction to Her Religion.* New York: Crossroad Publishing Co., 1983.

Plaskow, Judith. *Sin, Sex, and Grace: Women's Experience and the Theologies of Reinhold Niebuhr and Paul Tillich.* Lanham, Md.: University Press of America, 1980.

Raitt, Jill. "Structures and Strictures: Relational Theology and a Woman's Contribution to Theological Conversation." *Journal of the American Academy of Religion* 50 (March 1982): 3–17.

Ruether, Rosemary Radford. *Sexism and God-Talk: Toward a Feminist Theology.* Boston: Beacon Press, 1983.

———. *Woman-Church: Theology and Practice of Feminist Liturgical Communities.* San Francisco: Harper & Row, 1985.

———. *Womanguides: Readings Toward a Feminist Theology.* Boston: Beacon Press, 1985.

Russell, Letty M. *Household of Freedom: Authority in Feminist Theology.* Philadelphia: Westminster Press, 1987.

Sanday, Peggy Reeves. *Female Power and Male Dominance: On the Origins of Sexual Inequality.* Cambridge: Cambridge University Press, 1981.

Schaef, Anne Wilson. *Women's Reality: An Emerging Female System in the White Male Society.* San Francisco: Harper & Row, 1985.

Schüssler Fiorenza, Elisabeth. *In Memory of Her: A Feminist Theological Reconstruction of Christian Origins.* New York: Crossroad Publishing Co., 1983.

Soelle, Dorothee. *The Strength of the Weak: Toward a Christian Feminist Identity.* Translated by Robert and Rita Kimber. Philadelphia: Westminster Press, 1984.

Spretnak, Charlene, ed. *The Politics of Women's Spirituality: Essays on the Rise of Spiritual Power Within the Feminist Movement.* Garden City, N.Y.: Doubleday & Co., 1982.

Starhawk, *The Spiral Dance: A Rebirth of the Ancient Religion of the Great Goddess.* San Francisco: Harper & Row, 1979.

Stone, Merlin. *When God Was a Woman.* New York: Harcourt Brace Jovanovich, 1976.

Suchocki, Marjorie Hewitt. *God, Christ, Church: A Practical Guide to Process Theology.* New York: Crossroad Publishing Co., 1982.

Trible, Phyllis. *God and the Rhetoric of Sexuality.* Philadelphia: Fortress Press, 1978.

———. *Texts of Terror.* Philadelphia: Fortress Press, 1984.

Weidman, Judith L., ed. *Christian Feminism: Visions of a New Humanity.* San Francisco: Harper & Row, 1984.

Welch, Sharon D. *Communities of Resistance and Solidarity: A Feminist Theology of Liberation.* Maryknoll, N.Y.: Orbis Books, 1985.

Index of Names